ROGER WILLIAMS AND HIS WORLD

THE **BROADVIEW SOURCES** SERIES

Roger Williams and His World

A HISTORY IN DOCUMENTS

edited by CHARLOTTE CARRINGTON-FARMER

BROADVIEW PRESS
Peterborough, Ontario, Canada

Founded in 1985, Broadview Press is a fully independent academic publishing house owned by approximately twenty-five shareholders—almost all of whom are either Broadview employees or Broadview authors. Broadview is supported by a collaboration with Trent University, a liberal arts university located in Peterborough, Ontario—the city where Broadview was founded and continues to operate. Broadview is committed to environmentally responsible publishing and fair business practices.

Library and Archives Canada Cataloguing in Publication

Title: Roger Williams and his world : a history in documents / edited by Charlotte Carrington-Farmer.
Names: Carrington-Farmer, Charlotte, editor.
Series: Broadview sources series.
Description: Series statement: The Broadview sources series | Includes bibliographical references.
Identifiers: Canadiana (print) 20240536223 | Canadiana (ebook) 20240536231 | ISBN 9781554816576 (softcover) | ISBN 9781770489356 (PDF) | ISBN 9781460408599 (EPUB)
Subjects: LCSH: Williams, Roger, 1604?-1683. | LCSH: Rhode Island—History—Colonial period, ca. 1600-1775—Sources. | LCSH: Colonization—History—17th century—Sources. | LCSH: Colonists—United States—17th century—Sources.
Classification: LCC F82 .R64 2025 | DDC 974.5/02—dc23

Broadview Press handles its own distribution in Canada and the United States:
PO Box 1243, Peterborough, Ontario K9J 7H5, Canada
555 Riverwalk Parkway, Tonawanda, NY 14150, USA
Tel: (705) 482-5915
email: customerservice@broadviewpress.com

Broadview Press books are imported and distributed in the United Kingdom and European Union by:
Gazelle Book Services Ltd.
White Cross Mills, Hightown, Lancaster, Lancashire, LA1 4XS
sales@gazellebookservices.co.uk

European Union – Responsible Person (for official use only):
eucomply OÜ
Pärnu mnt 139b14
11317 Tallinn, Estonia
hello@eucompliancepartner.com
+33757690241

Canada Broadview Press acknowledges the financial support of the Government of Canada for our publishing activities.

Copy-edited by Michel Pharand
Book design by Em Dash Design

PRINTED IN CANADA

2 3 4 5 6 7 8 9 10 25 26 27 28 29 30

CONTENTS

ACKNOWLEDGEMENTS

This book owes its existence to many wonderful people who have helped, supported, and inspired me over the years. Firstly, I'm thankful to John Coffey for introducing me to Roger Williams when I was an undergraduate student in his class back in 2001; I've been fascinated by Roger Williams and his world ever since. Coffey encouraged me to write about Williams for my undergraduate dissertation, and then Williams became part of my graduate work, a book chapter, a journal article, and (finally) this book. Support from Plimoth Patuxet Museums was instrumental to this book taking shape, particularly the invitation to create a staff manual and run training sessions on Williams, collaborating on grants, and co-directing the NEH "Ancient Stories, New Neighbors" K-12 institute. Most notably, Richard Pickering at Plimoth Patuxet Museums has championed my work on Williams, and I'm lucky to count him as a colleague and friend. He is an inspiration and I'm humbled by his knowledge and kindness.

Getting a job in 2012 at a university named after Roger Williams seemed like fate, and my greatest joy is sharing my passion for our namesake with my students. Thanks to Jason Jacobs for leading the efforts at Roger Williams University to create a First Year Seminar on Roger Williams, which pushed me to conceptualize this edited collection. The wonderful students in the FYS in the Honors Program have been a driving force behind this book, and I've also received endless support from fellow Roger Seminar faculty, colleagues in the History Department, and the School of Humanities, Arts, and Education. Funding from Roger Williams University enabled me to complete research for this project, and I spent part of my sabbatical in 2020 researching both Roger and Mary Williams.

Over the last decade, countless collaborations with historian, archeologist, and former National Park Ranger, John McNiff, have helped me to understand Williams in new ways. McNiff's knowledge of Williams is second to none, and learning from him is something I always treasure. I've been lucky to take students from Roger Williams University on two study abroad classes with McNiff to England to "Retrace Roger Williams in England," and these trips reshaped my understanding of Williams' early life. Taking students to sites connected to Williams around New England also helped me to visualize Williams' world, including Smith's Castle (Williams' trading post), the Rhode Island State House, NPS Roger Williams National Memorial, Plimoth Patuxet Museums, and various monuments dedicated to Williams (including the (in)famous Rumford site!). Working with McNiff and Julie Fisher on "Reading Roger Williams" events in collaboration with the Rhode Island Historical Society and Roger Williams University brought Williams' writings to life for me. I have been privileged to be made an honorary member of the Roger Williams Family Association, and I thank my "cousins" from the RWFA for their continued encouragement.

I could not have written this book without support from the Providence Early American Group, and I owe a huge shout out to Edward Andrews, Adrian Weimer, Owen Stanwood, and Linford Fisher, who offered wonderful feedback and fabulous friendship as this book took shape. Many people graciously read different versions of this book, including Courtney Garrity, Rebecca Farias, Richard McGee, Stanley Lemons, Lane Sparkman, and Charlie Hartman. I'm deeply grateful to William Doherty for his help with early transcription efforts, and to all of the scholars whose work on Williams influenced this book, most notably Glenn LaFantasie's incredible editorial work on Williams' correspondence and the *Tomaquag Edition of A Key into the Language of America*. Stephen Latta at Broadview Press has been the best editor I could have asked for; his knowledge, kindness, and encouragement made the publication of this book an enjoyable process, which is no mean feat! Tara Lowes at Broadview also played an instrumental role in pulling the book together. Michel Pharand worked tirelessly on the copy edits, and his talent as a wordsmith transformed this book.

Trying to reimagine the Indigenous worlds that Williams lived in was the most challenging part of this project, and I owe a deep debt of gratitude to Lorén Spears (enrolled Narragansett Tribal Nation Citizen and Executive Director of the Tomaquag Museum), who offered important feedback, powerful perspectives, and friendship along the way. Brad Lopes (Aquinnah Wampanoag Citizen and Program Manager, Native American Teacher Retention Initiative) pushed me to reconsider Williams' role in the process of settler-colonialism when we collaborated on the National Endowment for the Humanities institute "Ancient Stories, New Neighbors: *Decolonizing Indigenous Homelands and 17th-Century New England*" in 2022.

Lastly, cheers to my family! Thank you to my husband, John Farmer, for supporting my love of history, from the big to the small—from crossing an ocean to be with me, to listening to me give impromptu lectures when we visit historical sites. I look forward to teaching our future family about Williams as we continue to grow our lives in our adopted home of Rhode Island. To my parents, Audrey and David Carrington, none of this would have been possible without you. Thank you for everything—for all of the sacrifices you've made, for inspiring my love of learning from an early age (often in the most unique ways), and for being my biggest champions; knowing you are proud of me is the best feeling in the world.

PREFACE

Roger Williams is arguably the most written about person of seventeenth-century New England, and countless books and articles cover every aspect of his life, ideas, and legacy.[1] Just when it seems as if there is nothing new to say about Williams, scholars come up with new interpretations that reframe our understanding.[2] Beyond the academy, public recognition of Roger Williams, especially in Rhode Island, is everywhere: a university, hospital, streets, parks, and a zoo named after him, and a dedicated Roger Williams National Memorial administered by the National Park Service. While Williams never sat for a portrait, sculptors and artists have drawn on all kinds of inspiration—from the baseball player Ted Williams to surviving descendants through the Roger Williams Family Association—to imagine what he looked like. Statues based entirely on imagined depictions of Williams are found all over Rhode Island, the US Capitol, and on the Reformation Wall in Geneva. Williams even appeared on a postage stamp in 1936.

Williams' life was complex and multifarious, but most histories of Williams focus on his most famous/infamous moments: his banishment from Massachusetts Bay, relationship with Indigenous Peoples, and advocacy for religious freedom and the separation of church and state. Some traditional biographies of Williams depict him as being ahead of his time, both in his dealings with Indigenous Peoples and his calls for religious liberty. But, as the sources in this book show, this was not the case: Williams was not a man out of his times nor indeed ahead of them. While he had many

1 See, for example, Perry Miller, *Roger Williams: His Contribution to the American Tradition* (Indianapolis: Bobbs-Merrill, 1953); John Barry, *Roger Williams and the Creation of the American Soul: Church, State, and the Birth of Liberty* (New York: Viking, 2012); Ola Elizabeth Winslow, *Master Roger Williams: A Biography* (New York: Macmillan, 1957); W. Clark Gilpin, *The Millenarian Piety of Roger Williams* (Chicago: University of Chicago Press, 1979); Edmond Morgan, *Roger Williams: The Church and the State* (New York: W.W. Norton & Company, 1967); Edwin Gaustad, *Liberty of Conscience: Roger Williams in America* (Valley Forge, PA: Judson Press, 1999); Samuel H. Brockunier, *The Irrepressible Democrat* (New York: Ronald Press Co., 1940); Cyclone Covey, *The Gentle Radical: A Biography of Roger Williams* (New York: Macmillan, 1966); and James Warren, *God, War, and Providence: The Epic Struggle of Roger Williams and the Narragansett Indians against the Puritans of New England* (New York: Scribner, 2018).

2 For some of the more recent and innovative scholarship on Williams and his work, see Julie Fisher, "Roger Williams and the Indian Business," *The New England Quarterly* 94, no. 3 (Sept. 2021): 352–93; Linford Fisher, J. Stanley Lemons, and Lucas Mason Brown, *Decoding Roger Williams: The Lost Essay of Rhode Island's Founding Father* (Waco, TX: Baylor University Press, 2014); Jonathan Beecher Field, "A Key for the Gate: Roger Williams, Parliament, and Providence," *The New England Quarterly* 80, no. 3 (Sept. 2007): 353–82; J. Stanley Lemons, "Roger Williams Was Not a Seeker but a 'Witness in Sackcloth,'" *The New England Quarterly* 88, no. 4 (Dec. 2015): 693–714; and Teresa M. Bejan, *Mere Civility: Disagreement and the Limits of Toleration* (Cambridge, MA: Harvard University Press, 2017).

remarkable ideas (and founded a revolutionary colony), his feet were very firmly planted on the English or Narragansett earth he resided on.

Williams is notoriously hard to read. Even though many historians have written about him, reading Williams in his own words is difficult because of the nature of seventeenth-century sources, Williams' complex ideas, and his writing style. This book combines his correspondence, published works, and non-textual sources in an accessible way, so that you can read Williams for yourself. This collection frames Williams within his wider world, covering all aspects of his life—from the famous to the lesser-known.

Roger Williams was complicated. He proclaimed that Indigenous People were equal in God's eyes, but also referred to them as proud and filthy barbarians. He described how he longed to convert Indigenous Peoples to Christianity, but later changed his mind and declared that forced religious worship was so offensive to God it stunk in His nostrils. He proclaimed religious freedom but detested the Quaker religion. He described the love Indigenous Peoples had for their children and then took an unfree Pequot boy away from his mother and siblings. One of Williams' enemies asked, "What is Roger Williams?" deliberately saying *what* rather than *who*. This collection enables you to interpret the primary sources and decide for yourself who (or what) Roger Williams was.

INTRODUCTION

As he neared his eightieth year, an elderly Roger Williams reflected on his life's accomplishments. He was proud of Rhode Island's Royal Charter, as it not only excelled "all" in New England but also the World "as to the Souls of Men."[1] Williams was right: the 1663 Charter was nothing short of revolutionary, as it cemented Williams' vision of religious freedom. In a time when state religion ruled and dissenters faced imprisonment, banishment, and corporal and capital punishment, the small colony of Rhode Island and Providence Plantations was arguably the freest place in the western world. When Williams founded the colony in 1636, he pioneered an experiment in **religious liberty** and the separation of church and state. He had grown up in England, where the official state religion changed on the whim of a monarch and **heretics** were burned alive for their dissenting beliefs. Across the Atlantic, Williams created something different.

Williams arrived in Boston, the nucleus of the **Puritan**-led Massachusetts Bay Colony in 1631. Williams' first few years in New England were turbulent, and he was unable to settle in one place, both geographically and spiritually. Immediately upon arrival, he turned down the position of Teacher of the Boston Church and moved to Salem, and then quickly on again to Plymouth, where he lived from 1631 to 1633. He returned to Salem in 1633, and by 1635 Williams had become an outspoken critic of persecution. He was judged to be in "great contempt of authority" and banished for his "new & dangerous opinions" on liberty, land, and the church.[2] Williams fled Massachusetts Bay and crossed into **Narragansett** homelands, where the **Sachems**, Canonicus and Miantonomi allowed him to settle.[3] He named the settlement Providence, as he believed that it was God's providence that had carried him to safety. The 1636/38 land evidence represented the first step in Williams' plan to create a radical new settlement. While he had no patent from England, he had the permission of the Narragansett citizens, which allowed him to put theory into practice. Williams' ideas were formalized in a parliamentary patent in 1644 and again in 1663 with a Royal Charter

religious liberty: In religious matters, the state had no role to play other than to guarantee the free exercise of religion.

heretics: Someone who disagreed with the established religion. To their supporters, heretics were seen as martyrs when they were executed.

Puritan: Protestants who believed that the Church of England retained too many Catholic elements and wanted to purify it. This term was viewed as an insult at the time.

Narragansett: Indigenous Nation in whose homelands Williams settled. Historically, Narragansett would have been pronounced *Nahahegansuck* as the language has no "l" or "r" sounds; the name means "The People of the small point." The Narragansett Indian Tribe remains a vibrant community today, with many citizens residing in their ancestral homelands. They are currently the only federally recognized Nation in the state of Rhode Island.

Sachems: Indigenous leaders. Williams wrote extensively about two Narragansett sachems, Canonicus and Miantonomi, who were dual leaders as uncle and nephew.

1 Roger Williams to the Town of Providence, 15 January 1682, in *The Correspondence of Roger Williams*, ed. Glenn LaFantasie, 2 vols. (Providence, RI: Rhode Island Historical Society, 1988), 2:774–76 (hereafter referred to as *Williams Corres.*).

2 Nathaniel B. Shurtleff, ed., *Records of the Governor and Company of the Massachusetts Bay in New England* (Boston: William White, 1853), 1:160–61.

3 For more on the traditional spelling and pronunciation of the Narragansett language, see Dawn Dove, Sandra Robinson, Lorén Spears, Dorothy Herman Papp, and Kathleen J. Bragdon, eds., *The Tomaquag Museum Edition: Roger Williams, A Key into the Language of America* (Yardley, PA: Westholme, 2019), especially the introduction and p. 25.

Indigenous: The past five hundred years have seen myriad terms used as referents to the Indigenous Peoples of the Americas. This work will use specific tribal names when possible and then use the following terms interchangeably: Indigenous, Native, Indian, and Ninnimissinuok. The collective term Ninnimissinuok gained traction in Kathleen Bragdon's *Native People of Southern New England 1500–1650* (Norman: University of Oklahoma Press, 1996).

Ninnimissinuok: Variation of Ninnimissinnûwock, Ninnimissinuok is a Narragansett word for Indigenous Peoples collectively. It refers to Indigenous Algonquian-speaking residents of Southern New England. Williams recorded the definition as "Men, Folke, or People" in *A Key into the Language of America*. Narragansett Peoples still use the term Ninnimissinuok today to mean The People, i.e., Indigenous People. Ninnimissinuok is used to describe multiple groups, including Nipmuck, Wampanoag, Narragansett, and Massachusett, but it does not imply a homogeneity of social forms or motivations among different tribes and nations, as Southern New England was (and is) home to a complex variety of communities.

settler-colonists: People who migrated to a new region and imposed their own political, legal, social, and cultural systems at the expense of (or with

from King Charles II.[4] Albeit only a small corner of the English Atlantic world, Rhode Island was a revolutionary place that offered shelter to the "poor and persecuted."[5]

Williams wrote extensively on the idea of religious freedom in both his published works and private letters. His most famous defense of religious liberty, *The Bloudy Tenent of Persecution* (1644), was viewed as one of the most dangerous books of the time.[6] As Williams discovered, living with and within the reality of religious freedom was easier said than done. His struggles with the Quakers, Samuel Gorton, William Harris, and the domestic violence case of the Verin family illustrate this clearly. Williams' radical ideas cost him dearly. He was banished. His masterpiece on religious freedom, *The Bloudy Tenent*, was burned. His neighbors fought. He had to live alongside those he despised. His colony was viewed with contempt. His long-term acquaintances wished him dead. His house and town were burned down. He lived his final years in poverty. However, in the face of opposition and hardship, Williams created something different in Rhode Island.

Much of the scholarship on Williams has focused on his work separating church and state and championing religious freedom, but as the sources in this collection show, Williams' life was also defined by his trading, business, and political interactions with his Narragansett, Wampanoag, Pequot, Niantic, Mohegan, and other **Indigenous** neighbors. Williams was closer to the **Ninnimissinuok** than most other **settler-colonists**[7] of his time, and he went to great lengths to learn the Narragansett language. After over a decade of studying it, he published *A Key into the Language of America* in 1643. The book was a groundbreaking Narragansett-English dictionary and phrase book, but also included Williams' ethnographic observations on Indigenous customs, manners, and worship.[8]

When he first arrived in New England, Williams hinted that he was interested in converting the Ninnimissinuok to Christianity, but he eventually opposed coercive conversion efforts. Williams directly objected to the work of the Bay Colony's chief missionary, John Eliot, who translated the

4 John Clarke played an instrumental (and often overlooked) role in writing and securing the charter. Williams had been back in Providence for almost a decade when the charter was secured. *Rhode Island Royal Charter* (1663), Charter Museum, Rhode Island State House, Providence, RI.

5 Roger Williams to Major John Mason and Governor Thomas Prence, 22 June 1670, *Williams Corres.*, 2:609–20.

6 Roger Williams, *The Bloudy Tenent of Persecution, for cause of Conscience, discussed in A Conference betweene Truth and Peace* (London, 1644).

7 For more on the concept of settler-colonialism and its nuances in the context of early American history, see Trevor Burnard and Agnès Delahaye, "Settler Colonialism and Early American History," in *Agents of European Overseas Empires: Private Colonisers, 1450–1800*, ed. Agnès Delahaye, Elodie Peyrol-Kleiber, L.H. Roper, and Bertrand Van Rumbeke (Manchester: Manchester University Press, 2024), 153–78.

8 Roger Williams, *A Key into the Language of America* (1643).

Bible into **Wôpanâôt8âôk** and set up **Praying Towns** to pioneer conversion to Christianity. Williams published his views in *Christenings make not Christians* (1645) but also wrote about it in short-hand.[9] As a diplomat, Williams worked hard to mediate conflict between the settler-colonists and Indigenous Peoples and to keep peace in the region, especially during the **Pequot War**. However, Williams' life was full of contradictions. Just one year after Providence was founded on the premise of freedom, he had an **unfree** Indigenous child living in his house, a boy taken from his mother and siblings, who was then renamed. Williams' diplomatic efforts ultimately failed during **King Philip's War** and Native forces burned Providence to the ground. After the war, the townspeople in Providence, including Williams, sold some Indigenous captives into slavery. The Pequot War and King Philip's War were part the all-encompassing "**War for New England**."[10] Williams was simultaneously a scholar of the Narragansett language, an interpreter, trader, scribe, diplomat, captor, and enslaver.[11] This was Roger Williams' world: a complex place, with competing impulses and tensions.

RELIGIOUS PERSECUTION IN ENGLAND

Williams was born in London, England in approximately **1603**. He grew up in a world of religious turmoil, where the "official" state religion changed on the whim of a monarch and religious terrorism posed a real and present danger. From 1534, when **King Henry VIII** broke away from the **Catholic** Church and made England a **Protestant** country, anyone who did not embrace the official state religion was not only a religious heretic, but also liable for treason against the monarch. Following the **Reformation**, England switched back and forth between Protestantism and Catholicism, before settling uneasily into Protestantism when Williams grew up under **King James I**. In England, Williams witnessed first-hand how the state could pollute the church, for example when "unspiritual" bishops were appointed by the crown. Such practices impacted Williams' revolutionary vision for Rhode Island.

Childhood and Education

Williams grew up in the Smithfield district of London, and close to his home on Cowes Lane there was livestock market, a bustling hub of Dutch traders,

9 Roger Williams, *Christenings make not Christians* (London, 1645).

10 Lorén Spears (Executive Director of the Tomaquag Museum and Narragansett Citizen), email correspondence with author, August 2024.

11 Julie Fisher, "Roger Williams and the Indian Business," *The New England Quarterly* 94, no. 3 (Sept. 2021): 352–93.

the purpose of) displacing or destroying an existing Indigenous society.

Wôpanâôt8âôk: Wampanoag Language, which is one of more than three dozen languages belonging to the Algonquian language family.

Praying Towns: Towns set up by settler-colonists to spread Christianity and erase Indigenous cultures and religions. Massachusetts Bay established approximately 14 Praying Towns and residents were known as Praying Indians.

Pequot War: Conflict between the English and their Indigenous allies against the Pequot based in modern-day Connecticut between 1636 and 1638.

unfree: A term used to classify someone who is not free, especially if their status as enslaved or indentured is unclear.

King Philip's War: Conflict between the settler-colonists and Wampanoag Peoples and their allies between 1675 and 1676, although the war did not end until 1678 in northern Indigenous territories.

War for New England: Lorén Spears (Executive Director of the Tomaquag Museum and Narragansett Citizen) describes the conflict as the "War for New England" as the settler-colonists wanted to break the sovereign power of Indigenous nations and create a "new" England.

1603: The estimated year Williams was born. Williams' baptism records were destroyed in the Great Fire of London. Williams referenced his age several times in later life, but each pinpointed his birth to a slightly different year.

King Henry VIII: Ruler of England from 1509 until his death in 1547. He broke England's long-standing connection with the Catholic Church in 1534 to divorce his first wife, Catherine of Aragon, and marry Anne Boleyn, making England a Protestant country.

Catholic: Catholicism was the official religion in England from the sixth century until 1534. Key Catholic beliefs include the authority of the Pope, that your good deeds can impact your salvation, and Mary as the "Mother of God." Catholics embrace mystery, hierarchy, rituals, liturgy, structure, and symbolic worship.

Protestant: Protestantism is a branch of Christianity that originated in the sixteenth-century Reformation. Key Protestant beliefs are that you cannot influence your salvation with your actions, the priesthood of all believers, and the supremacy of the Bible. Protestant worship is plain and straightforward, with a focus on scripture.

Reformation: A sixteenth-century religious revolution that became the basis for Protestantism. Martin Luther and John Calvin were important leaders.

King James I: King of England from 1603 to 1625, he was also King of Scotland (known as King James VI in Scotland). The first monarch of the Stuart

Newgate prison, and the Smithfield execution site. Williams' parish church, St. Sepulchre-without-Newgate, was the closest church to the prison and execution site. St. Sepulchre, a medieval church, was partially destroyed in the **Great Fire of London**, which resulted in the loss of Williams' baptism records. However, the tower, porch, and outer walls survived (and still stand today), as has the specially commissioned **execution bell**. Williams was aware of the long history of persecution in his neighborhood, and in *The Bloody Tenent Yet More Bloody* (1652) Smithfield gained further notoriety not only when many Protestants were burned alive there under **Queen Mary I**, but also because it was the site of the final burning of a religious heretic/martyr in 1612.[12] That execution happened when Williams was approximately eight years old and an enormous crowd watched as Bartholomew Legate, who was branded an "incorrigible" heretic (for being a **Separatist**), was burned to ashes.[13]

The awful stench of burning human flesh filled the air as victims suffered for up to 45 minutes before dying. The process was deliberately slow, with three separate wood-fires being lit and then extinguished, forcing victims to pray for mercy and more fire to end their torment. Accounts describe how the person suffered, as their lips turned black, hair singed, fingers fell off, and arms melted into their breast as they clutched their heart. Others who were spared the horrors of burning rotted in Newgate prison, a stone's throw from Williams' house. Thomas Helwys met his demise in Newgate in 1616 (when Williams was approximately 13 years old) for arguing for the very thing that Williams eventually went on to create in Rhode Island: a place where religion was separate from the state. Helwys proclaimed that "the Magistrate is not to meddle with religion or matters of conscience, nor to compel men to this or that form or religion."[14] Williams' childhood neighborhood revealed the long and bloody history of state persecution for religion's sake.

Williams grew up in a middle-rank household. His father, James, was a merchant tailor who imported and traded in textiles and made bespoke suits. The London docks were a hub of international exchange, with hotly contested negotiations in multiple languages, and a place where personal connections mattered—all of which Williams eventually put into practice at his own trading post in Narragansett homelands. Roger had three siblings: Sydrach, Catherine, and Robert. When Roger's father, James, died in 1621, his will included bequests to his wife, Alice, his children, and money and

12 Roger Williams, *The Bloody Tenent Yet More Bloody* (London, 1652).

13 Thomas Fuller, *Church History of Britain* (London, 1656), book 10, 63–64.

14 John Barry, *Roger Williams and the Creation of the American Soul: Church, State, and the Birth of Liberty* (New York: Viking, 2012), 319.

bread to the poor in struggling London parishes. Roger's mother, Alice, went on to run a successful inn, and upon her death in 1634 she bequeathed ten pounds yearly for twenty years to Roger.[15] Alice also knew that she had a one-year-old grandchild, Mary, in New England, as she further provided that if Roger predeceased her, his wife and daughter would receive the remainder.[16]

As a youth, Williams caught the eye of **Edward Coke**, one of the most important men in England. A leading jurist and eventual Chief Justice, Coke took Williams on as his amanuensis, tasking him with taking shorthand notes in sermons and speeches in the **Star Chamber** and at court and Parliament.[17] Coke eventually challenged the authority of King James I, using the **Magna Carta** of 1215 to argue that nobody (including the King) was above the law. This was a direct affront to the King, who believed that God had chosen him to rule, and royal orders (backed by divine authority) could potentially overrule legal decisions. Coke was imprisoned in the **Tower of London** as punishment, which may have impacted a young Williams, who witnessed his mentor's persecution by the state firsthand. As Williams turned away from the Church of England, his relationship with Coke deteriorated.

On Coke's patronage, Williams attended Charterhouse school, which had been founded by Sir Thomas Sutton in 1611. Charterhouse was a short five-minute walk from Williams' home, cutting through the notorious Smithfield execution site. A plaque to Williams, erected in 1899, is still on display at Charterhouse today. It honors him as the founder of Rhode Island and as a "pioneer of religious liberty in America."[18] After Charterhouse, Williams enrolled at Pembroke College at the University of Cambridge in 1623. He received a scholarship based on financial need and academic excellence. The scholarship targeted students who were "well affected towards religion and the ministry" and were skilled in Latin, Greek, and Hebrew. It also prioritized students from certain geographic areas, including Williams' hometown of London, and the "poorest" were "preferred."[19]

---

15 Williams did not receive it because he refused to swear an oath in God's name in court.

16 For more on Williams' family background, see Ola Elizabeth Winslow, *Master Roger Williams: A Biography* (New York: Macmillan, 1957).

17 For more on Williams' time in England and the connection to Coke, see Barry, *Roger Williams and the Creation of the American Soul.*

18 The plaque to Roger Williams at Charterhouse was placed by Oscar S. Straus in 1899. Straus, an American politician and diplomat, was the first Jew to serve in a US president's cabinet. In 1894 he published a biography of Williams and in 1891 named his son Roger Williams Straus.

19 Williams' matriculation record is curious. Unlike other entries, which include details about the student, Williams' entry simply reads "Jun. 29. 1623. Williams." It does not even include his first name. Pembroke College Matriculation Register, COL/4/3/1/1, Pembroke College Archives, Cambridge, UK; Pembroke College Registrum Magnum II, B β 2, Pembroke College Archives, Cambridge, UK; Matthew Wren Note Book, A α Pembroke College Records, Pembroke College Archives, Cambridge, UK.

dynasty and a Protestant, he commissioned a new English translation of the Bible, known today as the King James Bible.

Great Fire of London: A fire that started in Pudding Lane in 1666, and burned 436 acres of the city, including 13,200 houses and 87 churches.

execution bell: A special bell purchased in 1605 by merchant, John Dowe, to be rung at executions.

Queen Mary I: Ruler of England from 1553 to 1558. She was Henry VIII's daughter from his first marriage to Catherine of Aragon. She switched England back to Catholicism and earned herself the nickname "Bloody Mary" for the number of Protestants she put to death.

Separatist: Protestants who believed the Church of England retained too many Catholic practices and could not be fixed; separation was the only solution.

Edward Coke: A leading barrister, judge, and politician. He led the prosecution in several important cases including the one against the Gunpowder Plot conspirators, who planned to blow up Parliament and King James I in 1605.

Star Chamber: An English court that sat at the Royal Palace of Westminster.

Magna Carta: A document declaring that the king was not above the law, written in 1215 in response to King John's abuse of power. Magna Carta is Latin for "Great Charter."

Tower of London: Built in the eleventh century, it was used as a prison in the early modern period to house people considered a threat to national security.

private chaplain: Wealthy Puritan families often hired private chaplains to guide their worship at home.

Jane Whalley: The daughter of Richard Whalley of Nottinghamshire and Frances Cromwell. After her mother's death, Jane moved in with the Barringtons at Broad Oak in Essex and came under the care of her aunt, Lady Joan Barrington, before moving in with her cousin, Elizabeth Masham, at Otes.

Lady Joan Barrington: A wealthy, powerful, and well-connected woman who controlled of the estates at Broad Oak and Hatfield Priory. Her late husband, Sir Francis Barrington, was a baronet, who sat in Parliament from 1601 to 1628.

Move to High Laver, Essex

Williams was ordained as an Anglican priest, but as his spiritual journey indicates, his views on the established church rapidly changed. Cambridge, a hotbed of Puritanism, certainly affected Williams, and upon graduation in 1627, he took a job as chaplain to a wealthy Puritan family in High Laver, Essex. Sometime before 1628, Williams moved to Otes Manor, Sir William Masham's household and a hub of non-conformity. As a newly minted twenty-something graduate, Williams was employed as **private chaplain** by the Masham family. Upon arrival, Roger fell immediately in love with one **Jane Whalley**. He waxed lyrical about Whalley and declared how there was "none in the world I more affect."[20] These affirmations of love for Whalley, from April 1629 onwards, are among his earliest surviving correspondence.

As Williams contemplated his love life, he also pondered his career options. By this point, he had made a name for himself in Puritan circles, turned down two church livings, and held off officially accepting a position in New England until his betrothal to Whalley was secured.[21] However, the union was not to be, as Whalley's aunt, **Lady Joan Barrington**, forbade it due to Williams' "low-ebb." While Williams admitted that he was "altogether unworthy & unmeet for such a proposition" and that it was indecorous of Whalley to condescend to his "low-ebb," he did not take the rejection well. He lamented that although the Lord had denied their union on Earth, he hoped that he and Whalley would live together in Heaven. He expressed his displeasure in no uncertain terms to Lady Barrington, warning her that the Lord had a quarrel against her and ungraciously pointing out her gray hair![22]

Mary Bernard arrived at Otes Manor around the same time as Williams. She was surely aware of Williams' courtship of Whalley, especially as she knew Whalley through her father's connections from her childhood in Nottinghamshire.[23] Mary Bernard was there to nurse Williams through his rejection, and they were married just seven months after Williams declared his undying love for Whalley. Mary Bernard was employed as a companion-in-waiting to Joanna Altham, Lady Masham's daughter by her

---

20 Roger Williams to Lady Joan Barrington, April 1629, *Williams Corres.*, 1:1–3.

21 In the letter asking for Jane's hand in marriage, Roger acknowledged the other offers: "Poor yet as I am I have some few offers at present, one put into my hand, person and present portion worthy." Roger left the offers to "stand they still at door, and shall, until the fairest end the Lord shall please to give to this [Jane Whalley's hand], shall come to light." Roger Williams to Lady Joan Barrington, April 1629, *Williams Corres.*, 1:1–3.

22 Roger Williams to Lady Joan Barrington, 2 May 1629, *Williams Corres.*, 1:4–7.

23 Roger Williams to Lady Joan Barrington, April 1629, *Williams Corres.*, 1:1–3.

first marriage.[24] Mary Bernard's father, Richard Bernard, was a clergyman, and her position was typical for daughters of the clergy.

Born in 1609, Mary Bernard spent the first few years of her life living in the gatehouse of the old Worksop Priory, Nottinghamshire, where her father, **Richard Bernard**, was the vicar. Nestled in the east midlands of England, the area was a hub of political and religious non-conformity. Richard Bernard spent much of his life walking the line between conformity to the Church of England, Puritanism, and Separatism.[25] The Bernard family moved to Batcombe, Somerset in 1613 following Richard's move for work. Richard continued to network with Puritans and Separatists and had several personal connections to New England. He published more than thirty volumes on a wide range of topics, from witchcraft to ministering to prisoners. His best-selling book, *The Isle of Man* (1626), was in print for 200 years and went through ten editions in his lifetime.[26] Richard's network was extensive, and he had connections to scholars, churchmen, landowners, and even Charles I as **Royal Chaplain in Extraordinary** in 1628.[27]

Richard Bernard: Mary Bernard Williams' father (1568–1641). A clergyman, Bernard at times dissented from the Church of England and also published many important books.

Royal Chaplain in Extraordinary: A chaplain appointed to the household of the British Crown; used mostly by the Stuart dynasty in the seventeenth century.

Richard Bernard's views on his daughter's marriage to Williams have not survived, but presumably he supported the union. Mary Bernard and Roger Williams were married at All Saints Church, High Laver, Essex, and the record reads: "Roger Williams **Clerk** and Mary Barnard were married thee 15th day of December anno domini 1629."[28] All Saints, High Laver still stands today with minimal changes to its interior and exterior, maintaining the plain white walls and predominantly clear and plain stained-glass windows, which the newly wed Williamses would have seen in 1629. Mary Bernard Williams may have played second fiddle to Jane Whalley at first, but her support of (and lifelong commitment to) her husband over almost fifty years of marriage enabled many of his radical ideas to become a reality. Mary Bernard Williams was someone who lived with and understood the implications of religious controversy, first with her father and then with her husband.

Clerk: Someone who was educated, literate.

24 Jane later apologized to her aunt, before marrying a Puritan clergyman, William Hooke, and moving to New England. Jane and her husband settled in Taunton, MA and then moved to New Haven, before returning to England in the 1650s.

25 For more on Bernard, see Amy G. Tan, *The Pastor in Print: Genre, Audience, and Religious Change in Early Modern England* (Manchester: Manchester University Press, 2022).

26 Richard Bernard, *The Isle of Man: or, The legall proceeding in Man-shire against sinne* (London, 1626).

27 Hugh Adlington, Tom Lockwood, and Gillian Wright, eds., *Chaplains in Early Modern England: Patronage, Literature and Religion* (Manchester: Manchester University Press, 2013); Tan, *The Pastor in Print*, 94, 137.

28 1629 Marriage Record, All Saints Church, High Laver, Essex, Ref: D/P 111/1/1, Essex Record Office, Chelmsford, UK. A letter from Lady Masham to her mother described how "Mr Williams is to marrye Mary barnard, Jug. Altham's made." Lady Elizabeth Masham to Lady Joan Barrington, undated but likely late autumn 1629, Mss. 2650, folio 292, Barrington Correspondence, Egerton Manuscripts, British Library, London. John Locke is buried at All Saints High Laver.

Predestination: God had preselected those who were going to heaven, and nothing one did on Earth could affect this decision.

covenant of works: A Catholic belief that your good works on Earth could impact your entrance to heaven.

covenant of grace: A Protestant-Puritan belief that only God's grace determined your entrance to heaven and that nothing you did on Earth could influence your entrance to heaven.

TULIP: Total depravity: Man is utterly corrupted by the fall of Adam and Eve; Unconditional election: some people (the elect) are predestined (without regard for their worthiness) for salvation because of Christ's sacrifice; Limited atonement: Christ's sacrifice does not apply to everyone, Some people are damned; Irresistible grace: If God grants you Grace, you can't refuse it; Perseverance of the Saints: For the elect, God's gift of grace could not be revoked even if they sinned: once saved, always saved.

Archbishop Laud: Appointed Archbishop of Canterbury by King Charles I in 1633. Bishops in England owed their appointments to the King and often used their influence to back royal interests. Laud was an advocate for King Charles I's reforms, including highly ritualist elements which Puritans despised.

Massachusetts Bay Colony: Founded in 1630 by John Winthrop and other Puritans, with Boston as its

Migration

Williams' decision to leave England was a mix of push and pull factors. After his failed courtship of Whalley, he and his new wife likely wanted a fresh start. Given the conflict with Lady Joan Barrington, Williams had outstayed his welcome at Otes. He became increasingly connected in Puritan circles, building a reputation as a budding theologian, and turned down at least two church livings in England because they came into conflict with his Puritan beliefs. Puritans were Protestants who sought to "purify" the Church of England of all aspects of Catholic worship.[29] They were preoccupied with determining God's will, especially what God expected *of* them and what He would do *to* them. Puritan beliefs were complex, and an important focus was the afterlife, in particular the doctrine of **Predestination**. In contrast to Catholics, who believed in a **covenant of works**, Williams embraced a **covenant of grace**. The mnemonic **TULIP** is helpful for understanding some of the key tenets of Puritanism: Total depravity, Unconditional election, Limited atonement, Irresistible Grace, and Perseverance of the Saints. As a Puritan, Williams sought simple worship and personal intimacy with God. However, under **Archbishop Laud**, Puritan ministers were compelled to use the Book of Common Prayer, wear the surplice, and lead congregations in what they deemed rote worship. Those who refused faced imprisonment or worse. Williams decided that England's religious climate was too dangerous, and as private chaplains were being rounded up, he feared he too would be taken.[30] The founding of the **Massachusetts Bay Colony** under **John Winthrop**'s vision of a "city upon a hill" in 1630 solidified Williams' call to New England.[31]

Roger and Mary Williams arrived in Boston on 5 February 1631 aboard the *Lyon*. Almost as soon as he stepped foot on American soil, Williams began to vocalize the problems he saw and his vision for what needed to change: all the churches in New England should fully separate from the Church of England, oaths for political loyalty should be banned, and the patent for

---

29 Puritanism was part of a wider movement of radicalism, which included Quakers, General Baptists, Levellers, and other groups. For more on this topic, see Christopher Hill, *The World Turned Upside Down: Radical Ideas during the English Revolution* (London: Penguin, 1991).

30 Roger Williams to Anne Sadleir (undated, but likely April 1652), *Anne Sadleir, Collection of letters, drafts, and other papers*, R.5.5. letters 31 and 32, Wren Library, Trinity College, Cambridge University, UK.

31 Abram C. Van Engen examines the origin of the famous sermon that Winthrop gave, along with its biblical references, and the importance (or lack thereof) we should attribute to the term "city upon a hill." Van Engen argues that for the migrating Puritans the question was not *whether* they would be a city upon a hill, but *how* they would be seen. Abram C. Van Engen, "Origins and Last Farewells: Bible Wars, Textual Form, and the Making of American History," *New England Quarterly* 86, no. 4 (Dec. 2013): 576.

Massachusetts Bay should be returned to the King, as it was fraudulent. Consequently, Williams turned down the post of Teacher of the Boston Church because he did not want to "officiate to an **unseparated people**."[32] Winthrop described how Williams refused to join the congregation at Boston because they would not make a public declaration of their repentance for having communion with the churches of England (even when they lived there). According to Winthrop, Williams also began to deny the authority of the civil magistrates to punish "breach of the Sabbath" or any offense that violated the religious injunctions of the **first table**, other than those offenses that broke only the civil peace. After a brief spell in Boston, Williams headed north to Salem.[33] By the end of the year, the Williams family removed again, this time south to Plymouth. In just one year, Roger and Mary had crossed the Atlantic, arrived in Boston, moved to Salem, and relocated again to Plymouth. The decision to settle in Plymouth, a Separatist colony, was tied to a range of factors, namely Williams' move towards Separatism but also Mary's connections through her father's networks.[34]

Plymouth and Salem

Conflict quickly arose in **Plymouth Colony**. Williams was disgruntled that even though Plymouth professed to be a Separatist colony, many settlers continued their communication with parishes in England.[35] In October 1632, John Winthrop, **John Wilson**, and others from Massachusetts Bay visited Plymouth, and Williams headed a debate with other leaders including **William Bradford** and **William Brewster**.[36] Williams was clearly critical of Plymouth's affairs, but, at least initially, Bradford was willing to accept Williams' sharpest admonitions and reproofs. However, by 1633 things had changed, and Bradford believed that Williams had some "strange opinions" that had started to cause controversy within the church which prompted

nucleus. This marked the start of the "great migration," with over 20,000 colonists arriving during the next 10 years.

John Winthrop: A Puritan and a leading figure in the Massachusetts Bay Colony. He served as governor for 12 of the colony's first 20 years. His writings, especially his journal, *A History of New England*, have shaped the way historians understand the founding of the colony.

unseparated people: A congregation that had not formally broken away from the Church of England.

first table: The first three of the Ten Commandments, which describe how people should live in relation to God.

Plymouth Colony: Founded in 1620 by William Bradford and other Separatists who arrived on the *Mayflower*.

John Wilson: A Puritan clergyman and the minister of the Boston Church in the Massachusetts Bay Colony.

William Bradford: A Separatist and governor of Plymouth Colony for many years between 1621 and 1657. His journal, *Of Plymouth Plantation*, is an important primary source describing the founding of the colony.

William Brewster: A Separatist who arrived on the *Mayflower*, he was an elder in the church and leader in Plymouth Colony.

---

32 Roger Williams to John Cotton, Jr., 25 March 1671, *Williams Corres.*, 2:627–30.

33 In April 1631, Winthrop recorded that "Salem had called Mr. Williams to the office of teacher," but the job offer never came to fruition as the Boston leaders intervened to prevent it. As a fellow Calvinist, Winthrop agreed that the civil and religious spheres should be separate, but he thought mandating Sabbath observance was part of the role civil magistrates played in maintaining the well-being of the commonwealth. For Winthrop's issues with Williams, see John Winthrop, *History of New England, 1630–1649* (Winthrop's Journal), ed. James Kendall Hosmer (New York: Charles Scribner's Sons, 1908), 1:49–50, 61–63, 116–17, 119, 149, 154, 157, 162–63 (hereafter referred to as Winthrop, *History of New England*).

34 For more on Bernard's networks, see Tan, *The Pastor in Print*.

35 Roger Williams to John Cotton, Jr., 25 March 1671, *Williams Corres.*, 2:627–30.

36 Winthrop, *History of New England*, 1:93.

Williams to leave abruptly.[37,38] The Williamses readied themselves to return to Salem—just as Mary was about to give birth to their first child. Mary Jr., was born in Plymouth the "first week in August 1633," and the new family of three relocated back to Salem that autumn.[39] The journey from Plymouth to Salem is just over 60 miles as the crow flies, and the Williams family most likely traveled on foot, by dug-out canoe, or on a small sailing craft, perhaps in combination and staying with friends along the way—all with a new-born baby.[40]

In Salem, Williams' ideas gained traction, and with a growing number of supporters, his earlier rejection of royal patents for land grants cemented. Building upon an earlier treatise to Bradford at Plymouth, Williams exhorted Massachusetts Bay to return their royal patent to England. The original treatise (which Williams wrote in Plymouth) has not survived, but other sources reference how it was a large four-part book that charged the King with a "solemne public lie" in claiming New England. According to Williams, the King could not claim New England as it was a "sin of unjust usurpation upon others possessions."[41] Williams' views on Indigenous land ownership were radical, but he did not go as far as accusing his fellow settler-colonists of evicting the Ninnimissinuok. In practice, his views centered on his theological and theoretical conflict with monarchs using Christianity as a justification to take Indigenous land.[42] The situation was further complicated by the fact just a few years prior to the arrival of the *Mayflower*, Indigenous populations in the **Dawnland** were depleted by 60–90 percent by European

Dawnland: New England shore in Indigenous cultures, meaning the place where the sun rises. The inhabitants of the Dawnland are the People of the First Light.

37 William Bradford, *History of Plymouth Plantation 1620–1647* (Boston: Massachusetts Historical Society, 1912), 2:161–64.

38 There is only one surviving letter from Williams from this period, a letter that he sent from Plymouth to John Winthrop in Boston in the second half of 1632, which addressed whether a person could simultaneously be a minister and magistrate. Nathaniel Morton later chronicled how Williams asserted "his own singular opinions" on Plymouth church members, but lacking support, he requested to be dismissed. Bradford, *History of Plymouth Plantation*, 2:161–64; Nathaniel Morton, *The New-England's Memorial: or, A Brief Relation of the Most Memorable and Remarkable Passages of the Providence of God, Manifested to the Planters of New-England in America: with Special Reference to the First Colony Thereof, Called New Plymouth* (Cambridge, MA: 1669), 78–82; Roger Williams to John Winthrop, Jr., 19 August 1669, *Williams Corres.*, 2:591–93.

39 The First Book of the Town of Providence, Long Book, *Early Records of the Town of Providence, 1633–1832*, RG100, City of Providence Archives, Providence, RI.

40 While horses had arrived in New England a few years earlier, it is unlikely that the Williams family traveled on horseback or in a carriage. For more on horses in early New England, see Charlotte Carrington-Farmer, "The Rise and Fall of the Narragansett Pacer," *Rhode Island History Journal* 76, no. 1 (Winter/Spring 2018): 1–38. For more on the saltwater geography of Indigenous New England, see Andrew Lipman, *The Saltwater Frontier: Indians and the Contest for the American Coast* (New Haven, CT: Yale University Press, 2017).

41 John Winthrop to John Endicott, 3 January 1634, *Winthrop Papers 1631–1637* (Boston: Massachusetts Historical Society, 1943), 3:146–49; Winthrop, *History of New England*, 1:145; Roger Williams, *Bloody Tenent Yet More Bloody* (London, 1652).

42 Winthrop to Endicott, 3 January 1634, *Winthrop Papers*, 3:147; Roger Williams, *Christenings make not Christians* (London, 1645).

diseases brought over by fishing vessels and traders. Accounts describe how the situation was so bleak in Wampanoag Pawtuxet homelands (the site of Plymouth Colony) that there was nobody left to bury the dead. This fundamentally changed the balance of power for Native tribes and nations, especially as the Narragansett were not impacted by illness in the same way as their Wampanoag neighbors.

Other disputes arose during Williams' time in Salem, including over whether women should wear a veil during public assemblies and their right to speak in church.[43] In November 1634, Salem became embroiled in further discord as some residents cut out the red cross of St. George from the new **King's Standard** believing it was a "relic of the antichrist," the Pope. While John Endicott was behind the order, some saw it as an indirect result of Williams' role in turning Salem into a hotbed of extremism.[44] Massachusetts Bay required all men over the age of sixteen to swear an oath of fidelity to the colony; Williams outright refused. He believed that swearing by God made the oath a prayer, as it was sworn in God's name. Thus, forcing someone to proclaim an oath (when they may not fully believe the words they were proclaiming) was akin to the magistrates forcing a spiritual practice. In April 1635, Williams appeared in the General Court for refusing to take the oath of submission to the governor and magistrates, as "a magistrate ought not to tender an oath to an **unregenerate** man" (forcing them to break the commandment of taking the Lord's name in vain).[45] Williams' refusal gained traction, and others followed suit. Williams stopped attending the Salem church entirely, as they refused to separate from the Church of England and other New England churches; instead, he held meetings in his own home with an ever-growing group of followers.

King's Standard: A new ensign, a solid red flag with a white canton containing the red cross of St. George.

unregenerate: Someone who had not experienced God's saving grace through a conversion experience.

The situation in Salem was further complicated by the fact that Mary was pregnant as the disputes played out. Mary had become pregnant likely in late January or early February 1635, just as her husband's conflict escalated. According to a later report by Nathaniel Morton, Mary continued to participate in services at the Salem Church after her husband stopped attending. As a result, Roger "withdr[e]w all private religious communication" from her as she held "communion with the church there." Morton further noted that Roger refused to "pray nor give thanks at meals with his own wife nor any of his family"

43 For a discussion of the conflict and the sources, see LaFantasie, "Road to Banishment Editorial Note," *Williams Corres.*, 1:12–23.

44 William Hubbard, *General History of New England from the discovery to MDCLXXX* (Boston: Charles C. Little and James Brown, 1848), iii, 165, 205.

45 Winthrop, *History of New England*, 1:188; Nathaniel B. Shurtleff, ed., *Records of the Governor and Company of the Massachusetts Bay in New England* (Boston: William White, 1853), 1:137.

as they "went to the church assemblies."[46] Morton's account is repeated and collaborated by a later account by Cotton Mather, who described how Roger would not "hold any Communion in any exercise of Religion with any Person, so much as his own wife, that went up unto their Assemblies."[47] Mary's final months of pregnancy were spent watching her husband stand trial for his controversial ideas—all while being excluded from religious services in her own home. Mary's final few weeks in Salem eerily foreshadowed what would become a defining theme in her life: separation from her husband.

Banishment and Removal

John Cotton: The "Teacher" of the Boston Church; he would publish many pamphlets criticizing Roger Williams.

Williams remained steadfast in his opinions, even when Bay Colony ministers, including **John Cotton**, tried to convince him of his errors. He doubled down and renounced all communion with their churches. By October 1635, his ideas had been deemed "erroneous, and very dangerous." Williams laid bare how Winthrop's vision for a city upon a hill had failed, in both its legal and religious aims. Williams charged the magistrate with injustice and extreme oppression and all the churches in the colony with being "full of antichristian pollution."[48] Williams declared that there should be "unlimited toleration of all religions," and that if anyone was punished for "matters of his conscience" it was "persecution." By default, Williams' attack on the church extended to the Church of England and its head, King Charles I. Williams was not only a political liability to Massachusetts Bay, but he also put their royal charter in jeopardy. A later account by William Hubbard chronicled how Williams had spoken "dangerous words against the Patent," the governmental foundation of the colony.[49] This was not simply a theoretical fear, as there were forces at work in England seeking to revoke the charter, especially if Massachusetts Bay could not control its people.

In October 1635, Massachusetts Bay banished Williams from the colony for his "new and dangerous opinions."[50] Initially, the implementation was deferred to the spring as Williams was ill, winter was approaching, and Mary had just given birth to their second child, a daughter named Freeborn.[51] However, when Williams continued to meet with other like-minded

---

46 Nathaniel Morton, *The New-England's Memorial: or, A Brief Relation of the Most Memorable and Remarkable Passages of the Providence of God, Manifested to the Planters of New-England in America: with Special Reference to the First Colony Thereof, Called New Plymouth* (Cambridge, MA, 1669), 78–82, 96–99.

47 Cotton Mather, *Magnalia Christi Americana* (London, 1702), VII:8.

48 Winthrop, *History of New England,* 1:154, 162–63.

49 Hubbard, *General History of New England,* 206.

50 Shurtleff, ed., *Records of the Governor and Company of the Massachusetts Bay,* 1:160–61.

51 The First Book of the Town of Providence, RG100, City of Providence Archives; Shurtleff, ed., *Records of the Governor,* 1:160–61.

individuals in his home and share his ideas, the magistrates ruled to seize him immediately and banish him to England. Williams was tipped off about the arrest from Winthrop and he escaped amid a blizzard in the winter of 1635–36. Without help from the Ninnimissinuok, who guided and sheltered him, Williams would have perished. He later observed that it was a "strange truth" that he had found "more free entertainment and refreshing" among the Ninnimissinuok than "amongst thousands that call themselves Christians."[52]

By spring of 1636, Williams and his followers from Salem had started to build a settlement along the Seekonk River, in present-day Rumford, Rhode Island. However, Plymouth asserted that the land was within their jurisdiction, which meant that Williams could be arrested and shipped back to Massachusetts for banishment. Even though Williams and his followers had already begun to erect houses and plant crops, they crossed the Seekonk River and settled in a place that lay beyond Plymouth's boundaries.[53] After rounding the river, they crossed into Narragansett homelands, and Canonicus and Miantonomi aided Williams by permitting him to settle. Williams symbolically named the settlement **Providence**. In allowing Williams to take up residence, the Sachems not only reinforced their sovereignty but also their leadership over their lands and waters, where their people have resided since **time immemorial**.

Providence: Williams believed it was God's providence that had carried him to safety. The first mention of the name "Rhode Island" in connection with Narragansett Bay is in a 1524 letter by Italian explorer Giovanni da Verrazzano. He likened the area to the Greek island of Rhodes in the Aegean Sea, and the name was officially first applied on 13 March 1644: "Aquidneck shall be henceforth called the Isle of Rhodes or Rhode-Island." In 1663 the name "Colony of Rhode Island and Providence Plantations" was adopted in the Royal Charter granted by King Charles II.

time immemorial: Beyond memory or record. Indigenous Peoples often use this phrase to describe the temporal depth of their connections with ancestral lands.

BUILDING NEW PROVIDENCE

Narragansett Peoples and the Providence Land Evidence

Providence represented the first step in Williams' plan to put his "new and dangerous" ideas into practice, and the Narragansett Sachems made this possible by allowing him to live in their homelands.[54] From a Narragansett perspective, Williams' settlement was a tributary to the Narragansett nation.[55] The earliest surviving written land evidence for Providence (from March 1638) detailed how Canonicus and Miantonomi had "**sold**" the land to Williams two years ago, establishing and confirming the agreement in writing.[56] It reaffirmed the bounds of the settlement from the lands and

sold: While the Sachems signed the document, it was a colonial record, as is not interpreted the same way by the Narragansett.

52 Williams, *A Key into the Language of America.*

53 For more on the exact timing of when Providence was founded in 1636, see Linda MacLaughlan, "When Was Providence Founded?" *Rhode Island History Journal* 71, no. 1 (Winter/Spring 2013): 21–29.

54 Shurtleff, ed., *Records of the Governor and Company of the Massachusetts Bay*, 1:160–61.

55 Lorén Spears (Executive Director of the Tomaquag Museum and Narragansett Citizen), email correspondence with author, August 2024.

56 Lorén Spears (Executive Director of the Tomaquag Museum and Narragansett Citizen), email correspondence with author, August 2024.

meadows upon the two fresh rivers, Mooshausick and Wanasqutucket, from the river and fields at "Pautuckqut, the great hill of Notquonckanet" to the northwest, and the town of "Maushapogue" to the west.[57]

During his time in Plymouth and Salem, Williams built his relationship with Narragansett Peoples, learning their language, trading with them, and sending them gifts—all of which contributed to their willingness to allow the settlement.[58] Put simply, without the express permission of the Narragansett Sachems, Williams would not have been able to settle in their territory, which would become Providence. From a Native perspective, the land was likely gifted as part of a trade pact with the expectation that Williams would return the favor on a yearly basis through trade or contributions to the nation of which he was a tributary.[59] To further foster the trading agreement, Canonicus "with his own hands" also granted Williams a trading post "at Narragansett," which was readily accessible by land and water.[60]

Williams later recounted (somewhat idealistically) that it was not "price nor Money" that enabled the settlement; it was "obtained by Love."[61] Since his arrival in 1631, Williams had worked to build the foundation of his relationship with the Indigenous People whose homelands he resided on. Williams related how he spared no cost towards them with gifts, tokens, and presents. However, gifting was only part of the agreement, and over the years, Williams worked as a diplomat, scribe, and trader, writing at length about how he was "as a Right hand unto them" to his own cost and travail.[62] He not only offered transport for up to 50 tribal members simultaneously, but also lodged 50 people at a time at his **home**.[63] On his deathbed, Canonicus sent for Williams and wanted to be buried with a cloth that Williams had given him.[64] In 1661, the town of Providence reaffirmed that Williams had secured the settlement with "language, acquaintance, and favor" with the Narragansett, not with money. Williams "bore the charges and ventures of

home: The Williams family home in Providence was a one-room dwelling, but how or if this worked is unclear.

---

57 1638 Deed for Providence, Unmarked Hollinger Box (Founding Documents), Providence City Archives, Providence, RI.

58 Williams also built relations with the Massasoit Ossamequin, Sachem of the Pokanoket Wampanoag.

59 Lorén Spears (Executive Director of the Tomaquag Museum and Narragansett Citizen), email correspondence with author, August 2024.

60 Roger Williams to an Assembly of Commissioners, undated but likely on or before 17 November 1677, *Williams Corres.*, 2:749–53.

61 Roger Williams to [General Court of Commissioners of Providence Plantations?], 25 August 1658, *Williams Corres.*, 2:485; Roger Williams to an Assembly of Commissioners, undated but likely on or before 17 November 1677, *Williams Corres.*, 2:749–53.

62 Roger Williams to John Whipple, Jr., 8 July 1669, *Williams Corres.*, 2:586–88.

63 Roger Williams to an Assembly of Commissioners, undated but likely on or before 17 November 1677, *Williams Corres.*, 2:749–53.

64 Ibid.

all the gratuities" that were given to the "great sachems, and other sachems and natives round about us" in "loving and peaceable neighborhood."[65]

The town was surrounded (and vastly outnumbered by) Indigenous Peoples for most (if not all) of Williams' life; right in the heart of Indian country, it was an important site of long-held traditions of trading and gathering.[66] While Williams described his view and interpretation of the agreement several times throughout his life, one of the frustrating gaps in the surviving sources is the lack of perspective on this agreement from the Narragansett Sachems themselves, in their own words. By combining what Williams wrote with archeological findings and Indigenous oral histories, it seems likely that the Narraganset leaders calculated the political and diplomatic advantages in allowing Williams to settle in Providence. The archival silence of Native voices directly affects the scope of this volume. As you read the sources, try to reframe what Williams wrote from diverse Indigenous perspectives, keeping in mind that the Narragansett, Wampanoag, Pequot, Mohegan, Niantic, Nipmuck, and other Indigenous views of the same event were likely different.

Williams Family Home

From Williams' perspective, the Narragansett sachems gifted the land solely to him, and these proprietary rights in English, as well as colonial precedent, gave him political control over the settlement. But Williams did not heed that precedent; he relinquished nearly all his land to a town common stock and forfeited any special political rights, giving himself a vote equal to others. In designing the physical layout of the town, he also wanted to do something different. Unlike other New England towns, Providence was not designed around a meetinghouse, and all lots were equal, with the head of each house getting a vote. This was an unusual (even utopian) design for the time.[67] The original plots sat along what is now North Main Street and were a long thin strip of land that ran from around Brook Street over the top of the hill down to the river and freshwater spring. The Williamses' lot was no bigger than any of their neighbors, and the house was simple, with one all-purpose room and a small loft. The story-and-a-half high dwelling had a large fireplace and a stone chimney at the end, turned towards the hill. Archaeological excavations on the home in 1906 concluded that the fire room, lower room, or hall was 15 or 16 feet by 17 and about 6.5 feet

65 Memorandum of original agreement for Providence, 20 December 1661, *Records of the Town of Providence*, RG 100, Providence City Archives, Providence City Hall, Providence, RI.

66 Roger Williams to the General Court of Massachusetts Bay, October 5, 1654, *Williams Corres.*, 2:409.

67 Sydney V. James, *The Colonial Metamorphoses in Rhode Island: A Study of Institutions in Change*, ed. Shelia L. Skemp and Bruce C. Daniels (Lebanon, NH: University Press of New England, 2000).

high, with a very steep roof. The foundations were shallow, and if there was a cellar under the house, it was a simple hole to keep potatoes and other items from freezing.[68]

At times the Williamses faced financial hardship. When Plymouth's Governor **Edward Winslow** visited Providence in its early days, he "put a piece of Gold" into Mary's hands for the family's sustenance.[69] Their hardships were in part connected to debts from their time in Plymouth and Salem. Williams had hoped to make a profit on the sale of the family's house in Salem, which never materialized.[70] While the family was in Plymouth, Williams had consigned goods to George Ludlow to sell in Virginia, which resulted in a legal dispute with Ludlow in 1637. Williams described how he had "many debts" and used "many means" trying to recover them.[71] He humbly begged for "what helpe" was available and wrote several times about the family's financial woes.[72] Perhaps some of his claims of poverty were simply in relation to how much money he *could* have made had he joined his neighbors in trading guns and alcohol to Native Peoples.[73]

Edward Winslow: A Separatist who traveled on the *Mayflower* and wrote several important pamphlets. He was a key figure in Plymouth Colony and served in several governmental positions, including governor and assistant governor.

Civil Authority

As the seventeenth century progressed, three additional communities emerged beyond Providence: Portsmouth, Newport, and Shawomet (later Warwick), communities that were often in conflict with one another.[74] As it grew as a home for those **distressed of conscience**, more people who faced banishment joined the experiment, with approximately just under 1,000 people in residence by the 1640s. Williams quickly got to work constructing the apparatus to govern the settlement with a commitment to ensuring the separation of church and state. Unlike England and the rest of New England, the colony had no established church that received tax support. People were free to worship as they chose, which included not worshiping at all if they so desired. The colony's civil compact, which was adopted in August 1637, included the mandate that matters concerning the "public good" be made

distressed of conscience: People who were persecuted for their religious beliefs.

68 Access to the cellar was either on the outside from the lower ground of the sloping hillside, or most likely from within by a trap door (against prowling animals) outside. Norman Isham, "The House of Roger Williams," *Rhode Island Historical Society Collections* 18, no. 2 (April 1925): 33–39; Norman Isham and Albert Brown, *Early Rhode Island Houses: An Historical and Architectural Study* (Providence, RI: Preston & Rounds, 1895).

69 Roger Williams to Major John Mason and Governor Thomas Prence, 22 June 1670, *Williams Corres.*, 2:609–20.

70 *Williams Corres.*, 1:124, footnotes 4 and 5.

71 Roger Williams to Richard Collicut, 12 September 1637, *Williams Corres.*, 1:121–22.

72 Roger Williams to John Winthrop, before 26 October 1637, *Williams Corres.*, 1:125.

73 For more on Williams' relations with Indigenous Peoples, see Fisher, "Roger Williams and the Indian Business."

74 For more on the conflict, see Dennis Allen O'Toole, *Exiles, Refugees, and Rogues: The Quest for Civil Order in the Towns and Colony of Providence Plantations* (Newport, RI: Cosmopolite Press, 2014).

by "major consent," and that the government have authority "only in civil things."[75] Williams' decision to omit any reference to God was deliberate, evincing his belief that it was profane for humans to assume that God embraced any other state than ancient Israel.[76]

The colony's government structure was "Democratic ... a government held by the free and voluntary consent of all, or the greater part of the free inhabitants."[77] To Williams, the government got its power from the consent of the people—and the majority ruled.[78] Officeholders did not have to pass any religious or social test, as Williams was determined to prove that a person's religious beliefs had no bearing on their ability to serve in public office. In *The Bloudy Tenent* (1644), Williams summarized his vision: "The government of the civil Magistrate extended no further than over the bodies and goods of their subjects, not over their souls."[79] This commitment to democracy stood in contrast to policy in England and the rest of New England. King Charles I rejected democracy to reaffirm the monarchy, concluding that the "ills of democracy are tumults, violence and licentiousness."[80] John Winthrop, Governor of Massachusetts Bay, agreed and declared that: "Democracy is, amongst most civil nations, accounted the meanest and worst form of government."[81] John Cotton, Teacher of the Boston Church, concurred: "Democracy, I do not conceive that ever God did ordain as a fit government either from church or commonwealth."[82] Cotton asked: "If the people be governors who shall be governed?"[83] Williams' answer was clear: "the sovereign, original, and foundation of civil power lies in the people."[84] Williams knew first hand that the quest for religious uniformity did not ensure social stability and peace. He demonstrated the fallacy of trying to have only "true" Christians serve as magistrates. According to Williams,

---

75 John Bartlett, ed., *Records of the Colony of Rhode Island and Providence Plantations* (Providence, RI: A Crawford Green, State Printer, 1856), 1:14.

76 For more on Williams' religious beliefs, see W. Clark Gilpin, *The Millenarian Piety of Roger Williams* (Chicago: University of Chicago Press, 1979) and Edmond Morgan, *Roger Williams: The Church and the State*, 2nd ed. (New York: W.W. Norton & Company, 2007).

77 *Report of Arbitrators at Providence containing proposals for a form of government* (1640), Bartlett, ed., *Records of the Colony of Rhode Island*, 1:22–28; 156.

78 Williams, *The Bloudy Tenent.*

79 Ibid.

80 King Charles I, *His Maiesties Answer to the XIX Propositions of Both Houses of Parliament* (London, 1642).

81 Cited in Francis J. Bremmer, *John Winthrop: America's Forgotten Founding Father* (Oxford: Oxford University Press, 2003).

82 Cotton and others in the Bay Colony discussed the idea of an elected, represented government, but did not go as far as to call for full democracy. John Cotton, letter to Lord Say and Sele (1636) in Thomas Hutchinson, *History of the Massachusetts Bay Colony*, 2nd ed. (London, 1765), vol. 1, Appendix 3.

83 Ibid.

84 Williams, *The Bloudy Tenent.*

churches were tasked with nurturing religion; thus it was impossible for mere mortals (representing the state) to do the same job, as they could easily err. In his reasoning, the church could only be successful if it distanced itself from coercive politics.

Parliamentary Patent (1644) and Rhode Island Charter (1663)

As the New England colonies grew in the 1640s, so too did their imperialistic desire for land. Williams' settlement had a prime position along the shores of Narragansett Bay, making it a desirable hub for trade and export. While Williams made settlement and trading agreements with Canonicus and Miantonomi, the other New England colonies did not respect his rights to the land. Thus, Williams sailed to England in 1643 to retroactively get an English charter. He arrived in England amid **civil war** as King Charles I fought against Parliament. Williams drew on his influential connections, including **Oliver Cromwell**, to share his ideas wherever he could, whether it was in Parliament's lobbies, in taverns, or in private homes.[85] Parliament's Committee on Foreign Plantations granted Williams a patent, which confirmed that the colony had to adhere to English laws as far as the "Nature and Constitution of the place" allowed.[86] However, they had had full power and authority to govern and rule themselves by a civil government by "voluntary consent of all."[87] In leaving decisions to majority rule, the committee effectively allowed religious liberty to rule.

civil war: English civil wars and political conflicts between the Royalists (headed by King Charles I) and Parliamentarians between 1642 and 1651. During the conflict, Puritans fought on the side of Parliament.

Oliver Cromwell: A Puritan who led the Parliamentarians in the English Civil War. Following the execution of King Charles I in 1649, Cromwell ruled England as Lord Protector between 1653 and 1659.

The 1644 patent was revolutionary; however, its long-term impact was hampered by turmoil on both sides of the Atlantic. Williams' colony had begun as a collection of three (eventually four) towns—Providence, Portsmouth, Newport, and later Warwick—and each town guarded its independence. Other colonists played important roles in the founding of towns beyond Providence. In April 1651, William Coddington returned to Rhode Island with a commission as governor-for-life of the island, where Newport and Portsmouth were located. Williams and others were duly concerned about Coddington's takeover. Amidst this tumult, Williams sailed back to England again with **John Clarke** of Newport in 1651 to try to revoke Coddington's patent and secure a stronger charter for the colony.[88] Following the execution of King Charles I in 1649, England had bigger

John Clarke: Baptist minister and physician who played an important role in founding the towns of Portsmouth and Newport on Aquidneck Island. Clarke crafted and secured the 1663 charter.

---

85 Barry, *Roger Williams and the Creation of the American Soul*, 13.

86 The document is recorded using the original seventeenth-century calendar, 1643 Parliamentary Patent, Land and Public Notary Records, C#0481, Rhode Island State Archives, Providence, RI, 3:344–49.

87 Ibid.

88 For more on Clarke's role, see Sydney V. James, *John Clarke and His Legacies: Religion and Law in Colonial Rhode Island, 1638–1730*, ed. Theodore Dwight Bozeman (University Park, PA: Penn State Press, 2008).

governing issues to resolve than dealing with a small colony of radicals across the Atlantic. Williams returned to Rhode Island in 1654, but Clarke diligently remained in England for another decade to defend Rhode Island's interests against the efforts of other New England colonies and to try to get an improved charter.[89]

During this time, Clarke witnessed England's bloody transformation from monarchy to commonwealth and back again. Rhode Island was clearly not at the forefront of England's concerns during the 1650s. With the **restoration of the monarchy** in 1660, the king voided all actions taken by Parliament in the absence of the monarch, including Williams' 1644 patent. A new charter had to be obtained to prevent the colony from being swallowed up by its neighbors. The issue was finally resolved when **King Charles II** approved the charter in July 1663. The King's royal authority dominated the opening of the charter physically and in the text. King Charles II, whose own father had been executed by a Parliament headed by Puritans in 1649, allowed Rhode Island to be a testing ground.[90] For the King, the colony was far enough away and small enough to demonstrate the lived reality of religious liberty and separation of church and state.[91]

restoration of the monarchy: The restoration of the Stuart monarchy took place in 1660 when King Charles II returned from exile in Europe to assume the throne.

King Charles II: King of England from 1660 to 1685.

Writing in 1670, Williams still held onto the legal and symbolic importance of the document, which he described as a "jewel" and the King's "extraordinary favor" with his endorsement. In the seventeenth century, the concept of "freedom" was something that a person was born with, and "liberty" was how those rights were expressed in the law. Williams, a legal stickler, fully understood the implications when the King "declared himself that he would experiment whether Civil Government could consist with such a Liberty of Conscience." Though only a small corner of the English Atlantic world, the colony offered refuge to "the poor and persecuted." The King's approval allowed "all the World" to see the "Royal promise" which provisioned that nobody in the colony could be "molested or questioned" over religious matters provided they kept the civil peace.[92] Williams' used the King's approval of Rhode Island's system as a club against his neighboring

89 Before returning to Rhode Island, Williams anonymously published *The Fourth Paper, Presented by Major Butler* (London, 1652) and *The Examiner Defended in a Fair and Sober answer* (London, 1652). He also published an attack on the mandatory public support of clergy in *The Hirelings Ministry None of Christs* (London, 1652).

90 Scholars have debated whether King Charles II saw the 1663 charter as a way of intentionally provoking Massachusetts Bay, where some regicides were hiding in plain sight. For an exploration of King Charles II using the 1663 Charter to create a potential royalist base to hedge in the Bay, especially during the 1665 visit by the Royal Commissioners, see Adrian Weimer, *A Constitutional Culture: New England and the Struggle against Arbitrary Rule in the Restoration Empire* (Philadelphia: University of Pennsylvania Press, 2023).

91 *Rhode Island Royal Charter* (1663).

92 Roger Williams to Major John Wilson and Governor Thomas Prence, 22 June 1670, *Williams Corres.*, 2:616.

colonies that persecuted Quakers, Baptists, and other dissenters. Williams' praise for King Charles II stands in direct contrast to the disparaging remarks he made about the King's father, King Charles I, who Williams described as "vicious," a "Swearer from his youth," and an "oppressor and persecutor of Good Men."[93] King Charles II granting the charter changed everything for Williams, and the year before he died he reflected that "Our Charter Excels all in New England or the World, as to the Souls of Men."[94] Williams' greatest contribution to religious freedom was not that he simply espoused the theory of liberty, but that he created a geographical space where those principles could be lived. Without an instrument of civil government for Rhode Island and Providence Plantations, Williams' laudable opinions would have remained simply theoretical.

Mary Williams: Maintaining Providence

great man: The "great man" approach to history, popular in the nineteenth century, argued that most of history can be explained by the influence of male leadership. New approaches to history from the 1960s onwards, including social and cultural history, women's history, and bottom-up history, have fundamentally challenged the flaws in the "great man" approach.

The traditional "**great man**" historical narrative depicts Roger as a lone hero in the grand founding of Providence, but none of his accomplishments would have been possible without Mary Williams. For months and even years at a time, Mary was the head of the Williams family—not only in the immediate aftermath of Roger's banishment, but also once they settled in Providence. While there is only one surviving example of Mary's handwriting, creative reading of other sources demonstrate that Mary Williams was a force to be reckoned with in her own right.[95] Throughout almost half a century of marriage, Mary alone made many of the decisions for her family and the wider community, as her husband traveled far and wide, from the depths of Indian country to traversing the Atlantic.[96] Mary played a central role in key matters in the colony, from providing medical knowledge to confirming crucial land evidence. She spent large swaths of time away from Roger but refused to rejoin him on a three-year trip to England, even though he begged her.[97] By the time Roger returned to Providence in June 1654, Mary had been managing the Williams family affairs alone in Providence for almost three years. With Roger gone, Mary played an important role in keeping Rhode Island's "lively experiment" alive.[98]

---

93 Roger Williams to Anne Sadleir, Winter 1652/53, *Williams Corres.*, 1:374.

94 Roger Williams to the Town of Providence, 15 January 1682, *Williams Corres.*, 2:775.

95 Charlotte Carrington-Farmer, "More Than Roger's Wife: Mary Williams and the Founding of Providence," *The New England Quarterly* 97, no. 3 (Sept. 2024): 308–44.

96 Laurel Thatcher Ulrich explores the immense burdens and the considerable power of a New England housewife's domestic life in *Good Wives: Image and Reality in the Lives of Women in Northern New England, 1650–1750* (New York: Alfred Knopf, 1982).

97 For more on using sources creatively to write women's history, see Laurel Thatcher Ulrich, "Of Pens and Needles: Sources in Early American Women's History," *Journal of American History* 77, no. 1 (June 1990): 200–07.

98 *Rhode Island Royal Charter* (1663).

Williams and Harris

Williams' experiment in liberty was not a fairytale-like happy-ever-after story. On the ground, Rhode Island's experimental system of governance led to chronic dysfunction, internal disputes, and chaos. Men elected to office refused to serve, towns refused to pay taxes, and land ownership disputes rocked the colony. Contemporaries described how Rhode Islanders were "brawling continually in Mr. Williams meadow." Even the Dutch in New Amsterdam referred to Rhode Islanders as "scum." Outsiders insulted Rhode Island with a colorful plethora of slurs, including "Rogues Island," the receptacle for "all sorts of riff-raff," and the "sewers (*latrina*) of New England."[99]

Founding and maintaining a colony where all were welcome if they obeyed the civil laws tested Roger Williams to the maximum, and one such example was his strife with William Harris. Harris hated Williams so much that he could not even acknowledge Williams was human, asking rhetorically, on several occasions, what (not who) Roger Williams was.[100] Harris accused Williams of unscrupulously taking Providence in his own name, deceitfully making profits on land sales, and inciting conflict between Providence and Pawtuxet. According to Harris, Williams was a fool, ass, simple dunce, knave, liar, thief, cheater, hypocrite, drunkard, traitor, deceiver of Jesus, madman, glutton, blasphemer, traitor, and "a whore monger" with Native women—quite the list! One by one, Williams dismissed all of Harris' claims as "Unrighteous and Ridiculous."[101] Williams also lobbed back several insults, accusing Harris of being a rogue, a thief, and a liar.

Williams and Harris had traveled together on the same ship from England in 1631 and both had settled in Salem. When Williams was banished and removed to Providence, Harris promptly followed him. Harris was one of the original proprietors of the land evidence in Providence, but later moved to Pawtuxet and held a number of important roles in the General Court. It is hard to pinpoint when and why the conflict started, but by the mid-1650s their mutual dislike was evident. Over time, land disputes dominated the Williams–Harris conflict, coming to a head between 1660 and 1678. Harris sought to extend Pawtuxet's boundary westward by requesting confirmation land evidences from the Narragansett, causing much controversy. Williams fundamentally disagreed, believing Harris simply wanted the extra land for his own personal profit.

Harris tried all kinds of tactics to win the land dispute and garner political power after being ousted from office. The land conflict spewed into

99 LaFantasie, editorial note "Samuel Gorton in Providence," *Williams Corres*, 1:211; Barry, *Roger Williams and the Creation of the American Soul*, 13, 309; Warren, *God, War, and Providence*, 75, 172.

100 Roger Williams to John Whipple, Jr., 8 July 1669, *Williams Corres.*, 2:586–88.

101 Roger Williams to an Assembly of Commissioners, undated but likely on or before 17 November 1677, *Williams Corres.*, 2:749–53.

the political arena, and town meetings were not only divisive, but riotous—at times literally so. The dispute rapidly escalated soap-opera style, with an attempt to stop townsmen voting in the annual election, a refusal to turn over town records, and Harris going as far as setting up a rival town meeting. However, the most dramatic plot twist was the accusation of treason that followed. In August 1668, Williams composed a petition to the Rhode Island magistrates denouncing Harris for his abuse of King Charles II's "Name and Authority" and his shameful oppression of his majesty's loyal and peaceable subjects in Providence. The list of charges against Harris addressed his foul tongue, dissembling tactics, and "dirt of Reproach and Threatening."[102] Williams even wrote a poem about Harris and shared his disapproving "presentation in Verse" about Harris at a town meeting.[103] Williams was furious that other Providence residents, such as **John Whipple, Jr.**, sided with Harris. Harris went back to England multiple times to advocate for his land claim, even presenting his case before the Privy Council. After facing prison due to conflict in Connecticut and controversy over the Providence–Pawtuxet land disputes, Harris boarded a ship once again bound for England in 1679. However, he was captured and held captive in Algiers by pirates for two years. Upon release, he eventually made it back to England but died shortly after arrival. The Williams–Harris contretemps offers a different perspective on the well-known story of Williams' life and legacy and illustrates the very real issues Williams faced on the ground. The conflict with Harris forced Williams not only to clarify the original boundaries of Providence but to justify its very existence.

John Whipple, Jr.: An early settler in Providence. He migrated to Massachusetts with Roger Williams on the *Lyon* in 1631. He lived with his family in Dorchester, Massachusetts before moving to Providence.

INDIGENOUS PEOPLES

A Key into the Language of America

Williams' language skills set him apart and defined his life. With a command of Latin, Greek, Hebrew, French, Dutch, and Narragansett, his linguistic ability was exceptional.[104] Immediately upon arrival in the Dawnland, Williams set about learning and trying to understand the Algonquian language family. Looking back, he reflected (perhaps naively) that his "Soules desire was to do the Natives good" and "to that End to learn their

---

102 Town of Providence to Governor and Council of Rhode Island, 31 August 1668. Cited in LaFantasie, "Partisan Politics and the Pawtuxet Controversy: Editorial Note," *Williams Corres.*, 2:556–70.

103 Sadly, the poem has not survived. Early Records of Providence, 3: 139. Cited in ibid.

104 Fisher, "Roger Williams and the Indian Business," 356.

Language."[105] Williams repeatedly catalogued his "Constant" and "Zealous desire" to "dive into the Natives language," which began when he lived in Plymouth and Salem. He related the lengths he went to "gain their Tongue," and how his "Painful, Patient spirit" drove him to lodge with Native Peoples in their "filthy Smoky holes." Although Williams had doubts at times about his fluency, he recorded how he was known to all Wampanoag and Narragansett for his work as a public speaker, debating them "at great Measure" in their own languages.[106]

Williams published his groundbreaking work, *A Key into the Language of America*, in 1643. In it, Williams not only offered translations of Narragansett words and phrases, but also **ethnographic observations**. In the introduction, Williams listed the names that the English settlers used to collectively describe Indigenous Peoples, which included Natives, Indians, Savages, Wild-men, Pagans, Barbarians, and Heathens. He noted that his Indigenous neighbors often asked him why the English called them "Indian Natives," and when Williams explained they began to "call themselves Indians, in opposition to English." But he reminded his readers that prior to European settlement, Native Peoples did not have "any Names to difference themselves from strangers," but used *Ninnimissinnûwock* (or Ninnimissinuok) as a collective term for "the People" and then "particular names, peculiar to several Nations" such as Narragansett, Pequot, Massachusett, etc. Williams reported how within a 200-mile radius of Providence, Algonquian dialects "exceedingly differ." He clarified that the dialects were understandable in many ways, and he hoped that *A Key* would help settlers "converse with thousands of Natives all over the Country." While the book was "framed chiefly" after the Narragansett dialect (according to Williams, the "most spoken in the Country"), with attention to the variations in peoples and dialects, the guide could be useful in "all parts of the Country." On the front cover, Williams addressed his hopes for the book, namely that it would be of "special use (upon all occasions) to all the English" in New England, while also being "pleasant and profitable" to "all men."

ethnographic observations: In this context, refers to Williams studying Indigenous culture through an anthropological lens. Williams was a white Protestant man, and his understanding of Narragansett culture was fundamentally shaped by his own bias and world view.

At its core, the book is a dictionary and phrase book with the practical purpose of enabling conversation with Algonquian speakers, but Williams also had other goals for the book. His declaration that it would be useful for all the English in New England was a dig at his Puritan neighbors for their lack of effort to learn the language (and culture) of the land's original inhabitants. As the cover suggested, Williams also believed the book had a wider appeal outside of New England. Moreover, by publishing it in London,

105 Roger Williams to an Assembly of Commissioners, undated but likely on or before 17 November 1677, *Williams Corres.*, 2:749–53.

106 Ibid.

he hoped it would also help to secure a charter for Rhode Island.[107] Williams used his ethnographic observations to remind other New Englanders that Native People were equal in God's eye. Williams famously declared, "Nature knows no difference between *Europe* and *Americans* in blood, birth, bodies, &c." He exhorted his countrymen: "Boast not proud English, of thy birth & blood" as "Thy brother Indian is by birth as Good."[108]

Careful reading of *A Key* provides a glimpse of Native perspectives on interactions with settler-colonists. Williams recorded how his Indigenous neighbors often asked him, "Why come the *Englishmen* hither?" He shared their conclusion that it was because the English "burnt up the *wood* in one place ... and so to remove to a fresh new place for the *woods* sake." He also offered Native perspectives on English clothes, and how "Our English clothes are so strange unto them." Williams explained the Narragansett word for Englishmen, "Waútacone-nûaog," meaning "Coat-men," i.e., clothed men. *A Key* relates a "solemn Oration" between Canonicus and Williams on the trustworthiness of the English. Canonicus made it clear that "if the *Englishmen* speak true" then he would go to his "grave in peace," knowing that the English and Narragansett lived "in love and peace together." Williams replied that Canonicus had no reason to doubt the English settler-colonist's faithfulness, friendship, and trustworthiness. Canonicus promptly took a stick and broke it into ten pieces, and related how each stick represented an instance that gave him cause to fear the English. Descriptive passages such as this offer some insight into Narragansett perspectives of the devastating effects of settler-colonization. But, in practice, *A Key* and indeed Williams had their limits: as a white English man, who had a particular goal for his publication, there was only so much he could (and perhaps should) understand.

Tomaquag Museum: Rhode Island's only museum dedicated to telling the stories of the Indigenous cultures of the Dawnland (Southern New England). Established in 1958, the museum is Indigenous-led and tells first-person histories through engagement and shared dialogue to reconcile the past and empower present and future generations.

Lorén Spears: Enrolled Narragansett Tribal Nation citizen and Executive Director of the Tomaquag Museum.

The ***Tomaquag Museum*** *Edition: Roger Williams, A Key into the Language of America* (2019) assesses Williams' success in this endeavor. For the book, Narragansett citizens, culture keepers, and scholars collaborated to offer a new edition of Williams' 1643 work. With a thoughtful preface by **Lorén Spears** and footnotes identifying Narragansett perspectives on Williams' translations and ethnographic observations, the *Tomaquag Edition* offers a unique way to recenter Narragansett perspectives in Williams' writings. The preface acknowledges the importance of Williams' work: "Along with the passing down of language through the generations by our ancestors and Elders, Roger Williams' documentation of the Narragansett language is key

107 Jonathan Beecher Field, "A Key for the Gate: Roger Williams, Parliament, and Providence," *The New England Quarterly* 80, no. 3 (Sept. 2007): 353–82.

108 Williams, *A Key*.

to its survival into the twenty-first century."[109] Sources such as the *Tomaquag Edition* offer a glimpse of the dark side of Williams' role in subverting Native Worlds, pitted against Indigenous survival, resistance, and agency.

Trade

Williams' daily life revolved around sustained complex interactions with the Ninnimissinuok at his home, trading post, in their **wetuash**, and beyond. To this point, historian, Julie Fisher calculates that 70 percent of his extant correspondence references Native Peoples, with at least 85 Indigenous individuals specifically named.[110] Even when Williams was in England on charter business, Indigenous news and politics were still central facets of his world and feature in his correspondence. Williams' work as a trader enabled and fostered his relationship with Native Peoples. Canonicus "with his own hands" granted Williams permission to set up his trading post in a mutually beneficial spot in Narragansett homelands, which was readily accessible by land and water.[111] Williams' trading post at Cocumscussoc was an economic success, and he recorded how it yielded £100 per year.[112] Williams operated the trading post for just over a decade, and Glenn LaFantasie suggests that when the trading post was at its peak in the late 1640s, Williams was there from late summer to the late spring, with only brief visits back to Providence.[113]

wetuash: A Wampanoag home is called a wetu, and wetuash means homes (plural).

Williams' trading post was regularly abuzz with activity—as Native Peoples came to trade wampum, pelts, corn, and other items for English goods including kettles, metal utensils, and cloth. Williams' family sometimes came to visit, as did English and Dutch traders. The site was also a place of refuge for Williams away from the political disputes that embroiled Providence.[114] Williams' trading post was profitable, but it was not as profitable as it could have been, as (unlike many of his peers) he refused to trade munitions and alcohol.[115] The trading post was not simply a site for economic

---

109 Dawn Dove, Sandra Robinson, Lorén Spears, Dorothy Herman Papp, and Kathleen J. Bragdon, eds., *The Tomaquag Museum Edition: Roger Williams, A Key into the Language of America* (Yardley, PA: Westholme, 2019), xi–xiii.

110 Williams was not the only settler-colonist to learn Narragansett nor the only one offering services such as writing letters and petitions on behalf of Indigenous Peoples. Fisher, "Roger Williams and the Indian Business," 354.

111 Roger Williams to an Assembly of Commissioners, undated but likely on or before 17 November 1677, *Williams Corres.*, 2:749–53.

112 Ibid.

113 Glenn LaFantasie, "A Day in the Life of Roger Williams," *Rhode Island History Journal* 46, no. 3 (1987): 99.

114 Ibid., 100.

115 Williams eventually sold his trading post to fund his voyage back to England to pursue a royal charter for the colony. Fisher, "Roger Williams and the Indian Business," 382–84; LaFantasie, "A Day in the Life of Roger Williams," 101.

interactions, it played a central role in diplomatic negotiations and social interactions with various **Native Nations**.[116]

Native Nations: According to Lorén Spears (Enrolled Narragansett Tribal Nation citizen and Executive Director of the Tomaquag Museum), using the word Nation rather than "tribe" reinforces Indigenous sovereignty and pushes back against settler-colonial vocabulary.

Conversion

Williams' experiment in religious freedom had implications for his interactions with the Ninnimissinuok, and his views on converting Native Peoples to Christianity evolved during his life. Corresponding with John Winthrop, Jr. in 1632, Williams indicated that he longed for "natives Soules."[117] However, he later changed his mind and famously declared that "forced Worship stinks in Gods Nostrils."[118] It is not clear if Williams actively tried to convert any Indigenous Peoples to Christianity prior to founding Providence, and he likely feared false conversions. Moreover, Williams did not believe in imposing Christian beliefs or English culture upon Native Peoples against their will. Williams upheld that no person nor any earthly church had a monopoly on religious truth and he exhorted First Peoples to "seek the truth."[119] Williams simultaneously upheld that Natives conjured the Devil and were pagans and labored in "spiritual darkness" with their "barbarous" behavior as heathens while also trying to learn all he could about their spiritual and temporal worlds.[120] In *A Key*, Williams noted that Narragansett Peoples had a "modest Religious persuasion" and did not "disturb any man, either themselves *English, Dutch*, or any in their Conscience, and worship."[121]

Williams consolidated his views in *Christenings make not Christians* (1645).[122] By this point, following his own **believer's baptism**, Williams was convinced that a valid baptism needed knowing consent.[123] Thus, he not only questioned the validity of infant baptism but increasingly the missionary efforts to convert Native Peoples to Christianity. Williams contended that baptizing Natives was false because they did not truly understand scripture and thus relied on another person's translation and interpretation. Despite his effort to learn Narragansett, he lamented that conversion was not possible and "it is out of question to me, that I may not pretend a false conversion."[124]

believer's baptism: The practice of baptizing those who are able to make a conscious profession of faith, unlike infant baptism.

116 Lorén Spears (Executive Director of the Tomaquag Museum and Narragansett Citizen), email correspondence with author, September 2024.

117 Roger Williams to John Winthrop, Jr., July and December 1632, *Williams Corres.*, 1:8.

118 Roger Williams to Major John Wilson and Governor Thomas Prence, 22 June 1670, *Williams Corres.*, 2:671.

119 James Warren, *God, War, and Providence: The Epic Struggle of Roger Williams and the Narragansett Indians against the Puritans of New England* (New York: Scribner, 2018), 46–47.

120 Warren, *God, War, and Providence*, 46.

121 Williams, *A Key*.

122 Williams, *Christenings make not Christians*.

123 For more on Williams' own religious views, see J. Stanley Lemons, "Roger Williams Was Not a Seeker but a 'Witness in Sackcloth,'" *New England Quarterly* 88, no. 4 (2015): 693–714.

124 Williams, *Christenings make not Christians*.

In light of these views, it is unsurprising that Williams objected to the work of the Bay Colony's chief missionary, **John Eliot**. Eliot had no qualms about leading efforts to translate the Bible into Wôpanâôt8âôk (Wampanoag) and setting up Praying Towns to push conversion efforts along with cultural and religious erasure.[125] Williams' lived political reality also influenced his thoughts on conversion. He was aware of why the Narragansett Sachems allowed him to settle in their homelands, the terms of that agreement, and how his settlement was surrounded and outnumbered by his Ninnimissinuok neighbors. While Williams did have theological concerns about conversion, his reluctance also came from the time he spent in Indian country. Archival silences mean that we do not have perspectives written by Native Peoples and thus can only speculate on what they thought about Williams' efforts to learn their language and then publish it, his trading practices, and his ideas about religion. In this respect, works such as the *Tomaquag Edition* of *A Key* are invaluable resources offering Indigenous perspectives of the past and how it connects to the present.

John Eliot: Puritan missionary in Massachusetts who tried to convert Indigenous Peoples to Christianity, set up "Praying Towns," and translated the Bible.

Diplomacy, War, and Enslavement

Williams had his own economic, political, and ideological goals in New England, which at times directly conflicted with Native Peoples and their worlds. William played various roles in the two key wars for New England: the Pequot War (1636–38) and King Philip's War (1675–76).[126] Williams wrote letters and brokered deals as a diplomat throughout both wars, but at the end of each, he was directly involved in the enslavement of Native Peoples. The Pequot War was a defining moment for Native Peoples in Southern New England, when the Pequot fought against the settlers and their Indigenous allies. Hundreds of Pequot lost their lives in the conflict, particularly in the massacre at Mystic when the English surrounded the Pequot village, set it alight, and slayed anyone (including women and children) who fled. Survivors were either executed, enslaved, or indentured, and being Pequot was made **illegal**. Despite the settler-colonist's efforts to wipe out the Pequot, the Tribal Nation adapted, survived, resisted, and remain on their **ancestral homelands** today. Acknowledging that Indigenous Peoples are not a conquered or vanished people is one small part of wider decolonization efforts.

Williams chronicled his "hazardous and weighty" role in negotiations between the English and the Narragansett when the Pequot tried

illegal: The Treaty of Hartford (1638) stipulated that the name Pequot could not be used. In practice, this did not happen and within a few years, colonial records would include the name Pequot.

ancestral homelands: The Mashantucket (Western) Pequot Tribal Nation homelands are in what is now Connecticut.

125 John Eliot, *The Holy Bible: Containing the Old Testament and the New Translated into the Indian Language* (Cambridge, MA, 1663). For information on how the Eliot Bible has been used to revive the spoken Wôpanâak language today, see "Wôpanâak Language Reclamation Project," http://www.wlrp.org.

126 Scholarship is divided on the exact end of King Philip's War, as the fighting continued for several years further north.

(unsuccessfully) to recruit the Narragansett as allies. Williams did not mince his words, describing how this "almost ended" his "work and life together."[127] Williams claimed that he was involved in "all the great Transactions of War or Peace between the English and the Natives." He did not shy away from reminding (and shaming) those who had banished him from Massachusetts Bay how he had not spared "Purse, nor Pains nor Hazards (very many times)" so that the "Whole Land English and Natives might sleep in peace Securely."[128] According to Williams, Canonicus and Miantonomi invited him to operate as a "Counselor and Secretary in all their Wars," including with the "Pequts Monhiggins Long Islanders Wampanoogse."[129] Although Williams wrote at length about his work as a diplomat in Indian country, accounts from the perspective of the Narragansett Sachems have not survived. Given their diplomatic prowess and power, recruiting Williams to aid with affairs was on their own terms and for their own purposes. Even if Williams only partly understood Indigenous politics, his letters shed light on the dynamic and far-reaching nature of intra- and inter-tribal and national politics.

Williams' position as a diplomat was put to the test in the immediate aftermath of the Pequot War, when a former soldier and servant, Arthur Peach, murdered a Nipmuck trader, Penowanyanquis. Williams mediated with Plymouth and Massachusetts Bay to bring Peach to justice.[130] Williams' efforts to get justice for Penowanyanquis casts him as a "friend" to Native Peoples, something Williams repeatedly reaffirmed himself: "I have been and am a friend to the Natives."[131] However, Williams was a white English settler-colonist, who at times, put his own interests (and those of his countrymen) above different Native interests. Moreover, he made it clear that despite his close relationship with the Narragansett, he had not "turned Indian."[132]

Williams' household changed in the wake of the war with the addition of an unfree Indigenous boy in the summer of 1637. As the English and their Native allies debated what to do with the Pequot captives (mostly women and children), Williams dashed off a letter to the Massachusetts Bay Governor asking to keep one of the children. Williams had set his eye on one particular boy, but he made it clear he would take any of the Pequot

---

127 Roger Williams to the General Court of Massachusetts Bay, 5 October 1654, *Williams Corres.*, 2:408–13.

128 Ibid.

129 Roger Williams to an Assembly of Commissioners, undated but likely on or before 17 November 1677, *Williams Corres.*, 2:749–53.

130 Roger Williams to John Winthrop, ca. 1 August 1638, *Williams Corres.*, 1:170–73.

131 Roger Williams to the General Court of Massachusetts Bay, 5 October 1654, *Williams Corres.*, 2:408–13

132 Roger Williams to John Winthrop, 14 June 1638, *Williams Corres.*, 1:162–65.

children.[133] Williams got the boy he requested, observing that the boy's father was of Sasquakit, and the boy's mother and two siblings were with Winthrop in Massachusetts Bay. As he closed his letter, Williams had one more request for Winthrop: to name the boy.[134] It is ambiguous whether the child was enslaved or indentured, but nonetheless, just one year after the founding of Providence, Williams had an unfree Indigenous child living in his house with his two young daughters.[135] Removing the child from his family and erasing his identity by renaming him underscores the harsh reality of conquest in the wake of the war.[136]

Williams' views on enslavement were complex and evolved during his life. After the war, Williams argued that perpetual slavery would be fully justifiable for Pequot survivors. However, he urged that after a period of training up to "labor, and restraint," the **enslaved** should be set free, but carefully monitored. In practice, the line between limited term and lifelong unfreedom was often blurred. A year later, Williams referred to "Will ... my Indian servant," most likely the same boy. Williams' correspondence reveals how Will worked as a mediator between Winthrop, the Narragansett, and the Connecticut authorities.[137] By 1639, the Williams family had another servant, Joshua Winsor, in their home.[138] Later, the family had a Dutch servant, John Clauson, living with them after he sought freedom from his indentureship in the New Netherlands in 1647. Williams described how Clauson had been lost, naked, and starving, and how Native friends sought Williams' help due to his fluency in Dutch. According to Williams, the family gave Clauson endless possible "Helpe and Favour" and "cherished him."[139]

enslaved: Using the term enslaved (rather than slave) emphasizes the humanity of an individual and acknowledges that the person was forcibly placed into the condition of slavery by another individual or group. Using the term enslaver (rather than owner or master) challenges hierarchical language and recognizes that the person actively enslaved other humans.

133 Roger Williams to John Winthrop, 30 June 1637, *Williams Corres.*, 1:88–89.

134 Roger Williams to John Winthrop, 31 July 1637, *Williams Corres.*, 1:108–09.

135 In 1637 the colony did not have a slave law in place, and no New England colony had a slave code until Massachusetts adopted one in 1651. The following year, Providence Plantations passed a law stating that "no black mankind or white" should be forced into slavery for more than ten years for adults, or until the age of twenty-four if enslaved prior to the age of 14. However, the 1652 law did not mention Indigenous Peoples and, in practice, was not enforced by the end of the seventeenth century.

136 For more on Indigenous enslavement and the reality of "stolen relations," see "Stolen Relations: Recovering Stories of Indigenous Enslavement in the Americas" https://indigenousslavery.org/about/.

137 Several genealogists have investigated claims that Mary and Roger had an additional indentured servant named Thomas Angell, who traveled from England on the *Lyon* with them in 1631. Some suggest that Angell was a cousin and/or a servant/hired hand, but documentary proof of this is scant. More research (especially using records in England) is needed to verify the status of Angell and his relationship to Williams.

138 Roger Williams to John Winthrop, ca. 1 August 1638, *Williams Corres.*, 1:170–73; Roger Williams to John Winthrop, ca. October 1638, *Williams Corres.*, 1:189–90.

139 On the night of 4 January 1661, Clauson (also spelt Clawson) was murdered by an Indigenous man identified as Waumaion, who confessed and was sentenced to be hanged. Since Clauson died intestate and without relatives, there was significant dispute about his estate. See From the Quarterly Court of Providence, 27 April 1661, *Williams Corres.*, 2:519; Roger Williams to the Town of Providence, 11 May 1661, *Williams Corres.*, 2:520–21.

Metacom: Sometimes referred to as Pometacom, the Sachem of the Pokanoket Wampanoag. He adopted the English name "King Philip."

Williams' diplomatic efforts ultimately failed in King Philip's War (1675–76). The war, named after **Metacom** ("King Philip"), was a multi-tribal and national collaboration to push back against the devastating effects of settler-colonialism. Though sparked by the murder of a Christian Native, tensions had been growing for decades as settler-colonists took Native lands and tried to erase Indigenous cultures, religions, and traditional ways of life. The war was a bitter conclusion for Williams, and his efforts to live peaceably with his Native neighbors ultimately failed.[140] He lived his final years in poverty after his house and town were burned to the ground. After the war, a collective of Providence residents, including Williams, sold Indigenous Peoples into slavery in the Caribbean and around the Atlantic World.[141] Known leaders were executed, often publicly. One native leader, Chuff, was executed by firing squad in Providence under the watchful eye of Williams after he surrendered. Williams' son, Providence, "cleared the town by his vessel of all the Indians to the great peace and Content of the [English] Inhabitants." In other words, Providence transported enslaved Indigenous men, women, and children to the Caribbean. Residents, including Roger Williams, were rewarded with shares from the sale of Indigenous Peoples in slavery.[142] New scholarship acknowledges this terrible transformation of Williams' Indian business "from trading with Indians to trading Indians."[143]

cultural genocide: The systematic destruction of traditions, values, language, and other elements of Indigenous cultures and ways of life.

reunification powwow: In 2002 a delegation of Wampanoag, Pequot, and Narragansett citizens traveled to Bermuda to participate in a "Reconnection Indian Festival"; the reunification powwow has been held several times since.

Despite enslavement, forced removal, and attempted **cultural genocide**, just like the Pequot forty years earlier, the Wampanoag, Narragansett, Nipmuck, and their Indigenous allies survived, adapted, and persisted after the war. They remain on their ancestral homelands, retain traditional knowledge and language, and have made meaningful connections with their ancestors who were sold into slavery in the Caribbean via **reunification powwows**. They are still here—despite the devastating impact of settler-colonization in which Williams played his part.

---

140 For more on the war, see Jill Lepore, *In the Name of War: King Philip's War and the Origins of American Identity* (New York: Vintage, 1999); Lisa Brooks, *Our Beloved Kin: A New History of King Philip's War* (New Haven, CT: Yale University Press, 2019); Christine M. DeLucia, *Memory Lands: King Philip's War and the Place of Violence in the Northeast* (New Haven, CT: Yale University Press, 2019).

141 For more on slavery in seventeenth-century New England, see Wendy Warren, *New England Bound: Slavery and Colonization in Early America* (New York: Liveright, 2016).

142 The ties of bondage between New England and the West Indies were so strong that in 1676, the Assembly in Barbados passed an act to prohibit the importation of Indigenous People from New England. Linford Fisher, "'Dangerous Designes': The 1676 Barbados Act to Prohibit New England Indian Slave Importation," *The William and Mary Quarterly* 71, no. 1 (2014): 99–124.

143 Fisher, "Roger Williams and the Indian Business," 393.

The Theory and Practice of Religious Freedom and Separation of Church and State

Many statues of Williams mistakenly depict him clutching a book with the bold declaration of "Soul Liberty" on the front cover. To be clear, Williams never published a book with that title, but the idea of religious liberty was one of Williams' guiding principles. While some of Williams' contemporaries advocated for (and allowed some type of) toleration, Williams went further and put religious liberty (not simply toleration) into practice on the ground.[144] Williams abhorred any form of religious persecution, intrepidly declaring that any "souls compelled and forced into hypocrisy" of forced worship was akin to "spiritual and soul rape."[145] To Williams, religious liberty meant that there should be no laws "concerning Religion, God, the Soules of men." Put simply, the government should not take a position on religious issues.[146]

Williams was deeply religious by any standards, then and now, but he built a society where others could thrive apart from religious impositions by the government. Williams' vision meant that everyone could exercise their religion freely as they long as did not disrupt civic life and nobody could leverage governmental power to impose their beliefs (for both believers and non-believers). The civil and religious spheres were fully separate; there was no established church and no tax money went towards supporting any church. The colony also fully addressed the issue of ministers holding public office, and the colony's government could not impose the "first table" requirements.[147]

Williams did not simply advocate for religious toleration; he went further and created a place where religious freedom (not simply toleration) ruled, and church and state were fully separated. While other places in Europe had experimented with limited religious toleration, it was nothing compared to Rhode Island's bold experiment in religious freedom for all.[148] Williams

---

144 For a discussion of the key concepts and theories of toleration in the seventeenth century and the practice of toleration in Williams' time, see John Coffey, *Persecution and Toleration in Protestant England, 1558–1689* (New York: Routledge, 2000).

145 Williams, *Bloudy Tenent.*

146 Ibid.

147 In Rhode Island, the government could not prosecute heresy, and in some ways, the colony was agnostic about the origins of the laws; however, this did not prevent people from seeing them as God-ordained (if they so chose).

148 In 1555, the Peace of Augsburg allowed subjects within different territories of the Holy Roman Empire to emigrate to another territory if they objected to the religion their local leader adhered to. However, this applied only to Catholics and Lutherans. The Dutch moved consistently towards toleration, but only because they had to. Calvinists lived alongside Catholics following a fracturing from Spain in 1570, and thus the United Provinces chose *de facto* toleration. However, each Dutch province still had a state church and the Dutch persecuted Arminians after 1609. Barry, *Roger Williams and the Creation of the American Soul*, 317.

went against the grain of mainstream European political traditions and universal public opinion from the thirteenth to the seventeenth century, which demanded death for heretics.[149] And he was not the only person to write in favor of toleration; others, including **Sebastian Castellio** and **Hugo Grotius**, advocated for toleration, but they (unlike) Williams simply theorized about it. Williams also went beyond what his famed contemporaries **John Milton** and **John Locke** called for regarding tolerance.

Sebastian Castellio: A sixteenth-century French preacher and theologian, he was an early proponent of religious toleration and freedom of conscience after witnessing the burning of heretics as part of the French Inquisition.

Hugo Grotius: A seventeenth-century Dutch legal scholar and philosopher, he argued that theological doctrines should be a matter of private conscience.

John Milton: A seventeenth-century English poet and author who famously wrote *Paradise Lost*. He wrote extensively on the idea of religious toleration, as well as on his opposition to state-sanctioned religion and tyranny.

John Locke: An English philosopher and important Enlightenment thinker who argued for religious tolerance in *Letters Concerning Toleration* (1689–92).

wall of separation: A metaphor invoked by President Thomas Jefferson to describe the First Amendment and its restriction on the legislative branch of the federal government.

For many Americans, the defining moment separating church and state came much later with Thomas Jefferson's "**wall of separation**." However, its key features were present in Rhode Island almost 150 years earlier.[150] Long before James Madison averred that religious freedom was in the interest of civil peace, Williams had made that idea a reality.[151] But Williams' vision was different: he wanted separation of church and state to protect the church, not the state. What is more, Williams did not support religious freedom because he was a multiculturalist who was ahead of his time; he supported it as someone who was a religious fanatic by any measure, then and now. One scholar has termed this "mere civility," as everyone had to be tolerated because they were potential converts.[152] Williams despised the Quaker theology and thought that Catholics served the Antichrist. He refused to watch Indigenous religious rituals for fear of being "an eyewitness, Spectator, or looker on" in case he was mistaken for a partaker in Satan's "Inventions and Worships."[153] He considered all these religions false, but he defended their proponents' right to hold and practice their beliefs without state interference.

In 1644 in London, Williams published one of the most significant defenses of religious liberty in western history: *The Bloudy Tenent of Persecution, for cause of Conscience, Discussed, in A Conference betweene Truth and Peace*. It was not submitted to the censor for approval, nor was it licensed,

---

149 The intellectual and public opinion went back to Augustine, who justified death for unyielding heretics. Aquinas also argued that the sin of heresy was so great that heretics deserved to be separated from the Church by excommunication, but also shut off from the world by death. Once in power, neither Luther nor Calvin disputed this.

150 In Williams' seventeenth-century world, there was a spectrum of separation, which came into sharp focus with the differences between Massachusetts Bay and England. In Massachusetts Bay, church and state were not fully merged and prosecution almost always ensued when heretical ideas were expressed along with loud contempt for magistrates and ministers. More specifically, John Cotton advocated for some form of separation of civil and spiritual spheres, addressing directly whether a member of the clergy could hold civil office, which was shocking in England where bishops routinely served in this capacity. However, even though Puritans in Massachusetts Bay rejected the Church of England, they replaced it with another form of state-supported church.

151 As James Calvin Davis notes, "[e]ven now, Williams does not receive the kind of popular attention reserved for the architects of the First Amendment ... and the near rock-star status ... Revolutionary War heroes enjoy." James Calvin Davis, "Introduction: Roger Williams and the Birth of an American Ideal," in James Calvin Davis, ed., *On Religious Liberty: Selections from the Works of Roger Williams* (Cambridge, MA: Belknap Press of Harvard University Press, 2008), 38.

152 Bejan, *Mere Civility*, 13–14, 54, 64.

153 Williams, *A Key*.

but it sold rapidly, and a second edition appeared within weeks. Williams left for Providence before his book had come off the printing press, leaving many who read it outraged. In August 1644, Edmund Calany ordered the public hangman to burn it for "Tolerating of All Sorts of Religion."[154] Burning a book was not just a symbolic act of disapproval; it was a concerted attempt to extirpate the thought which that book contained. The following month, when Lazarus Seaman preached before Parliament on Fast Day, he exhorted that *The Bloudy Tenent* was one of the most dangerous books of the time. The sermon acknowledged that Williams' work had been "burnt by Order."[155] The waves that *The Bloudy Tenent* created stretched far and wide, and between 1644 and 1649 at least 60 publications directly addressed Williams and at least 120 more quoted him.[156] *The Bloudy Tenent* was bold from start to finish. Williams unflinchingly cited reason, religion, and experience to advocate for the separation of church and state throughout the book's 400 pages, using politics, economics, practical application, and theology to justify his views.[157] Politically, he rejected the prevalent view that religious uniformity was necessary for a good society, arguing that intolerance was destructive to civil peace.

Williams did not publish *The Bloudy Tenent* in a vacuum: it was part of a broader publication war between Williams and Massachusetts Bay minister John Cotton.[158] In *The Bloudy Tenent*, Williams interpreted many passages in the Old and New Testaments as limiting government interference in any religious matters. For him, it was abominable for people to interpret God's law, as they would inexorably err. He believed that Ancient Israel was not a blueprint for modern society, and he examined Jesus' example of teaching and exhortation. Williams made it clear that while the kings of Israel used violence and force to spread their message, Jesus did not. Jesus embodied the distinction between the types of the Old Testament and the antitypes of the New. Williams turned Puritan theology on itself from within.[159] He was able to do this because, like Cotton, he worshipped the **God of Calvin**, saw God

God of Calvin: John Calvin (1509–64) was a French theologian and pastor in Geneva during the Protestant Reformation. His doctrine (Calvinism) centered on predestination and God's absolute sovereignty in salvation.

154 Cited in Barry, *Roger Williams and the Creation of the American Soul*, 338.

155 Lazarus Seaman, *Solomons choice: or, A president for kings and princes, and all that are in authority* (London, 1644).

156 Barry, *Roger Williams and the Creation of the American Soul*, 339–40.

157 For more on Coke and Bacon, see Barry, *Roger Williams and the Creation of the American Soul*, 320–23.

158 For more on John Cotton and civil and religious liberty, see David Hall, *A Reforming People: Puritanism and the Transformation of Public Life in New England* (New York: Alfred A. Knopf, 2011). For more on the pamphlet wars between Roger Williams and John Cotton, see Davis, "Introduction," 27–28.

159 See John Calvin's *Institutes* of the Christian Religion, book 20, paragraphs 1–2, 9–10, for where Williams departs from the tradition. John Calvin, *Institutes* of the Christian Religion, ed. John T. McNeill, trans. Ford Lewis Battles (Philadelphia: Westminster Press, 1960).

in everything, respected the preeminent authority of the Bible, and sought to advance the kingdom of God. Their conflict centered on *how* to do this.

Conflict and Controversy

Less than two years after the founding of Providence, the practical implementation of religious freedom was tested by Williams' next-door neighbors Jane and Joshua Verin. The Verins knew the Williams family from Salem and were among the first settlers to join them in Providence in 1636. Joshua did not attend the religious meetings held in Williams' house, but Jane did—directly against her husband's wishes. The colony "molested him not" for his beliefs, but Joshua refused to offer his wife (whom Williams described as a "gracious and modest woman") the same liberty. Joshua, a "boisterous and desperate" man, punished Jane so "tyrannically and brutishly" that she feared for her life.[160] The Verin case posed several problems for Williams. He had founded Providence based on freedom of conscience, and Joshua's behavior prevented this.

Williams and his fellow townsmen debated the Verin case at length. Providence resident William Arnold declared that any intervention from the town would breach God's ordinance on the subjection of wives to their husbands.[161] Arnold's comments reflected the widely held belief that intelligence and understanding were given to men, not women. Even though women were a key part of the seventeenth-century household, they were viewed as intellectually and morally weak. After much debate, the town voted to disenfranchise Joshua and discard him from their "Civil Freedom." The decision made sense, as husbands on both sides of the Atlantic were punished by the courts for "excessively" correcting their wives. But it was no *typical* case of spousal abuse, and Joshua was not prosecuted for violently beating his wife: his punishment was for challenging her freedom of worship. The ruling held that Joshua would "be withheld from the liberty of voting ... for restraining of the liberty of conscience."[162] The Verin case put Williams' vision of religious freedom to the test and made it clear that soul liberty ruled in Providence.

Samuel Gorton tested Williams' vision in a very different way. Gorton, a self-taught lay preacher who rejected the formalism of the professional

160 Roger Williams to John Winthrop, 22 May 1638, *Williams Corres.*, 1:156.

161 Ibid.

162 Joshua Verin returned to Salem and compelled his wife to accompany him. Williams noted: "He will hale his wife with ropes to Salem, where she must needes be troubled and troublesome as differences yet stand. She is willing to stay and live with him or elsewhere, where she may not offend." Roger Williams to John Winthrop, 22 May 1638, *Williams Corres.*, 1:156. Jane Verin was expelled from the Salem church in 1640 and disappeared from the records. By 1663, Joshua had moved to Barbados, acquired land and enslaved peoples, remarried, and died in 1695. For more on the Verins, see Margaret Murányi Manchester, *Puritan Family and Community in the English Atlantic World: Being "Much Afflicted with Conscience"* (New York: Routledge, 2019).

clergy, gained followers with his charismatic and direct style. Gorton had strong antiauthoritarian beliefs, which stemmed from mystical theology. He despised the role of the government so much that he called ministers the Anti-Christ. Gorton was convinced of the indwelling of the Holy Spirit in all believers, which obscured the distinction between saint and sinner. He believed in a direct relationship with the Holy Spirit, arguing that gathered churches were tainted and their ceremonies formed a barrier against Christ. Williams countered that Gorton's radical religious and political ideas undermined the existing political alignments and the authority of the government. Gorton also advocated for a democratic ecclesiastical polity based on the equality of all—men as well as women.

Gorton arrived in New England in 1637, settling in Plymouth. After almost stirring up a mutiny in court, he was charged with heresy for his controversial religious views and behavior towards the ministers and magistrates and was quickly removed. He then relocated to the newly founded town of Portsmouth on Aquidneck Island, where more issues on the authority of magistrates surfaced, culminating in Gorton calling them "Just Asses." He was whipped and banished and moved on again, this time to Providence. When Gorton arrived there in late 1640 or early 1641, Williams was worried.[163] Gorton's timing could not have been worse, arriving just as land disputes flared up again. Williams was furious not only about Gorton's arrival, but at the traction he gained. Williams envisioned that the government in Providence should ensure "justice, peace and sobriety." If anyone argued that there should be no "commanders or officers" and "no laws nor orders, nor corrections nor punishments" because "all are equal in Christ, therefore no masters nor officers" were needed, then the government had full authority to "judge, resist, compel and punish such transgressors."[164] Gorton challenged all of these ideas and more.

Williams blocked Gorton from settling in Providence, and Gorton quickly moved south to settle along the Pawtuxet River.[165] He immediately became embroiled in even more conflict over his "insolent and riotous carriage," and other settlers in the region petitioned Massachusetts Bay for help by saying there was no established government in the region. At its core, the dispute revolved around settlements on Narragansett homelands. In 1643, Gorton

163 Roger Williams to John Winthrop, 8 March 1641, *Williams Corres.*, 1:215.

164 Roger Williams to the Town of Providence, ca. January 1655, *Williams Corres.*, 2:423–24.

165 For more on Samuel Gorton, see John Donoghue, *Fire under the Ashes: An Atlantic History of the English Revolution* (Chicago: University of Chicago Press, 2013); Jonathan Beecher Field, *Errands in the Metropolis: New England Dissidents in Revolutionary London* (Hanover, NH: University Press of New England, 2009); Philip F. Gura, *A Glimpse of Sion's Glory: Puritan Radicalism in New England, 1620–1660* (Middletown, CT: Wesleyan University Press, 1984); Michelle Burnham, "Samuel Gorton's Leveller Aesthetics and the Economics of Colonial Dissent," *William and Mary Quarterly* 67 (2010): 433–58.

acquired land from the Narragansett Sachem, Miantonomi. Conflict followed when two minor Sachems complained that Gorton had dealt with them unjustly. When Gorton was summoned to Massachusetts Bay to answer the charges related to land issues, he refused to go until soldiers forcibly escorted him to Boston. When he arrived in Boston in 1643, he was put on trial for heresy (not the land charges). After initially being sentenced to death, Gorton was ordered to wear bolts or irons to prevent his escape while doing hard labor. He was once again at liberty in the spring, and after a brief stint in Rhode Island, he sailed to England to secure a charter. In England, he obtained an order of protection from the Earl of Warwick and secured a charter for Shawomet (Warwick) from Parliament in 1646. Gorton published several works, most notably, *Simplicities Defence Against Seven-Headed Policy* (1646), in which he described his struggles to secure independence for Shawomet. Gorton invoked Indigenous political self-determination, as he sought Narragansett allies in his quest for a charter. Upon returning to Warwick, Williams and Gorton eventually put their differences aside and joined forces to block Massachusetts' claim to Shawomet. Gorton's inclusion in this collection highlights the complicated nature of settlements, politics, government, and religion in the colony—all of which came to bear directly on Williams.

Williams' belief in religious freedom was pushed to the limit with the Quakers, whose faith he despised. Quakers believed they were guided by an inner light that compelled them to spread their message to others (no matter what the consequence).[166] They gave dramatic speeches from the courthouse to the church and ignored common social conventions, from refusing to doff their cap to going to church naked! Widely seen as dangerous religious heretics, they preached that everyone (male and female, free and unfree) was of equal worth before God, and that because everyone had direct access to God, churches were obsolete. Quakers were so determined to spread their beliefs that Massachusetts Bay ordered jail cell windows to be boarded up. Despite the harsh penalties, many Quakers continued to return to Massachusetts and some, including **Mary Dyer**, went to the gallows for their beliefs. Quakers faced intense persecution in both England and New England. However, although Williams was deeply troubled by Quaker beliefs, they were offered sanctuary in Rhode Island.

Mary Dyer: A Quaker who was hanged in Boston in 1660 for repeatedly defying the law banning Quakers from the colony.

Death and Burials

The last known letters that Williams wrote give a sense of how he struggled in his final years. Writing in May 1682, he described how he was old and weak, bruised with rupture, weakened by colic, and lame in both feet.[167]

---

166 Roger Williams, *George Fox Digg'd out of his Burrowes* (Boston, 1676).

167 Roger Williams to Simon Bradstreet, 6 May 1682, *Williams Corres.*, 2:777–78.

Williams died the following year, aged approximately 80. In death, as in life, Williams' journey was not straightforward, and he has been buried in three different places. Originally, he was buried directly behind the family house, up the hill from what is now the Roger Williams National Memorial operated by the National Park Service. In the 1860s, amidst national and local debates about honoring founders and the 200th anniversary of the Rhode Island Charter, Providence residents, historians, and family descendants decided that Williams deserved a more fitting resting place. When they dug up his grave, they found several interesting things, including an apple tree root vaguely in the shape of a body—but no actual body. So they removed dust and earth from the site and moved this to a crypt at the North Burial Ground, where it remained until 1932, when it was moved again, waiting to be ceremoniously interred beneath a new monument at Prospect Terrace for the 300th anniversary of Providence's founding in 1936. However, the statue to Williams was not finished in time for that important occasion; he was finally laid to rest only on 29 June 1939. The inscription at the base of the statue reads, "HERE REPOSES DUST FROM THE GRAVE OF ROGER WILLIAMS."[168]

Interpreting Roger Williams

This collection enables you to consider Williams from different perspectives—from that of a religious radical who was banished and had his books burned to a husband who missed his wife. The sources are a mix of Williams' personal correspondence and published works, but the collection also includes sources by his contemporaries, which help frame Williams' wider world. These sources evidence the diverse worlds in which Williams lived: from a place of idealistic religious liberty to the very real tragedy of Native exploitation. This collection also balances out Williams' well-known works with lesser-known pieces. Williams was a complex person who lived in a period of radical upheaval, both in England and New England. All sources have been carefully selected to share Williams' ideas and world views while also contextualizing Williams as a dynamic human in historical context. Large swaths of Williams' correspondence are missing or lost; only a couple of letters have survived from the entire period Williams lived in England prior to migrating in 1631, and only one letter remains from his

---

168 Roger Williams Apple Tree Root, 1898.3.1, Rhode Island Historical Society, Providence, RI; Howard M. Chapin, *Report Upon the Burial Place of Roger Williams* (Providence, RI: Rhode Island Historical Society, 1918); Stanley Lemons (emeritus professor of History at Rhode Island College) email correspondence with author, June 2024; "Body, Body, Who's Got the Body? A Rhode Island Mystery … Where in the World IS Roger Williams?" *Rhode Island Historical Society Notes and News* (Spring/Summer 2008); author interview with NPS Park Ranger John McNiff at Roger Williams National Memorial, "Roger Williams: Death and Burial," January 2022.

most tumultuous time in Massachusetts Bay; all his letters are missing for almost four years between 1641 and 1645.

The most dramatic and impactful silence in this collection, however, is the lack of sources by Native Peoples describing Roger Williams in *their* words, and the life he lived in *their* homelands. Hence it is imperative to listen to and learn from Indigenous culture keepers and educators today as they share their perspectives. The lack of written seventeenth-century Indigenous perspectives is not unique to reconstructing Williams' life, and with the rise of social, cultural, and **ethnohistory**, scholars have reframed the traditional **westward facing** historical narrative.[169] Writing Indigenous history is a political act, and seventeenth-century histories have contemporary ramifications—from federal recognition to returning sacred lands. Amid **decolonization** efforts, it is important to acknowledge that the Native nations, tribes, and Peoples that Williams knew have not vanished.

The collection opens with a chronological structure, exploring Williams' childhood in England in Part I and the impact of England's bloody history of religious persecution on Williams. Following the chronological structure, Part II examines Williams' decision to leave England and relocate to New England and his conflict with the New England authorities, which lead to his banishment from Massachusetts Bay in 1635. Part III examines key moments in how and why Providence was founded and governed, including Williams' land agreements with the Narragansett Sachems, civil authority structure, parliamentary patent from 1644, and the 1663 charter. Part III also contextualizes the founding of Providence by including documents that examine Mary Williams' role in the colony and the conflicts between Roger Williams and William Harris over land and government. Part IV examines the different ways Williams interacted with his Indigenous neighbors, as linguist, cultural observer, and diplomat. Part IV also examines Williams' views on efforts to convert Natives to Christianity, and his diverse roles in the Pequot War and King Philip's War.

As students of **paleography** will attest, reading any seventeenth-century document is tricky; for example, the new year (and date change) began in March, spelling was not standardized, writers often used a "long S" that looks like the letter F, the letters U and V were used interchangeably (as were I and J), writers often used shorthand, and some folks just had downright messy handwriting. In addition, Williams' writing is often dense, disorganized, filled with biblical references, and rambling. This collection aims to maintain some of this complexity while at the same time enabling readability and accessibility. In this vein, documents that were written between January and

ethnohistory: A discipline blending anthropological, historical, and archaeological methods by foregrounding Indigenous oral histories, reading written sources by settler-colonists against the grain, and allowing the landscape itself to tell stories to reframe archeological findings.

westward facing: Traditional histories foreground the settler-colonists and begin in Europe, move westwards across the Atlantic, and continue westwards to the Pacific—with Native Peoples as side players in the grand narrative of the founding of the United States. The term "Facing East" was coined by historian Daniel Richter and puts Native Peoples front and center in the historical narrative by foregrounding them as they looked eastwards and saw the arrival of strangers from Europe. From this perspective, US history is Indigenous history.

decolonization: The repatriation of Indigenous land and life.

paleography: The study of deciphering and interpreting historical manuscripts.

169 Daniel Richter, *Facing East from Indian Country: A Native History of Early America* (Cambridge, MA: Harvard University Press, 2001).

March (old style) and were dated for the previous year have been modernized to reflect the following year (new style). For example, the parliamentary patent was dated 14 March 1643, but in practice this was 1644 by our modern calendar, where the new year now starts on 1 January. Seventeenth-century writers recorded words as they sounded, which meant that someone might record a particular word in several different ways (sometimes in the same document), as there was no such thing as a "correct" spelling. To make Williams' writings more accessible, this collection has standardized some of the more obscure spellings. However, this means that the reader loses the way the word sounded to Williams and the richness of seventeenth-century vocabulary. In contrast, Indigenous words, especially the names of nations, tribes, and places, have been mostly left with their original spelling intact to avoid further erasure of Indigenous dialects.

This book is an introduction to reading Roger Williams in his own words—a springboard to reading the original manuscript documents. As Williams hoped of his *A Key into the Language of America*, this collection also aspires to be a "little key [to] open a Box, where lies a bunch of keys"—a gateway to learning more about Roger Williams and his world, in his own words.[170]

170 Williams, *A Key*.

CHRONOLOGY

1603 (estimated)	Born in Smithfield, London (baptism records destroyed in 1666)
1618–21 (estimated)	Apprentice scribe/assistant with Sir Edward Coke
1621	Admitted to Charterhouse school on the patronage of Sir Edward Coke
1623–27	Studies at Pembroke College, University of Cambridge
1629	Begins working as a chaplain at Sir William Masham's manor house at Otes, High Laver, Essex
1629 (December)	Marries Mary Bernard at All Saints Church, High Laver, Essex
1630 (December)	Sails with his wife, Mary, on the *Lyon* to Boston
1631 (February)	Arrives in Boston
1631	Turns down the position of Teacher of the Boston Church Leaves Boston for Salem and then Plymouth
1631–33	Lives in Plymouth Colony
1633 (August)	Mary Jr. born in Plymouth
1633 (Fall)	Leaves Plymouth and returns to Salem
1635 (April)	Accepts position of teacher at Salem Church
1635 (October)	Son Freeborn born in Salem Banished by order of the General Court of Massachusetts Bay
1636 (likely January)	Flees Salem; spends winter months with Indigenous Peoples
1636 (Spring)	Settles in present day Rumford, Rhode Island Forced to abandon the settlement, as it was within Plymouth's jurisdiction

1636 (Spring/Summer)	Crosses the Seekonk River and founds Providence with the permission of the Narragansett Sachems and establishes Providence
1636–38	Pequot War
1638	Land evidence for Providence recorded with Narragansett Sachems
1638 (September)	Son Providence born in Providence
1639	Baptist church gathers in Providence, but Williams leaves after a few months
1639 (estimated)	With the permission and support of the Narragansett, opens trading post at Cocumscussoc (present-day Wickford, RI)
1640 (July)	Daughter Mercy born in Providence Williams and others in Providence agree to civil compact
1642 (Feb)	Son Daniel born in Providence
1643 (June/July)	Sails on a ship bound for England at the Dutch settlement, New Amsterdam
1643 (December)	Son Joseph born in Providence
1643	*A Key into the Language of America*, *Mister Cotton's Letter Examined*, and *Queries of the Highest Consideration* published in London
1644 (March)	Receives parliamentary patent for Providence Plantations
1644	*The Bloudy Tenent of Persecution* published in London (after Williams had left England) and ordered to be burned by Parliament
1644 (September)	Returns from England to Boston with a letter of safe passage to RI
1644–47	Serves as Chief Officer of Providence Plantations
1645	*Christenings make not Christians* published in London

1649	Is Deputy President of Providence Plantations
1651	Sells trading post to Richard Smith
1651 (November)	Sails with John Clarke and William Dyer for England
1652	*Fourth Paper, Presented by Major Butler*; *Hirelings Ministry None of Christ*; *Experiments of Spiritual Health*; *Bloody Tenent Yet More Bloody*; and *Examiner Defended* published in London
1654 (June)	Returns from England
1654 (September)	Elected President of Providence Plantations
1657 (May)	Retires from Presidency of Providence Plantations
1663 (July)	Charles II grants a royal charter to the colony of Rhode Island and Providence Plantations
1672	Debates Quakers in Newport and Providence
1675–76	King Philip's War. The war did not end until 1678 in northern Indigenous territories
1676 (March)	Providence burned down, including Williams' house
1676	*George Fox Digg'd out of his Burrowes* published in Boston
After 1676 (date unknown)	Mary Williams dies
1680 (estimated; between 1679–83)	Writes "A Brief Reply to a Small Book" in shorthand in the margins of *An Essay Towards the Reconciling of Differences Among Christians*
1683 (January–March)	Dies in Providence

PART I

Religious Persecution in England

DOCUMENT 1

Map of London as Roger Williams knew it, *Civitas Londinum* (1633)[1]

The map, *Civitas Londinum*, offers a bird's-eye view of the buildings and streets of London as Roger Williams would have known them growing up there in the early seventeenth century. It was first printed from woodblocks in 1561, and source 1 is from a modified version that was printed in 1633. The details show an overview of the city, Williams' neighborhood (Smithfield), his church (St. Sepulchre-without-Newgate), and his school (Charterhouse). Williams' neighborhood, Smithfield, was a notorious site for burning alive people who disagreed with the official state religion, which changed depending on the monarch. Williams grew up on Cowes Lane, and the map illustrates the proximity of his house and church to the Smithfield execution site. Smithfield was also a bustling international marketplace. Williams' father, a merchant tailor who traded fine cloths, likely took Roger to the docks on the River Thames to learn the trading business. This map is important, as it shows London before the landscape fundamentally changed in 1666 following the Great Fire of London. The fire destroyed part of Williams' parish church as well as his baptism records.

1 *Civitas Londinum*, https://mapoflondon.uvic.ca/index.htm. The map is widely known as the Agas map, due to a specious provenance to surveyor, Ralph Agas (ca.1540–1621).

Figure 1.1: An overview of London in 1633 with St. Sepulchre-without-Newgate identified

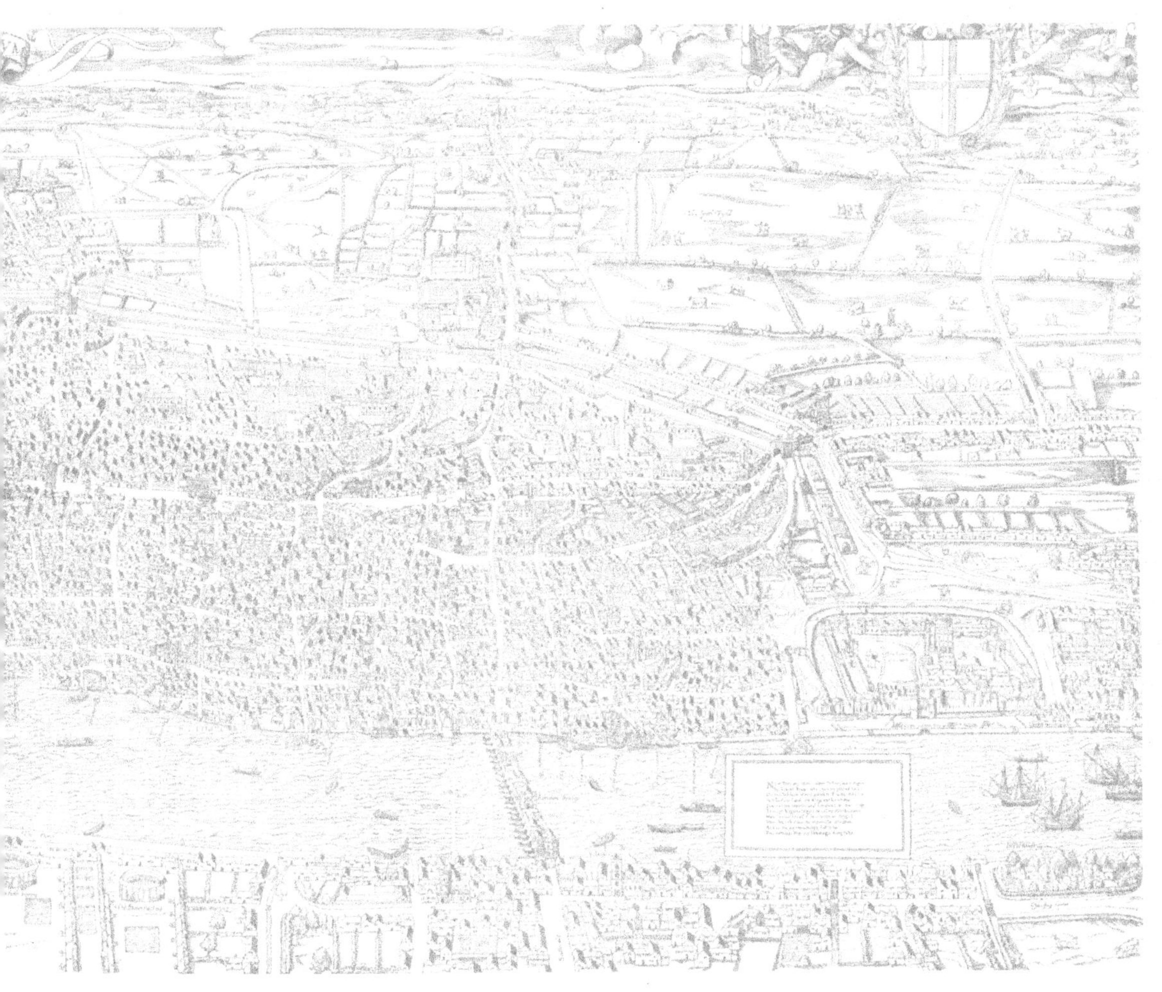

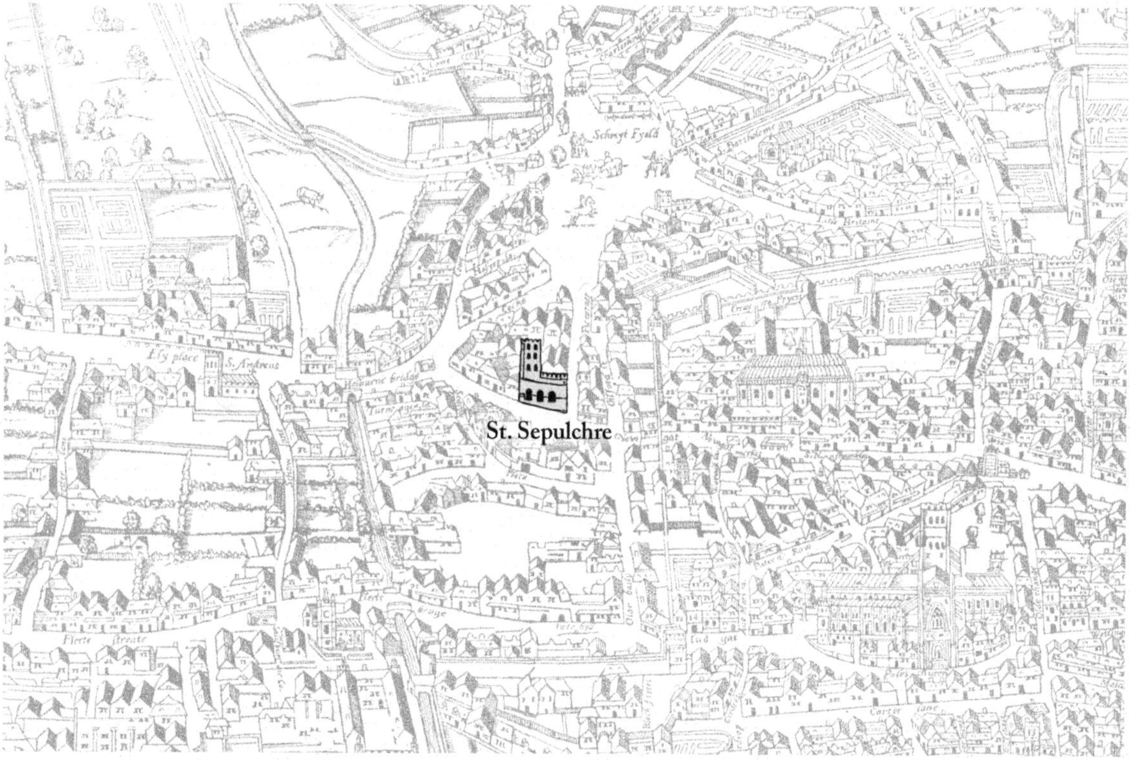

Figure 1.2: An overview of Williams' neighborhood in 1633

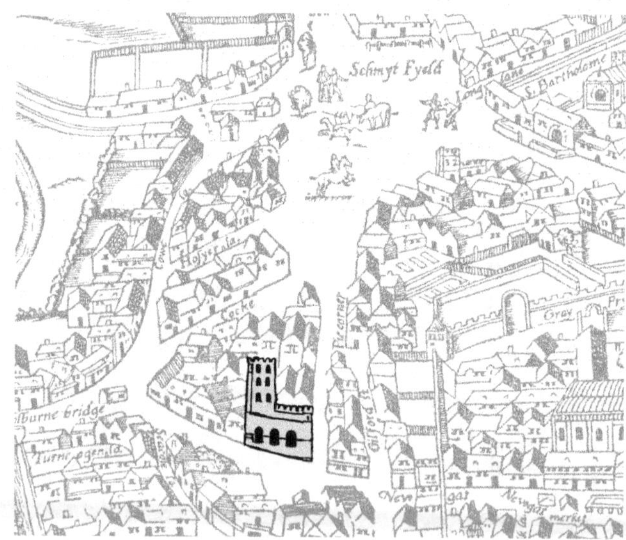

Figure 1.3: Close up of Williams' neighborhood in 1633, highlighting its proximity to "Schmyt Fyeld"

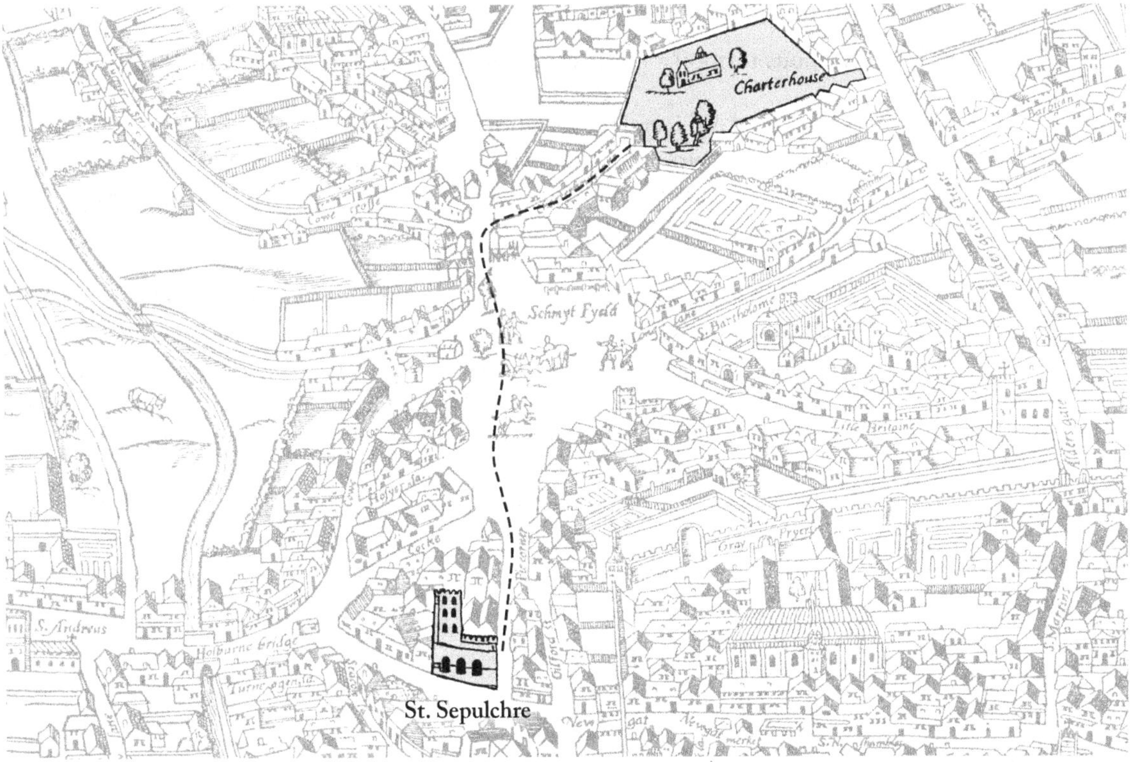

Charterhouse

St. Sepulchre

Figure 1.4: Imagined route between Williams' parish church and his school, Charterhouse

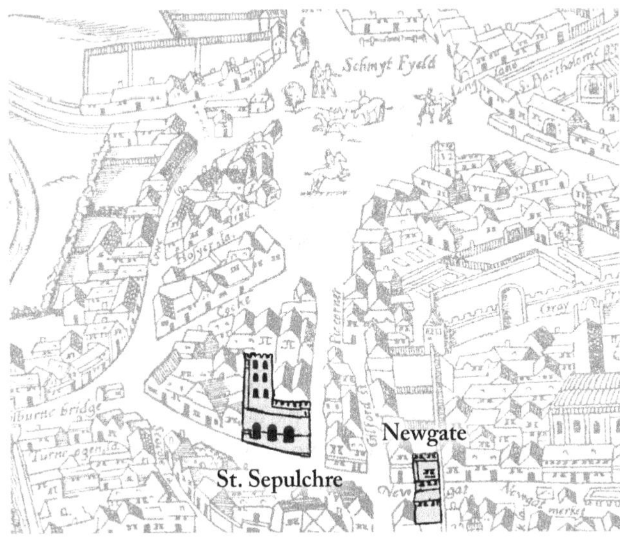

Figure 1.5: Site of Newgate prison in relation to St. Sepulchre

DOCUMENT 2

Religious turmoil and the execution of heretics at Smithfield

John Lambert: A Protestant who was burned to death in November 1538 at Smithfield. He was accused of heresy and put on trial for denying the presence of Christ in the bread and wine of the Eucharist (Transubstantiation), a Catholic belief.

***Foxe's Book of Martyrs*:** A highly influential book about the sufferings of Protestants under the Catholic Church written by John Foxe and published in London in 1563. Its full title is *Actes and Monuments of these Latter and Perillous Days, Touching Matters of the Church*, but it is popularly known as *Foxe's Book of Martyrs*.

Bartholomew Legate: Rejected the Church of England and argued that there was no "true" church or baptism. In 1611 he was arrested and charged with heresy with his brother, Thomas, and they were imprisoned at Newgate. Thomas died in prison and Bartholomew was burned alive in 1612 after he refused to recant.

Henry: King Henry VIII.

Marie: Queen Mary I.

Cromwell: Thomas Cromwell, a key advisor to King Henry VIII during the Reformation. In 1540 Henry ordered his execution for treason and heresy.

Cranmer: Thomas Cranmer, the first Protestant Archbishop of Canterbury under King Henry VIII. He was burned at the stake for heresy under Queen Mary I in 1556.

Smithfield, Williams' childhood neighborhood, was the site where many people were burned when their religious beliefs went against the state religion. Under Queen Mary I, many Protestants, including **John Lambert**, were put to death in Smithfield. Although Lambert was executed before Williams' time, Williams described the event in the *The Bloody Tenent Yet More Bloody* (1652); see excerpt (a). Excerpt (b) is from ***Foxe's Book of Martyrs*** (1563), which also describes Lambert's execution in detail and includes an image of him crying out "None but Christ." When Williams was approximately nine years old, **Bartholomew Legate** was burned a stone's throw from his house. In excerpt (c), Thomas Fuller reflects on Legate's execution in his 1656 publication, *Church History of Britain*. In Providence, Williams looked back on England's long and bloody history of changeable forced state worship, which switched direction like a "Weather-cock" on the whim of the monarch. In excerpt (d) from Williams' *Christenings make not Christians* (1645), Williams explores how forced worship due to fear of persecution led to false conversions.

a. Roger Williams on the burning of John Lambert in Smithfield in 1538, from *The Bloody Tenent Yet More Bloody* (1652)[2]

Tis true this bloudie Tenent of persecution was lamentably drunk with blood in the days of that **Henry**, as well as afterwards in the days of his bloodier daughter **Marie** ... I will rather produce an Instance in our Nation of England ... At that very time when King Henry himself disputed in so famous an Assembly against the blessed witness of Christ Jesus, John Lambert! ... Find we not then also holy and zealous **Cromwell** (at the Kings command) reading that bloodier Sentence of Death against that blessed Lambe of Christ Jesus ... This was that blessed Lambert, a true Follower of the Lamb of God Christ Jesus, who cried out in the midst of the Flames, None but Christ, None but Christ: and well might he so cry: Not **Cranmer**, not Cromwell, who after so much Light in Disputations, yet persisted in their Heresy and Idolatry, and partaking with violence against this holy man, that he might well cry out, None but Christ, None but Christ.

2 Roger Williams, *The Bloody Tenent Yet More Bloody* (London, 1652).

b. John Lambert's execution, from *Foxe's Book of Martyrs* (1563)[3]

Figure 2.1: John Lambert

Upon the day that was appointed for this holy martyr of God to suffer, he was brought out of the prison at eight o'clock in the morning ... showing no manner of sadness or fear. When the breakfast was ended, he was carried straightway to the place of execution, where he should offer himself unto the Lord, a sacrifice of sweet savor, who is blessed in his saints, for ever and ever. Amen. As touching the terrible manner and fashion of the burning of this blessed martyr, here is to be noted, that of all others which have been burned and offered up at Smithfield, there was yet none so cruelly and piteously handled as he. For, after that his legs were consumed and burned up to the stumps, and that the wretched tormentors and enemies of God had withdrawn the fire from him, so that but a small fire and coals were left under him, then two that stood on each side of him, with their **halberts** pitched him upon their **pikes**, as far as the chain would reach, after the manner and form that is described in the picture adjoined. Then he, lifting up such hands as he had, and his fingers' ends flaming with fire, cried unto

halberts: Two-handed polearm weapons; an axe blade topped with a spike and mounted on a long wooden shaft.

pikes: Long thrusting spears with a wooden shaft and an iron or steel spearhead affixed.

3 John Foxe, *Actes and Monuments of these Latter and Perillous Days, Touching Matters of the Church* (London, 1563).

the people in these words, "None but Christ, None but Christ"; and so, being let down again from their halberts, fell into the fire, and there ended his life.

c. Thomas Fuller on the burning of Bartholomew Legate at Smithfield in 1612, *Church History of Britain* (1656)[4]

cause: Religious beliefs.

Marian days: Reign of Queen Mary I.

Legate had long been in prison in Newgate ... the counsel ... [by] definitive sentence ... pronounced, decreed, and declared the foresaid Bartholomew Legate an obdurate, contumacious, and incorrigible Heretic ... Whereas King James ... gave order ... for the burning of the foresaid Legate ... To Smithfield he was brought to be burned. See here, it is neither the pain nor the place, but only the **cause** makes a Martyr. In this very Smithfield how many Saints in the **Marian days**, suffered for the testimony of Jesus Christ? Whereas now one therein dies in his own blood for denying him. Vast was the Conflux of people about him. Never did a scare-fire at midnight summon more hands to quench it, than this at noon day did eyes to behold it. At last, refusing all mercy, he was burned to ashes. And so we leave him, the first that for a long time suffered death in that manner: And, oh that he might be the last to deserve it!

d. Roger Williams on England's religious turmoil and false conversions, in *Christenings make not Christians* (1645)[5]

Henry the seventh: The first Tudor King, who ruled from 1485 to 1509 after taking the throne following the Wars of the Roses, a series of wars over the throne.

Papist: A derogatory term (along with popish and popery) meaning Catholic.

Edward the sixth: Henry VIII's son with his third wife, Jane Seymour, who ruled from 1547 to 1553. He was nine years old when he assumed the throne and England was governed by regency council. He died before he reached maturity.

Queen Elizabeth: King Henry VIII's daughter from his second marriage to Anne Boleyn, who ruled from 1558 to 1603. Elizabeth I was Protestant and was the last of the Tudor monarchs.

Yea what lamentable experience have we of the Turnings and Turnings of the body of this Land in point of Religion in few years? When England was all Popish under **Henry the seventh**, how easy is conversion wrought to half **Papist** half-Protestant under Henry the eighth? From half-Protestantism half-Popery under Henry the eight, to absolute Protestantism under **Edward the sixth** to absolute popery under Queen Mary (just like the Weather-cock, with ... every Prince) to absolute Protestantism under **Queen Elizabeth** & c. For all this, yet some may ask ... why have I not brought them [the Indigenous Peoples of New England] to such a conversion [to Christianity] as I speak of? I answer, woe be to me ... if I call that conversion unto God, which is indeed subversion of the souls of Millions in Christendom, from one false worship to another ... I may not pretend a false conversion, and false state of worship, to the true Lorde Jesus ... it must not be, (it is not possible it should be in truth) a conversion of People to the Worship of the Lord Jesus, by force of Arms and swords of steel.

4 Thomas Fuller, *Church History of Britain* (London, 1656), Book X, 63–64.

5 Roger Williams, *Christenings make not Christians* (London, 1645), 11–15.

DOCUMENT 3

Roger Williams on his decision to leave England, from letters to Lady Joan Barrington (1629) and Anne Sadleir (1652)

After studying at Charterhouse and Pembroke College under the patronage of Sir Edward Coke, Williams took a job as a private chaplain at Otes Manor in High Laver, Essex in 1629. While at Otes, he fell in love with Jane Whalley, but her aunt, Lady Joan Barrington, forbade the marriage on account of Williams' low social rank. Later that year, Williams married Mary Bernard, a lady-in-waiting at Otes. Excerpt (a) is from letters Williams sent to Lady Barrington; they reflect on his love life, disappointment at Lady Barrington's decision, early career, and his job prospects, all of which impacted his decision to move to New England. When Williams returned to England in the 1650s on charter business, he reached out to a former childhood friend, Anne Sadleir, Sir Edward Coke's daughter. In excerpt (b) Williams describes to Sadleir his relationship with Coke and how fear of persecution by Archbishop Laud played a role in his original decision to leave England.

a. Roger Williams to Lady Barrington (April/May 1629)[6]

(undated, April 1629)

Many & often speeches have long fluttered or flown abroad concerning your Ladyship's near kinswoman [Jane Whalley] & my unworthy self. Yet like a rolling snow-ball or some flowing stream ye report extends & gathers stronger & stronger ... I acknowledge my self altogether unworthy & unmeet for such a proposition ... Objections have come in about her spirit, much accused for [being] passionate & hasty, rash & unconstant, other fears about ... it being some Indecorum for her to condescend to my low Ebb ... Besides many former offers & that late New England call, I have since had 2 several livings proffered to me each of them £100 per annum ... Nor doe I seeke nor shall I be drawn on any terms to part (even to my last parting) from Otes. Poor yet as I am I have some few offers at present ... The kind affection of your dear Ladyship & worthy niece of better merit and desert. I shall add for the present I know none in the world I more affect ... oft I do pray ... for the everlasting peace and well fare of your kind Ladyship,

6 Roger Williams to Lady Joan Barrington, April 1629, *Williams Corres.*, 1:1–3; Roger Williams to Lady Joan Barrington, 2 May 1629, *Williams Corres.*, 1:4–7.

whose soul … The Lord that hath caried you from the womb to gray hairs crown those gray hairs by making your last days … rest fruitful … in old age.

(2 May 1629)

I doubt not but your good wisdom & love have fairly interpreted my carriage in ye late treaty, & I also trust, quieted & stilled the loving affections of your worthy niece [Jane Whalley]. We hope to live together in the heavens though ye Lord have denied that union on Earth … Good Madam it is not for nothing, that ye God of Heaven hath sent such thunderclaps of late and made such great offers at the door of your Ladyship's heart … Woe unto me if I hold my peace & hide that from you, which may seem bitter at present, it may be sweeter than honey at the latter end … your Ladyship only I beseech you to lay to heart these few considerations … Job 34.9 … He with whom we deal excepted not the persons of princes nor regarded the rich more than the poor for they are all the work of his hands … When birth greater, maintenance more ample, time longer and means of grace more plentiful, then a great account of the Lord is expected … I beseech you your candle is twinkling & glass near run ye Lord only knows how few minutes are left behind.

b. Roger Williams reflects on his decision to leave England, from a letter to Anne Sadleir (1652)[7]

dear Father: Anne Sadleir's father, Sir Edward Coke.

National Church: Church of England.

Ceremonies and Bishops: Williams and other dissenters objected to key elements of worship within the Church of England, including many ceremonies and the role of Bishops.

My much honored friend, That Man of Honor and Wisdom and piety your **dear Father**, was often pleased to call me his Son and truly it was as bitter as Death to me (when Bishop Laud pursued me out of this Land and my Conscience was persuaded against the **National Church** and **Ceremonies and Bishops** beyond the Conscience of your dear Father) I say it was as bitter as Death to me when I rode Windsor way to take ship at Bristol, and saw Stoke-House where that blessed man was and then I durst not acquaint him with my Conscience and my Flight. But how many thousand times since have I had honorable and precious remembrance of his person and the Life the Writings and Speeches and Examples of that Glorious Light? And I truly say that beside my natural Inclination to study and activity His Example Instruction and Encouragement have spured me on to a more than ordinary and industrious and patient Course, in my whole Course hitherto … And I would not tell Your self of this, but that you may acknowledge some Beams of his holy Wisdom and Goodness who hath not suffered all

7 Roger Williams to Anne Sadleir, R.5.5, Letter 30, Sadleir Collection, Wren Library, Trinity College, Cambridge University, UK. Undated, but before April 1652.

your own and Your Dear Fathers smiles to have bene lost upon so poor and despicable an object ... I hope for God, your honorable Father was wont to say He that shall harrow what I have sown must rise early.

QUESTIONS TO CONSIDER

1. How did growing up in England affect Roger Williams' later views on religious freedom and separation of church and state?

2. Why did Williams migrate to Massachusetts Bay in 1631?

PART II

New England Calling

DOCUMENT 4

The Vision for Massachusetts Bay (1629–30)

In 1620 a group of Separatists, headed by William Bradford, left England (after a stint in Holland) on board the *Mayflower* and founded Plymouth Colony. As Separatists they believed that the Church of England was too corrupt to save and wanted to separate themselves entirely from it. A decade later, they were joined by a group that included many Puritans, headed by John Winthrop in Massachusetts Bay. While the Puritans did not want to separate entirely from the Church of England, they agreed that it was too Catholic and wanted to purify it. In excerpt (a) Winthrop sets out his vision for Massachusetts Bay in his *Model of Christian Charity* speech. He declared that the new colony was going to be an example to the rest of the world, and that God would punish the colony if its members allowed sin to flourish. These Puritans left England to escape persecution, *not* because they believed in religious freedom. When King Charles I granted the Massachusetts Bay Colony a charter, he also allowed them to use a seal (source b), which they did from 1629 to 1686 and from 1689 to 1692. The seal features an Indigenous man holding a bow and arrow, with the words "**Come over and help us**" coming out of his mouth. The **seal** illustrates the settler-colonist's views of Indigenous Peoples, including their lack of respect for Indigenous land rights and their goal of religious conversion (arguably religious/cultural genocide). Williams moved to Massachusetts Bay one year after it was founded, after being offered the ministry of the Boston Church.

Come over and help us: Biblical reference to Acts 16:9–10: "And a vision appeared to Paul in the night; There stood a man of Macedonia, and prayed him, saying, Come over into Macedonia and help us."

seal: There is currently a commission to replace the Massachusetts seal and flag (based on the 1629 seal) as symbols of the historical oppression of Native Peoples.

covenant: Agreement.

Him: God.

a. John Winthrop, *A Model of Christian Charity* (1630)[1]

Thus stands the cause between God and us. We are entered into **covenant** with **Him** for this work. We have taken out a commission. The Lord hath given us leave to draw our own articles. We have professed to enterprise these and those accounts, upon these and those ends. We have hereupon besought Him of favor and blessing. Now if the Lord shall please to hear

1 John Winthrop, *A Model of Christian Charity* (1630), http://history.hanover.edu/texts/winthmod.html.

us, and bring us in peace to the place we desire, then hath He ratified this covenant and sealed our commission, and will expect a strict performance of the articles contained in it; but if we shall neglect the observation of these articles which are the ends we have propounded, and, dissembling with our God, shall fall to embrace this present world and prosecute our carnal intentions, seeking great things for ourselves and our posterity, the Lord will surely break out in wrath against us, and be revenged of such a people, and make us know the price of the breach of such a covenant …

The Lord will be our God, and delight to dwell among us, as His own people, and will command a blessing upon us in all our ways, so that we shall see much more of His wisdom, power, goodness and truth, than formerly we have been acquainted with. We shall find that the God of Israel is among us, when ten of us shall be able to resist a thousand of our enemies; when He shall make us a praise and glory that men shall say of succeeding plantations, "may the Lord make it like that of New England." For we must consider that we shall be as a city upon a hill. The eyes of all people are upon us. So that if we shall deal falsely with our God in this work we have undertaken, and so cause Him to withdraw His present help from us, we shall be made a story and a by-word through the world. We shall open the mouths of enemies to speak evil of the ways of God, and all professors for God's sake. We shall shame the faces of many of God's worthy servants, and cause their prayers to be turned into curses upon us till we be consumed out of the good land whither we are going … But if our hearts shall turn away, so that we will not obey, but shall be seduced, and worship other Gods, our pleasure and profits, and serve them; it is propounded unto us this day, we shall surely perish out of the good land whither we pass over this vast sea to possess it.

b. Seal of the Massachusetts Bay Colony (1629)[2]

Figure 4.1: Seal of the Massachusetts Bay Colony

2 Secretary of the Commonwealth of Massachusetts, Massachusetts Seal, Public Records, https://www.sec.state.ma.us/divisions/public-records/history-of-seal.

DOCUMENT 5

Roger Williams reflects on his conflict with Massachusetts Bay and Plymouth in a letter to John Winthrop, and William Bradford examines the conflict in *Of Plymouth Plantation* (1632–33)

Williams' letter to John Winthrop from 1632 is his only surviving piece of correspondence from the time of the controversy. In excerpt (a) Williams expresses his views that a person could not simultaneously be a civil magistrate and ruling elder. The letter also briefly mentions Williams' early views of and encounters with Natives. Williams was later opposed to converting Indigenous Peoples to Christianity, as he feared it would lead to false conversions; however, in this letter he described his longing for "native Soules." It is unknown whether Williams attempted to convert any Indigenous Peoples during his time at Plymouth. In excerpt (b) William Bradford discusses the conflict with Williams in Plymouth that prompted his removal and return to Salem.

a. Roger Williams reflects on his conflict with Massachusetts Bay and Plymouth in a letter to John Winthrop (1632)[3]

Only let me crave a word of explanation: among other pleas for a Young Counselor (which I fear will be too light in the balance of the holy One) you argue from **25** in a church **Elder**. Tis riddle as yet to me, whether you mean any Elder in these **New English churches**, or (which I believe not) old English, disorderly, functions, from whence our Jehovah of armies more and more redeem his Israel, or the **Levites**, who served from 25 to 50 ... I am no Elder in any church, no more nor so much as your worthy self, nor ever shall be if the Lord please to grant my desires, that I may intend what I long after, the natives Soules ... I crave interpretation ... You lately sent music to our Ears, when we heard, you persuaded ... our beloved **Mr Nowell** to **Surrender up one sword**: and you were preparing to seeke the Lord further: a duty not so frequent in Plymouth as formerly, but ***Spero meliora***.

25: Winthrop argued that ruling elders should be over 25 years old.

Elder: Lay member of the congregation who enforced proper behavior among parishioners.

New English churches: Following Calvinism, New England churches had a fourfold division of the ministry: a pastor, teacher, elders, and deacons.

Levites: Biblical reference to the Tribe of Levi, one of the tribes of Israel who had religious duties for the Israelites as well as political responsibilities.

Mr Nowell: Increase Nowell.

Surrender up one sword: Resign as either elder or magistrate; he elected to remain as a magistrate.

***Spero meliora*:** (Latin) I hope for better things.

3 Roger Williams to John Winthrop, between July and December 1632, *Roger Williams Corres.*, 1:8–9.

b. William Bradford examines the conflict with Roger Williams in *Of Plymouth Plantation* (1633)[4]

1633 ... Roger Williams (a man godly and zealous, having many precious parts, but very unsettled judgment) came over first to the Massachusetts, but upon some discontent left that place, and came hither [to Plymouth], (where he was friendly entertained, according to their poor ability,) and exercised his gifts amongst them, and after some time was admitted a member of the church, and his teaching well approved, for the benefit whereof I still bless God, and am thankful to him, even for his sharpest admonitions and reproofs, so far as they agreed with the truth. He this year began to fall into some strange opinions, and from opinion to practice; which caused some controversy between the church and him, and in the end some discontent on his part, by occasion whereof he left them some thing abruptly. Yet afterwards sued for his dismission to the church of Salem, which was granted, with some caution to them concerning him, and what care they ought to have of him. But he soon fell into more things there, both to their and the governments trouble and disturbance. I shall not need to name particulars, they are too well known now to all, though for a time the church here went under some hard censure by his occasion, from some that afterwards smarted themselves. But he is to be pitied, and prayed for, and so I shall leave the matter, and desire the Lord to show him his errors, and reduce him into the way of truth, and give him a settled judgment and constancy in the same; for I hope he belongs to the Lord, and He will show him mercy.

4 William Bradford, *History of Plymouth Plantation 1620–1647* (Boston: Massachusetts Historical Society, 1912), 2:161–64.

DOCUMENT 6

John Winthrop and Nathaniel Morton examine Roger Williams' escalating conflict in Plymouth and Salem in *Winthrop's Journal* (1631–36) and *New England's Memorial* (1669)

Upon arrival in Boston, Williams was offered the post of Teacher of the Boston Church, one of the most prestigious jobs in the entire colony. However, he turned the position down and headed north to Salem, where the Church mirrored his religious beliefs more closely. As his views moved towards Separatist theology, he relocated south to Plymouth Colony. However, Williams' opinions fell out of favor in Plymouth, and he removed back to Salem. By 1635 Williams was increasingly known as an outspoken critic of the churches and government in Massachusetts Bay. Williams attacked the religious policies of the churches, charged the magistrate with injustice, and questioned the legitimacy of settling on Indigenous homelands with a royal charter. Excerpt (a) is John Winthrop's account in his journal of the long-term conflict between Williams and the Massachusetts Bay colony, which had been brewing for several years prior to his banishment in 1635. Winthrop's journal also includes the explicit charges laid against Williams and his removal in 1636. Excerpt (b) is from a later account by Nathaniel Morton reflecting on the conflict between Williams and the Plymouth and Salem authorities.

a. John Winthrop records the long-term road to Roger Williams' banishment in his journal (1631–36)[5]

Mr. Endecott: John Endicott, longest-serving governor of the Massachusetts Bay Colony, who also held other elected and appointed positions throughout his life.

1631 ... At a court holden at Boston (upon information to the governor, that they of Salem had called Mr. Williams to the office of a teacher), a letter was written from the court to **Mr. Endecott** to this effect: That whereas Mr. Williams had refused to join with the congregation at Boston, because they would not make a public declaration of their repentance for having communion with the churches of England, while they lived there; and, besides, had declared his opinion, that the magistrates might not punish the breach of the Sabbath, nor any other offence, as it was a breach of the first table; therefore, they marveled they would choose him without advising with the council; and withal desiring him, that they would forbear to proceed till they had conferred about it.

5 John Winthrop, *History of New England, 1630–1649 (Winthrop's Journal)*, ed. James Kendall Hosmer (New York: Charles Scribner's Sons, 1908), 1:49–50, 61–63, 116–17, 119, 149, 154, 157, 162–63, 168, 179.

1633 … The governor and assistants met at Boston, and took into consideration a treatise, which Mr. Williams (then of Salem) had sent to them, and which he had formerly written to the governor and council of Plymouth, wherein, among other things, he disputes their right to the lands they possessed here, and concluded that, claiming by the king's grant, they could have no title, nor otherwise, except they compounded with the natives. For this, taking advice with some of the most judicious ministers (who much condemned Mr. Williams' error and presumption), they gave order, that he should be convented at the next court, to be censured. There were three passages chiefly whereas they were much offended: 1, for that he charges King James to have told a solemn public lie, because in his patent he blessed God that he was the first Christian prince that had discovered this land; 2, for he charges him and other with blasphemy for calling Europe Christendom, or the Christian world; 3, for that he did personally apply to our present king, Charles, these three places in the Revelations … the governor wrote to him to let him know what was done, wishing … Mr Williams to retract … Whereto he [Williams] returned a very modest and discreet answer. Mr Williams also wrote to the governor, professing his intent to have only written for the private satisfaction of the governor, etc., of Plymouth, without any purpose to have stirred any further in it, if the governor here had not required a copy him; withal offering his book, or any part of it, to be burnt. At the next court he [Williams] appeared penitently, and gave satisfaction of his intention and loyalty. So it was left, and nothing done in it.

1634 … with the advice of Mr. [John] Cotton and Mr. [John] Wilson, and weighing his [Williams'] letter, and further considering of the aforesaid offensive passages in his book, (which, being written in very obscure and implicative phrases, might well admit of doubtful interpretation), they [Wilson and Cotton] found the matters not to be so evil as at first they seemed. Whereupon they agreed, that, upon his retraction, etc., or taking an oath of allegiance to the king, etc., it should be passed over …

1634 … Mr Williams of Salem had broken his promise to us, in teaching publicly against the king's patent, and our great sin in claiming right thereby to this country, etc., and for usual terming the churches of England antichristian.…

1635 … The governor and assistants sent for Mr. Williams. The occasion was, for that he had taught publicly, that a magistrate ought not to tender an oath to an unregenerate man, for that we thereby have communion with a wicked man in the worship of God, and cause him to take the name of God in vain. He was heard before all the ministers, and very clearly confuted. Mr. Endecott was at first of the same opinion, but he gave place to the truth …

1635 … At the general court, Mr. Williams of Salem was summoned, and did appear. It was laid to his charge, that, being under question before the magistracy and churches for divers and dangerous opinions, viz, 1. That the magistrates ought not to punish the breach of the first table, otherwise than in such cases as did disturb the civil peace; 2. That he ought not to tender an oath to an unregenerate man; 3, that a man ought not to pray with such, though wife, child, etc.; that a man ought not to give thanks after the sacrament nor after meat, etc.; and that the other churches were about to write to the church of Salem to admonish him of these errors, notwithstanding the church had since called him to [the] office of a teacher. Much debate was about these things. The said opinions were adjudged by all magistrates and ministers (who were desired to be present,) to be erroneous, and very dangerous, and the calling of him to office, at that time, was judged a great contempt of authority. So, in fine, time was given to him and the church of Salem to consider of these things till the next general court, and then either to give satisfaction to the court, or else to expect the sentence; it being professedly declared by the ministers, (at the request of the court to give their advice,) that he who should obstinately maintain such opinions, (whereby a church might run into heresy, apostasy, or tyranny, and yet the civil magistrate could not intermeddle,) were to be removed, and that the other churches ought to request the magistrates so to do …

1635 [August] … Mr. Williams, pastor of Salem, being sick and not able to speak, wrote to his church a protestation, that he could not communicate with churches in the bay; neither would be communicate with them, except they would refuse communion with the rest; but the whole church was grieved herewith …

1635 [October.] At this general court, Mr. Williams, the teacher at Salem, was again convented, and all the ministers in the bay being desired to be present, he was charged with the said two letters,—that to the churches, complaining of the magistrates for injustice, extreme oppression, etc., and the other to his own church, to persuade them to renounce communion with all the churches in the bay, as full of antichristian pollution, etc. He justified both these letters, and maintained all his opinions; and being offered further conference or disputation, and a month's respite, he chose to dispute presently. So **Mr. Hooker** was appointed to dispute with him, but could not reduce him from any of his errors. So, the next morning, the court sentenced him to depart out of our jurisdiction within six weeks, all the ministers, save one, approving the sentence; and his own church had him under question

Mr. Hooker: Thomas Hooker, pastor at Newtown (later Cambridge), who later moved to Connecticut.

also for the same cause; and he, at his return home, refused communion with his own church, who openly disclaimed his errors, and wrote an humble submission to the magistrates, acknowledging their fault in joining with Mr. Williams in that letter to the churches against them, etc.

1636 [January] ... The governor and assistants met at Boston to consider about Mr. Williams, for they were credibly informed, that, notwithstanding the injunction laid upon him (upon the liberty granted him to stay till the spring) not to go about to draw others to his opinions, he did use to entertain company in his house, and to preach to them, even of such points as he had been censured for; and it was agreed to send him to England by ship then ready to depart. The reason was, because he had drawn above twenty persons to his opinion, and they were intended to erect a plantation about the Narragansett Bay, from whence the infection would easily spread into these churches (the people being, many of them, much taken with the apprehension of his godliness). Whereupon a warrant was sent to him to come presently to Boston, to be **shipped**, etc. He returned answer (and divers of Salem came with it), that he could not come without hazard of his life, etc. Whereupon a pinnace was sent with commission to **Capt. Underhill**, etc., to apprehend him, and carry him aboard the ship, (which then rode at Natascutt;) but, when they came at his house, they found he had been gone three days before; but whither they could not learn. He had so far prevailed at Salem, as many there (especially of devout women) did embrace his opinions, and separated from the churches, for this cause, that some of their members, going into England, did hear the ministers there, and when they came home the churches here held communion with them ...

shipped: Banished back to England.

Capt. Underhill: John Underhill, head of the colonial militia.

1636 [April] ... The church of Salem was still infect[ed] with Mr. Williams his opinions, so as most of them held it unlawful to hear in the ordinary assemblies in England, because their foundation was antichristian, and we should, by hearing, hold communion with them; and some went so far as they were ready to separate the church upon it. Whereupon the church sent two brethren, and a letter, to the elders of the other churches, for their advice in three points: 1. Whether (for satisfying the weak) they might promise not to hear in England any false church. This was not thought safe, because then they would draw them to the like towards the other churches here, who were all of the opinion, that it was lawful, and that hearing was not church communion. 2. If they were not better, to grant them dismission to be a church by themselves. This was also opposed, for that it was not a remedy of God's ordering; neither would the magistrates allow them to be a church, being but three men and eight women; and besides, it were dangerous to raise churches on such grounds. 3. Whether they ought then to excommunicate them, if they did withdraw, etc. This was granted, yet, withal, that if they did not withdraw or run into contempt, they ought, in these matters of difference of opinion in things not fundamental nor scandalous, etc., to bear each with other.

b. Nathaniel Morton examines Roger Williams' escalating conflict in Plymouth and Salem in *New England's Memorial* (1669)[6]

In the year 1634, Mr Roger Williams removed from Plymouth to Salem. He had lived about three years at Plymouth, where he was well accepted as an assistant in the ministry to Mr. Ralph Smith, then pastor of the church there, but by degrees venting of diverse of his own singular opinions, and seeking to impose them upon others, he not finding such a concurrence as he expected, he desired his dismission to the church of Salem, which though some were unwilling to, yet through the prudent counsel of Mr. Brewster (the ruling elder there) fearing that his continuance amongst them might cause divisions, and there being many able men in the bay, they would better deal with him than themselves could, and foreseeing (what he professed he feared concerning Mr. Williams, which afterwards came to pass) that he would run the same course of rigid separation and **anabaptistry**, which Mr. John Smith the separatist at Amsterdam had done; the church of Plymouth consented to his dismission, and such as did adhere to him were also dismissed, and removed with him, or not long after him to Salem.

anabaptistry: The belief that baptism is only valid when a person requests to be baptized; Anabaptists were opposed to infant baptism. For Puritans, "anabaptistry" was a slander and scare word connected to a sixteenth-century Anabaptist rebellion in the German city of Münster.

He came to Salem in the time of Mr. Skelton's weakness, who lived not long after Williams was come, whereupon after some time, the church there called him to office; but having in one year's time filled that place with principles of rigid separation, and tending to anabaptistry, the prudent magistrates of the Massachusetts jurisdiction sent to the church of Salem, desiring them to forbear calling him to office, which they hearkening to, was a cause of much disturbance; for Mr. Williams had begun, and then being in office, he proceeded more vigorously to vent many dangerous opinions, as amongst many others these were some: That it is not lawful for an unregenerate man to pray, nor take an oath, and in special, not the **oath of fidelity** to the civil government; nor was it lawful for a godly man to have a communion either in family prayer, or in an oath with such as they judged unregenerate: And therefore he himself refused the oath of fidelity, and taught others so to do also, that it was not lawful so much as to hear the godly ministers of England,

oath of fidelity: Oath to be taken by all freemen that consented and pledged fidelity to the authority of the civil government.

6 Nathaniel Morton, *The New-England's Memorial: or, A Brief Relation of the Most Memorable and Remarkable Passages of the Providence of God, Manifested to the Planters of New-England in America: with Special Reference to the First Colony Thereof, Called New Plymouth* (Cambridge, MA, 1669), 78–82, 96–99.

when any occasionally went thither, and therefore he admonished any church members that had done so, as for heinous sin; also he spoke dangerous words against the patent, which was the foundation of the government of the Massachusetts colony; also he affirmed that the magistrates had nothing to do in matters of the first table, but only the second; and that there should be a general and unlimited toleration of all religions, and for any man to be punished for any matters of conscience, was persecution.

And further he procured the church of Salem's consent unto letters of admonition, which were written and sent by him in their name, to the churches at Boston, Charlestown, Newtown, (now Cambridge) &c. accusing the magistrates, that were members of the respective churches, of sundry heinous offences, which he laid unto their charge; and though divers did acknowledge their error and gave satisfaction, yet Mr. Williams himself, notwithstanding all the pains that was taken with him by Mr. Cotton, Mr. Hooker, and many others, to bring him to a sight of his errors and miscarriages, and notwithstanding all the court's gentle proceedings with him, he not only persisted, but grew more violent in his way, in so much as he staying at home in his own house, sent a letter which was delivered and read in the public church assembly, the scope of which was to give them notice, That if the church of Salem would not separate not only from the churches of Old England, but the churches of New England too, he would separate from them.

The more prudent and sober part of the church being amazed at his way, could not yield unto him: Whereupon, he never came to the church assembly more, professing separation from them as anti-Christian, and not only so, but he withdraw all private religious communication from any that would hold communion with the church there, insomuch as he would not pray nor give thanks at meals with his **own wife** nor any of his family, because they went to the church assemblies, divers of the weaker sort of the church members, that had been thoroughly leavened with his opinions, of which numbers were divers women that were zealous in their ways, did by degrees fall off to him, insomuch as he kept a meeting in his own house, unto which a numerous company did resort, both on the sabbath day and at other times, in way of separation from, and opposition to the church assembly there; which prudent magistrates understanding, and seeing things grow more and more towards a general division and disturbance, after all other means used in vain, they passed a sentence of banishment against him out of the Massachusetts Colony, as against a disturber of the peace, both of the church and commonwealth.

own wife: Mary Williams, who continued to attend the Salem Church.

After which Mr. Williams sat down in a place called Providence, out of the Massachusetts jurisdiction and was followed by many of the members of the church of Salem, who did zealously adhere to him … keeping that one principle, that everyone should have liberty to worship God according to the light of their own consciences.

DOCUMENT 7

Roger Williams' banishment decree (1635) and Sir William Martin expresses his concerns about Roger Williams in a letter to Governor John Winthrop (1636)

In October 1635, Massachusetts Bay ruled to banish Williams from the colony for his "new & dangerous opinions" and he was "judged a great contempt of authority." Excerpt (a) is the official court record of his banishment. Initially, the implementation was deferred to the spring as Williams was ill, his second child had just been born, and winter was approaching. When Williams continued to meet with other like-minded individuals in his home and share his ideas, the magistrates ruled to seize him immediately and banish him to England. John Winthrop warned Williams, and he escaped amid a winter blizzard, surviving thanks to the Indigenous Peoples who provided him with shelter. In excerpt (b) **Sir William Martin** expresses his concern about Williams' increasingly radical ideas and removal.

Sir William Martin: A well-connected resident of Essex, England. Williams may have met Martin when he lived in High Laver, Essex.

a. Banishment Decree (October 1635)[7]

Whereas Mr. Roger Williams, one of the elders of the church of Salem, hath broached & divulged diverse new & dangerous opinions, against the authority of magistrates, as also write lies of defamation both of the magistrates & churches here, & that before any conviction, & yet maintains the same without retraction, it is therefore ordered, that the said Mr. Williams shall depart out of this jurisdiction within six weeks now next ensuing, which if he neglect to perform, it shall be lawful for the Governor & two of the magistrates to send him to some place out of this jurisdiction, not to return any more without license from the Court.

b. Sir William Martin expresses his concerns about Roger Williams in a letter to Governor John Winthrop (March 1636)[8]

I am sorry to hear of Mr. Williams' separation from you: His former good affections to you, and the plantations, were well known unto me and make me wonder now at his proceedings. I have wrote to him effectually to submit to better judgements, especially those whom formerly he reverenced and

7 Nathaniel B. Shurtleff, ed., *Records of the Governor and Company of the Massachusetts Bay in New England* (Boston: William White, 1853), 1:160–61.

8 Sir William Martin to Governor John Winthrop, 29 March 1636, in William Whitmore and William Appleton, eds., *Hutchinson Papers* (Albany, NY: Joel Munsell, 1865), 1:119–20.

admired; at least to keep the bond of peace inviolable. This hath always been my advice; and nothing conducts more to the good of plantations. I pray show him what lawful favor you can, which may stand with the common good. He is passionate and precipitate, which may transport him into error, but I hope his integrity and good intentions will bring him at last into the way of truth and confirm him therein. In the meantime, I pray God to give him a right use of this affliction. Thus leaving him to your favorable censures, and you to the direction of God.

DOCUMENT 8

Roger Williams reflects on his banishment, from letters to Major John Mason and Governor Thomas Prence (1670) and John Cotton, Jr. (1671)

Banishment was a mixed blessing for Williams; he was able to create a place where he put the theory of religious freedom and separation of church and state into practice, but it came at a price. Even after he was banished, Williams kept up a regular correspondence with many of the leaders in other New England colonies, describing how "My Letters are not Banished! May be welcome, may be seen and heard."[9] In excerpt (a), thirty-five years after his banishment, Williams reflects on the hardship of his removal. In excerpt (b) Williams addresses the conflict further in a letter to John Cotton, Jr.

a. Roger Williams to Major John Mason and Governor Thomas Prence (22 June 1670)[10]

Sir I am not out of hope, but that while Your aged Eyes and mine are yet in their Orbs, and not yet sunk down into their holes of Rottenness: We shall leave our Friends and Countrymen, our Children and Relations, and this Land in peace behind us ... First when I was unlikely and unchristianly (as I believe) driven from my house and land, and wife and children (in the midst of New England. Winter now about 35 years past) at Salem: That ever honored Governor Mr Winthrop privately wrote to me to steer my Course to the Narragansett Bay and Indians, encouraging me from the Freeness of the place from any English Claims or Patents. I took his prudent Motion as a Hint and voice from God, and (Waving all other Thoughts and Motions) I steered my Course from Salem (though in Winter snow which I feel yet) unto these parts ... I first pitched and begun to build and plant at Seekonk, (now Rehoboth). But I received a Letter from my ancient friend Mr [Edward] Winslow, then Governor of Plymouth, professing his own and others Love and respect to me, Yet lovingly advising me (since I was fallen into the Edge of their Bounds, and they were loath to displease the Bay) to remove but to the other Side of the Water, and then he said, I had the Country free before me, and might be as free as Themselves, and We should be loving Neighbors together ... in this respect and many other providences of the most holy and only wise, I called Providence. Sometime

9 Roger Williams to Governor John Endicott, August/September 1651, *Williams Corres.*, 1:337.

10 Roger Williams to Major John Mason and Governor Thomas Prence, 22 June 1670, *Williams Corres.*, 2:609–20.

Ousamaquin: Sachem of the Pokanoket Wampanoag.

after Plymouths great Sachim (**Ousamaquin**) upon occasion affirming that Providence was his land, and therefore Plymouth's Land, and Some resenting it … after due Examination it should be found true what the Barbarian said, Yet having (to my loss of a Harvest that year), been now … as good as banished from Plymouth as from … Massachusetts … I had quietly and patiently departed from them (at their Motion) … between those my Friends of [Massachusetts] Bay and Plymouth I was sorely tossed for … **14 weeks**, (in a bitter Winter Season) **not knowing what Bread or Bed did mean**. Besides the Yearly loss of no small matter in my trading with English and Natives, being debarred from Boston (the chief Mart and port of New England). God knows that many thousand pounds cannot repay the very temporary Losses I have Sustained … It pleased the Father of Spirits to touch many Hearts (dear to Him) with some Relenting: Amongst which that great and pious Soul, Mr. Winslow melted, and kindly visited me at Providence, and put a piece of Gold into the hands of my Wife for our Supply.

14 weeks: Very possibly an exaggeration, which covered the time from Williams' removal from Salem to settling in Providence. Williams likely made the journey from Salem to Pokanoket homelands in a week or two and spent the winter sheltering at Massasoit's winter encampment before relocating to modern-day Rumford in March.

not knowing what Bread or Bed did mean: Comforts of an English-style home.

Mahumetan: (Mohammedan) A follower of Muhammad, the Islamic prophet. It was used as noun and adjective; the terms Muslim or Islamic are more common today.

b. Roger Williams to John Cotton, Jr. (25 March 1671)[11]

I … received yours … and wonder not that Prejudice, Interest and passion have lift up your Feet thus to trample on me as some **Mahumetan** Jew or Papist, Some common Thief or Swearer, Drunkard or Adulterer, imputing to me the Odious Crimes of Blasphemies, Reproaches, Slanders Idolatries to be in the Devil's Kingdome, a Graceless man … I have now much above 50 years humbly and Earnestly begged of God to make me as vile as a dead Dog in mine own eye, so that I might not fear what Men should falsely say or Cruelly do against me: and I have long Experience of his merciful Answer to me in Men's false Charges and Cruelties against me … My great offence (you so often repeat) is My Wrong to Your dear Father [John Cotton] … But the truth is, the Love and Honor which I have always showed (in Speech and writing) to that Excellently learned and holy Man Your Father, have bene so great that I have been Censured by divers for it. God knows that for Gods Sake I tenderly loved and honored his person (as I did the persons of the Magistrates, Ministers, and Members whom I knew in old England) … The holy Eye of God hath seen this the Cause why I have not said nor writ what abundantly I could have done, but have rather chose to bear all Censures, Losses, and Hardships … Tis true, my first book the bloudy Tenent was burnt … [but] if your Selfe or any in public or private show me any failings against God or your Father in that Book, you shall find me diligent and faithful …

11 Roger Williams to John Cotton, Jr., 25 March 1671, *Williams Corres.*, 2:627–30.

Sir you Call my 3 proposals etc. abominable, false and wicked ... Your honored Governor tells me there is no Foundation for any dispute with Plymouth about those proposals for You force no men's Conscience ... You are pleased to count me Excommunicate and therein You deal more cruelly with me then with all the Prophane Protestants and Papists too ... you count me a slave to the Devil ... But Sir, the truth is (I will not say I excommunicated you but) I first withdrew Communion from Your Selves for halting between Christ and Antichrist, the parish Churches and Christian Congregations. Long after when you had Consultations of killing me, but Some rather advised of a Dry Pit of Banishment ... Sir You tell me my time is lost ... God knows I have much and long and conscientiously and mournfully weighed and dug into the Differences of the Protestants themselves about the Ministry ... He knows what Gains and preferments I have refused in Universities, City, Country and Court in Old England, and Something in New England. etc to keep my Soule undefiled ... God was pleased to show me much of this in Old England. And in New being unanimously chosen Teacher at Boston (before Your dear Father came divers years) I conscientiously refused and withdrew to Plymouth, because I durst not officiate to an unseparated people, as upon Examination and Conference, I found them to be. At Plymouth I spoke on the Lords day and week days, and wrought hard at the Hoe for my Bread (and so afterward at Salem) until I found them both professing to be separated people in New England (not admitting the most Godly to Communion without a Covenant) and yet Communicating with the parishes in Old [England].

QUESTIONS TO CONSIDER

1. Why and how was Massachusetts Bay founded? What were the goals of the colony?
2. Why was Roger Williams banished in 1635?

PART III

Building New Providence

DOCUMENT 9

Land Evidence for Providence, from the Narragansett Sachems Canonicus and Miantonomi (1636/38)[1]

Following his banishment and near arrest, Williams sought shelter with Indigenous allies as he made his way south. By spring of 1636, Williams and his followers from Salem started to build a settlement along the Seekonk River, in present-day Rumford, Rhode Island. However, Plymouth asserted that the land was within their jurisdiction, which meant that Williams could be arrested. Even though Williams and his followers had already begun to build houses and plant crops, they decided to cross the Seekonk River and settle in a place that lay beyond Plymouth's bounds. Williams made a verbal agreement with the Narragansett Sachems, Canonicus and Miantonomi, which allowed him to settle and trade in the area. He named the settlement Providence as he believed that it was God's Providence that had carried them to safety. Two years later, Williams recorded the particulars of the agreement. The evidence was signed by the Narragansett Sachems, Canonicus and Miantonomi, and two tribal members, Sotaash and Assotemeweit, witnessed the agreement. Rather than seeking a royal charter from the king in England, Williams dealt directly with the Narragansett. Williams went from theorizing that the king had no right to Indigenous lands to putting this belief into practice. While the perspective of the Narragansett Sachems has not survived in the written archive, oral histories and other sources suggest that the agreement likely benefited them based on trade and politics. Native Peoples of Southern New England had long acknowledged borders on their homelands, often using the natural landscape as a marker. However, this concept of land differed fundamentally from European ideas of "ownership." Interpreting the 1636/38 land evidence is further complicated by the fact that a later transcription had an additional forged paragraph. The document is recorded as 1636, for the oral agreement, which was confirmed in the written agreement below in 1638. However, this was not entered into the town records for another twenty years, and when it was, it had been tampered with amid land disputes in the colony. It was corrected and reentered in the town records in 1662.

1 1638 Deed for Providence, Unmarked Hollinger Box (Founding Documents), Providence City Archives, Providence, RI.

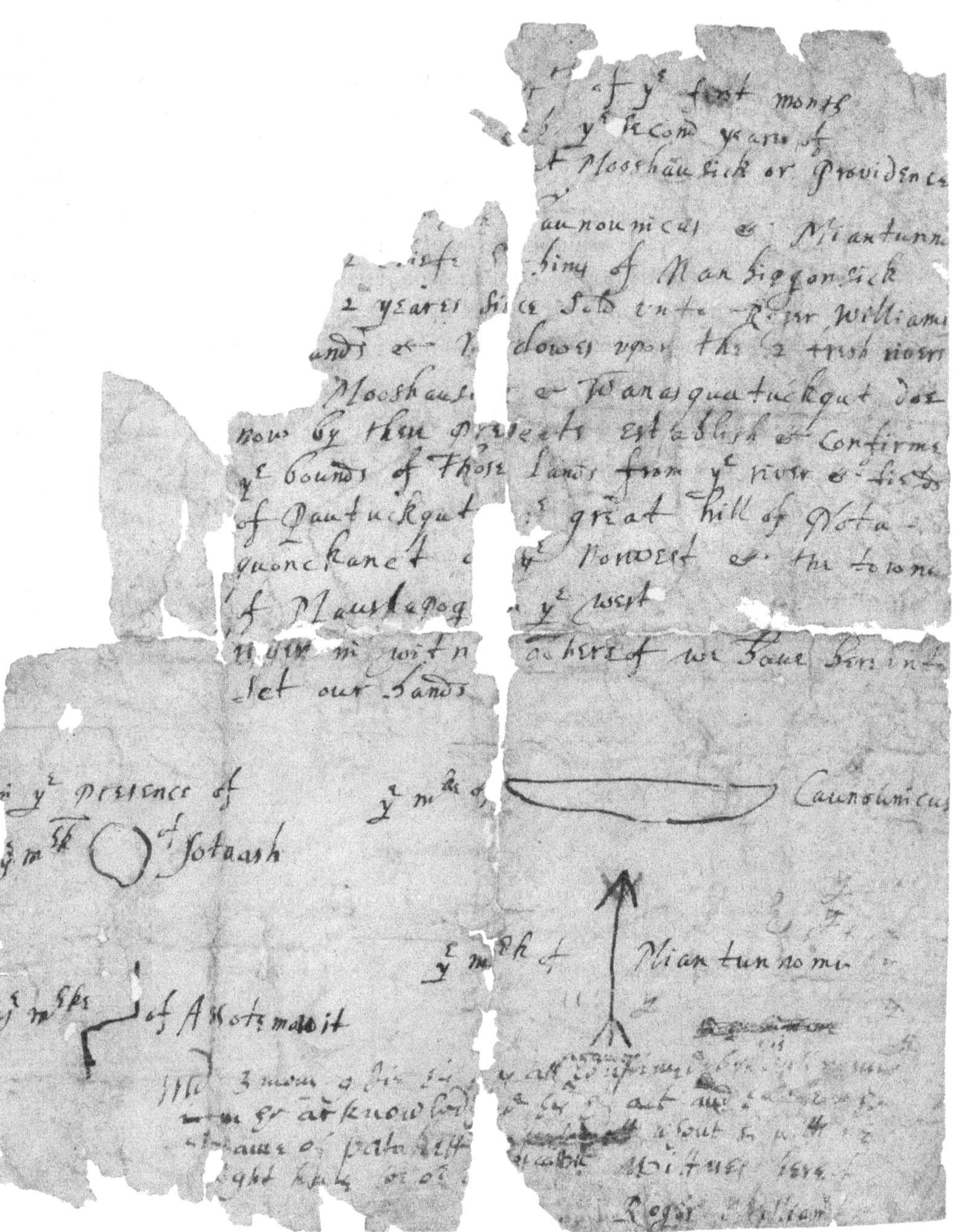

of ye first month
ye second yeare of
t Mooshausick or Providence
aunounicus & Miantunn
chiefe Sachims of Nanhiggonsick
2 yeares since sold unto Roger Williams
lands & meadows upon the 2 fresh rivers
Mooshausick & Wanasquatucket doe
now by these presents establish & confirme
ye bounds of those lands from ye river & fields
of Pautuckqut ye great hill of Nota-
quonckanet on ye Northwest & the towne
of Maushapog on ye west
witness whereof we have hereunto
set our hands

in ye presence of

ye mark of Canounicus

ye mark of Sotaash

ye mark of Miantunnomi

ye mark of Assotemewit

Roger Williams

Figure 9.1: Land Evidence for Providence from the Narragansett Sachems Canonicus and Miantonomi (1636/38)

Transcription

At Nanhiggansick, the 24th of the first month, commonly called March in ye second year of our plantation or planting at Mooshausick or Providence.

Memorandum, that we Cannaunicus and Miantunomi, the two chief sachems of Nanhiggansick, having two years since sold unto Roger Williams, ye lands and meadows upon the two fresh rivers, called Moshassuck and Wanasqutucket, do now by these presents, establish and confirm ye bounds of those lands, from ye river and fields at Pautuckqut, ye great hill of Notquonckanet, on ye northwest, and the town of Maushapogue on ye west.

In witness whereof we have hereunto set our hands.

Ye **mark** of CANNONNICUS.
Ye mark of MIANTUNNOMI.

In ye presence of

The mark of + Sotaash.
The mark of + Assotemeweit.

mark: Narragansett signatories used a mark to confirm the agreement in place of a formal signature. Miantonomi signed with an arrow and Canonicus with what is most likely a bow. Sotaash bore witness with a circle and Assotemeweit with a sideways "Z," possibly signifying a lightning bolt or branch.

DOCUMENT 10

Establishing a Civil Authority in Providence, from a letter to John Winthrop (1636)[2]

Following his banishment, Williams continued to correspond with John Winthrop on a wide range of issues. In this letter from 1636, Williams describes the problems of establishing an initial civil authority in Providence. Without a patent or charter from the king, the residents of Providence created a semblance of order among themselves using unofficial and inventive methods, with the head of the household serving as an officer at town meetings. There is no record of how or when this arrangement was instituted, although it may have been specified in an oral or written covenant.

The frequent experience of your loving ear ready and open toward me ... embolden me to request a word of private advise with the soonest Convenience if it may be, by this messenger. The Condition of my self and those few **families** here planting with me; you know full well. We have no patent: nor doth the face of Magistracy suite our present Condition. Hitherto, the masters of Families have ordinarily met once a fortnight and consulted about our common peace, watch, and planting: and mutual consent hath finished all matters with speed and peace. Now of late some **Young men** single persons (of whom we had much need) being admitted to freedom of Inhabitation, and promising to subject to the Orders made by the Consent of the House holders, are discontented with their estate, and seek the freedom of Vote also, and equalities etc. Besides, our dangers (in the midst of these **dens of Lyons**) now especially, call upon on us to be Compact in a Civil way and power. I have therefore had thoughts of propounding to my neighbors a double subscription, Concerning which I shall humbly crave your help.

The first Concerning ourselves the masters of families: thus We whose names are here under written, late Inhabitants of the Massachusetts (upon occasion of some difference of conscience) being permitted to depart from the Limits of that patent, under the which we came over into these parts, and being cast by the providence of the God of Heaven, remote from others of our Countriemen amongst the Barbarous in this Towne of New Providence, do with free and joint consent promise each unto other, that, for our common peace and Welfare (until we hear further of the Kings royal

families: There were roughly in Providence 32 inhabitants in the first year. The first arrivals were likely William Harris, Thomas Angell, John Smith, and Francis Weeks. These men, who started the temporary settlement along the Seekonk River, were then followed by the Arnold family, Hopkins family, and Carpenter family. Williams' family joined him in the spring.

Young men: Likely Thomas Angell and Francis Week. Edward Cope, William Reynolds, and John Throckmorton may have arrived at this time too.

dens of Lyons: A reference to the growing conflict with the Pequot.

2 Roger Williams to Deputy Governor John Winthrop, before 25 August 1636, *Williams Corres.*, 1:53–55.

pleasure concerning ourselves) we will from time to time subject ourselves in Active or passive obedience to such orders and Agreement, as shall be made by the greater numbers of the present Householders, and such as shall be hereafter admitted by their consent into the same privilege and Covenant in our ordinary meeting. In witness whereof we hereunto subscribe etc. Concerning those few young men, and any who shall hereafter … desire to plant with us: this: We whose names are here under written being desirous to inhabit in this Towne of New Providence, doe promise to subject ourselves in active or passive Obedience to such Orders and Agreements as shall be made from time to time, by the greater number of the present Householders of this Towne, and such whom they shall admit the same fellowship and privilege … Hitherto we chose one (named the officer) to call the **meeting** at the appointed Time. Now it is desired by some of us that the Householders by course perform that work, and also gather Votes and see the Watch go on … since the place I have purchased 2ndly at mine own charges and engagements the inhabitants paying (by consent) 30s a piece as they come until my charge be out for their particular lots: and 3rdly, that I never made any other Covenant with any person, but if I got a place, he should **plant** there with me. My query is this … Whither I may not lawfully desire this of my neighbors, that as I freely subject my self to Common Consent and shall not bring in any person into the Towne without their consent: so also that against my consent no person be **Violently** brought in and received …

I [do] not despise a Liberty, which the Lord seems to offer me if for mine own or others peace: and therefore have I been thus bold to present my thoughts unto you.

meeting: Assembled household heads made decisions, one head serving as an "officer" who could call meetings every two weeks.

plant: Williams likely distributed the first parcels of land among the other settlers in the summer of 1636. No written document has survived, and the initial agreements were likely oral.

Violently: Inappropriately.

DOCUMENT II

Parliamentary patent for Providence (1644)[3]

In 1643, seven years after Williams made an agreement with the Narragansett Sachems to found Providence, he sailed back to England to obtain a patent that would unite the towns of Providence, Portsmouth, and Newport and protect them from threats from neighboring colonies. However, due to his banishment decree, Williams was unable to sail from Boston and had to depart from New Amsterdam (modern-day New York City). Williams' timing was ripe, as a bloody civil war between King Charles I and a Puritan-led Parliament was brewing. Against this backdrop, Williams used his connections to publish many of his most important (and controversial) works, including *A Key into the Language of America* and *The Bloudy Tenent*. He successfully secured a patent from Parliament, which protected against encroachment from neighboring colonies, provided for self-government, and confirmed the colony's civil laws. It had no proviso about religion, reaffirming Williams' radical vision for the colony. The excerpt below addresses relations with Native Peoples, land boundaries, and structures of power. Williams returned to Boston not only with the patent but also a letter, endorsing his work and signed by several members of Parliament, which guaranteed his safe passage. He later remembered how "I went purposely to England and upon my Report and Petition, the Parliament granted us a charter of Government for these parts … And upon this the Country about us was more friendly … and treated us as an authorized Colony: only the differences of our Consciences much obstructed."[4]

WHEREAS by an Ordinance of the Lords and Commons, now assembled in Parliament … **Robert Earl of Warwick**, is constituted, and ordained Governor in Chief, and Lord High Admiral of all those Islands and other Plantations inhabited or planted by, or belonging to any His Majesty the King of England's subjects (or which hereafter may be inhabited and planted by, or belonging to them), within the Bounds, and upon the Coasts of America … And whereas there is a Tract of Land in the Continent of America aforesaid, called by the Name of the Narraganset-Bay; bordering Northward and Northeast on the Patent of the Massachusetts, East and

Robert Earl of Warwick: Robert Rich, 2nd Earl of Warwick, was a Puritan-sympathizer and colonial administrator and admiral. He led the Commission on Foreign Plantations and Warwick, RI was named after him.

3 The document is recorded using the original seventeenth-century calendar; *1643 Parliamentary Patent*, Land and Public Notary Records, C#0481, Rhode Island State Archives, Providence, RI, 3:344–49.

4 Roger Williams to Major John Mason and Governor Thomas Prence, 22 June 1670, *Williams Corres.*, 2:612.

Southeast on Plymouth Patent, South on the Ocean, and on the West and Northwest by the Indians called Nahigganneucks, alias Narragansets; the whole Tract extending about Twenty-five English Miles unto the Pequot River and Country.

And whereas divers well affected and industrious English Inhabitants, of the Towns of Providence, Portsmouth, and Newport in the tract aforesaid, have adventured to make a nearer neighborhood and Society with the great Body of the Narragansets, which may in time by the blessing of God upon their Endeavors, lay a sure foundation of Happiness to all America. And have also purchased, and are purchasing of and amongst the said Natives, some other Places, which may be convenient both for Plantations, and also for building of Ships Supply of Pipe Staves and other Merchandize. And whereas the said English, have represented their Desire to the said Earl, and Commissioners, to have their hopeful beginnings approved and confirmed, by granting unto them a free **Charter of Civil Incorporation and Government**; that they may order and govern their Plantation in such a Manner as to maintain Justice and peace, both among themselves, and towards all Men with whom they shall have to do. In due Consideration of the said Premises, the said Robert Earl of Warwick … Do, by the Authority of the aforesaid Ordinance of the Lords and Commons, give, grant, and confirm, to the aforesaid Inhabitants of the Towns of Providence, Portsmouth, and Newport, a free and absolute Charter of Incorporation, to be known by the Name of the Incorporation of Providence Plantations, in the Narraganset-Bay, in New-England. Together with full Power and Authority to rule themselves, and such others as shall hereafter inhabit within any Part of the said Tract of land, by such a Form of **Civil Government**, as by voluntary consent of all, or the greater Part of them, they shall find most suitable to their Estate and Condition; and, for that End, to make and ordain such Civil Laws and Constitutions, and to inflict such punishments upon Transgressors, and for Execution thereof, so to place, and displace Officers of Justice, as they, or the greater Part of them, shall by free Consent agree unto. Provided nevertheless, that the said Laws, Constitutions, and Punishments, for the Civil Government of the said Plantations, be conformable to the **Laws of England**, so far as the Nature and Constitution of the place will admit. And always reserving to the said Earl, and Commissioners, and their successors, Power and Authority for to dispose the general Government of that, as it stands in Relation to the rest of the Plantations in America as they shall conceive from Time to Time, most conducing to the general Good of the said Plantations, the Honor of his Majesty, and the Service of the State. And the said Earl and Commissioners, do further authorize, that the aforesaid Inhabitants, for the better transacting of their public Affairs to make and use a public Seal

Charter of Civil Incorporation and Government: The charter offered approval and protection from England.

Civil Government: The settlement was allowed to have its own civil government, with no rules about religion.

Laws of England: The settlement would have similar laws to England's but only when the "nature and constitution of the place will admit"; i.e., there would be no laws about religion.

as the known Seal of Providence-Plantations, in the Narraganset-Bay, in New-England. In Testimony whereof, the said Robert Earl of Warwick, and Commissioners, have hereunto set their Hands and Seals, the Fourteenth Day of March, in the Nineteenth Year of the Reign of our Sovereign-Lord King Charles, and in the Year of our Lord God, 1643.

DOCUMENT 12

Rhode Island Charter (1663)[5]

The implementation of Rhode Island's 1644 parliamentary patent was hampered by the English Civil War and the continued chaos in the four towns of Providence, Warwick, Newport, and Portsmouth. The towns had overcome William Coddington's resistance to the patent by 1647, but in 1651 Coddington secured a patent in England that made him governor-for-life over Aquidneck Island (where Newport and Portsmouth were located), thereby splitting the colony in two. Williams and John Clarke of Newport rushed to England to try to get Coddington's commission revoked and to secure a stronger charter for the colony.[6] They were able to restore the 1644 patent for the whole colony, but Williams remained in England for three years. Clarke stayed for another decade as an agent for Rhode Island to defend against the efforts by the United Colonies to dismantle the colony.[7] Following the restoration of the monarchy in 1660, King Charles II revoked all actions taken by Parliament in the absence of the monarchy, which meant that Williams' patent was voided. Securing a new charter was vital, but it took three years before King Charles II approved a charter for Rhode Island and Providence Plantations. The Charter described the colony as a "lively experiment," where individuals were free to worship as they chose, and where church and state were separate. These were radical ideas, especially in an era when religious war and persecution were the norm. The image of the charter shows the symbolic, ornate borders and how King Charles II's portrait dominates the charter. The charter declared that nobody could be "molested, punished, disquieted, or called in question, for any differences in opinion, in matters of religion." This famous line directly inspired later charters, including New Jersey's in 1664 and Carolina's in 1665.[8] The transcriptions below address the issues of religious freedom, separation of church and state, government structures, and relations with Indigenous Peoples.

---

5 *1663 Rhode Island Royal Charter*, Rhode Island State House, Providence, RI.

6 For more on Clarke's role, see Sydney V. James, *John Clarke and His Legacies: Religion and Law in Colonial Rhode Island, 1638–1730*, ed. Theodore Dwight Bozeman (University Park, PA: Penn State Press, 2008).

7 Before returning to Rhode Island, Williams anonymously published *The Fourth Paper, Presented by Major Butler* (London, 1652) and *The Examiner Defended in a Fair and Sober answer* (London, 1652). He also published an attack on mandatory public support of clergy, *The Hirelings Ministry None of Christs* (London, 1652).

8 In 1664, New Jersey used the same language to affirm that no person would be "molested, punished, disquieted, or called in question" for any differences in opinion, in matters of religion. The following year, King Charles II granted a charter for Carolina, which proclaimed that no one would be "molested, punished, disquieted, or called in question, for any differences in opinion of practice in matters of religious concernments." Edwin Gaustad, *Liberty of Conscience: Roger Williams in America* (Valley Forge, PA: Judson Press, 1999), 194.

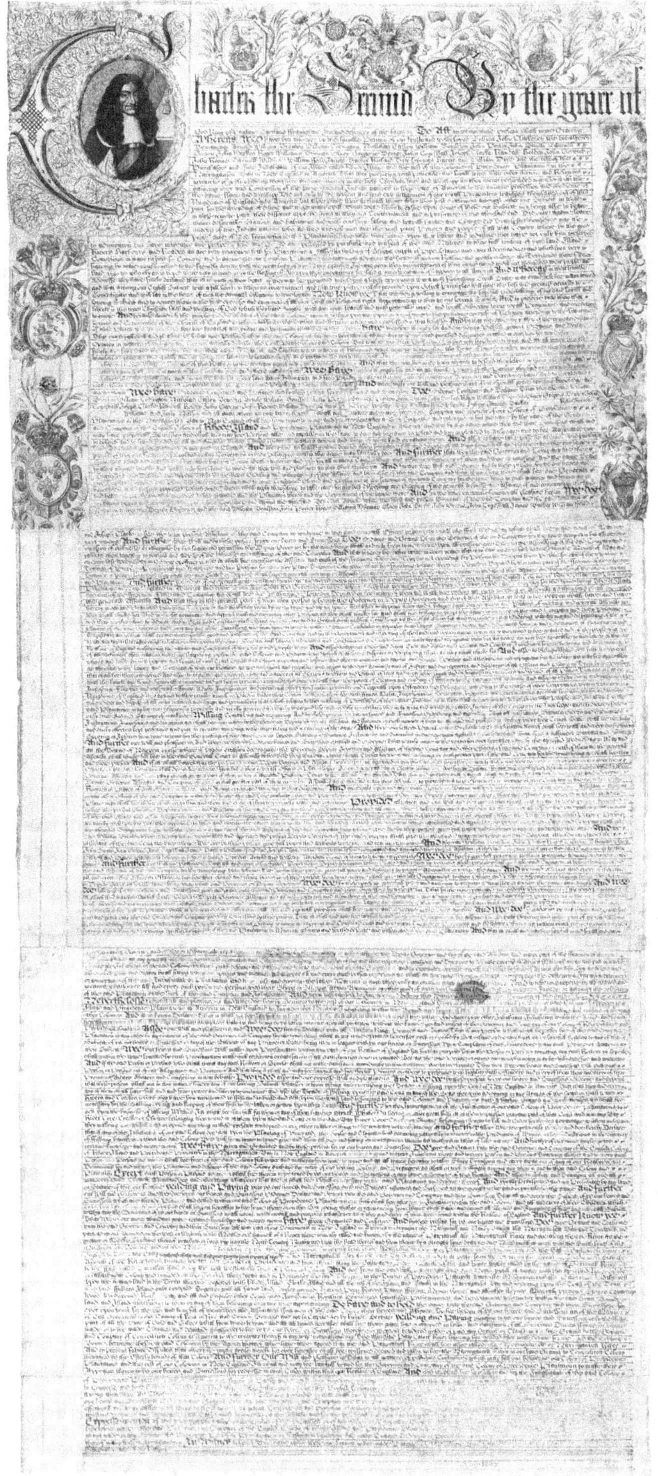
Charles the Second By the grace of

Figure 12.1: Rhode Island Charter

conversion: Attempts to convert Indigenous Peoples (described as "poor ignorant Indian natives") to Christianity. The language of converting "poor ignorant Indians" was boiler plate in the era, and Clarke likely had to include it to satisfy critics of the charter. While Williams himself was against conversion, this line in the charter demonstrates how the colony was part of the wider mechanism of settler-colonialism, which sought to take Indigenous land and eradicate Native religions.

encouragement of our royal progenitors: The New England colonies were not the result of royal encouragement; the colonists were pushed out because of religious persecution.

midst of the Indian natives: For most of the seventeenth century, Rhode Island was surrounded by Native Peoples. After the end of King Philip's War in 1676, their number rapidly declined.

purchase and consent of the said natives: The term "purchase" is complicated and the commodification of land problematic. Williams wrote at length about how he had acquired the land from the Narragansett Sachems through gifts and agreements; from a Narragansett perspective, the initial agreement was probably focused on trade and diplomacy.

lively experiment: In this context, experiment means demonstration. Rhode Island's charter demonstrated that one could have a civil society despite religious differences.

Charles the second by Grace of God, King of England, Scotland, France and Ireland, Defender of the Faith etc …

Providence plantations, in Narragansett Bay, in New England, in America that they, pursuing, with peaceable and loyal minds, their sober, serious and religious intentions, of godly edifying themselves, and one another, in the holy Christian faith and worship as they were persuaded; together with the gaining over and **conversion** of the poor ignorant Indian natives, in those parts of America, to the sincere profession and obedience of the same faith and worship, did not only by the consent and good **encouragement of our royal progenitors**, transport out of this kingdom of England into America, but also, since their arrival there, after their first settlement amongst other subjects in those parts, for the avoiding of discord, and those many evils which were likely to ensue upon some of those our subjects not being able to bear, in these remote parts, their different apprehensions in religious concernments, and in pursuance of the aforesaid ends, did once again leave their desirable stations and habitations, and with excessive labor and travel, hazard and charge did transplant themselves into the **midst of the Indian natives**, who as we are informed, are the most potent princes and people of all that country where; by the good Providence of God, from whom the Plantations have taken their name, upon their labor and industry, they have not only been preserved to administration, but have increased and prospered, and are seized and possessed, by **purchase and consent of the said natives**, to their full content, … they having near neighborhood to and friendly society with the great body of Narragansett Indians, given them encouragement of their own accord, to subject themselves, their people and lands, unto us whereby, as is hoped, there may, in time, by the blessing of God upon their endeavors[,] be laid a sure foundation of happiness to all America.

And whereas, in their humble address, they have freely declared, that it is much on their hearts (if they may be permitted) to hold forth a **lively experiment**, that a most flourishing civil state may stand and be best maintained, and among our English subjects, with a full liberty in religious concernments and that true piety rightly grounded upon gospel principles, will give the best and greatest security to sovereignty, and will lay in the hearts of men the strongest obligations to true loyalty. Now, know ye, that we, being willing to lay in the hearts of men the strongest obligations to true loyalty. Now, know ye, that we, being willing to encourage the hopeful undertaking of our said loyal and loving subjects, and to secure them in the free exercise and enjoyment of all their civil and religious rights, appertaining to them, as our loyal loving subjects and to preserve unto that liberty, in the true Christian faith and worship of God, which they have sought with so much travail, and with peaceable minds, and loyal subjection to our royal progenitors and ourselves, to enjoy; and become some of the people and inhabitants of the same colony cannot, in their private opinions, conform to the public exercise of religion, according to the liturgy, forms and ceremonies of the Church of England, or take or subscribe the oaths and articles made and established in that behalf; and for that the same, by reason of the remote distances of those places, will (as we hope) be no breach of the unity and uniformity established in this nation: Have therefore sought fit, and do hereby publish, grant, ordain and declare, that our royal will and pleasure is, that no person within the said colony, at any time hereafter shall be any wise molested, punished, disquieted, or called in question, for any differences in opinion in matters of religion, and do not actually disturb the civil peace of our said colony; but that all and every person and persons may, from time to time, and at all times hereafter, freely and fully have and enjoy his and their own judgements and consciences, in matters of religious concernments, throughout the tract of land hereafter mentioned, they behaving themselves peaceably and quietly, and not using this liberty to licentious and profaneness, nor to the civil injury or outward disturbance of others, any law, statutes, or clause therein contained, or to be contained, usage or custom of this realm, to the contrary hereof, in any wise notwithstanding. And that they may be in the better capacity to defend themselves, in their just rights and liberties, against all the enemies of the Christian faith, and others, in all respects, we have further thought fit, and at the humble petition of the persons aforesaid are graciously pleased to declare, That they shall have and enjoy the benefit of our late act of indemnity and free pardon, as the rest of our subjects in other our dominions and territories have; and to create and make a **body politic** or corporate, with the powers and privileges hereinafter mentioned …

body politic: Rhode Island would have its own government, meaning it would be self-governing.

That they the said William Brenton, William Codington, Nicholas Easton, Benedict Arnold, William Boulston, John Porter, Samuel Gorton, John Smith, John Weekes, Roger Williams, Thomas Olney, Gregory Dexter, John Cogeshall, Joseph Clarke, Randall Holden, John Greene, John Roome, William Dyre, Samuel Wildborne, Richard Tew, William Field, Thomas Harris, James Barker, [name missing] Rainsborrow, [name missing] Williams, and John Nickson, and all such others as now are, or hereafter shall be admitted and made free of the company and society of the colony … by the same name, they and their successor shall and may have perpetual succession, and shall and may be persons able and capable, in the law, to sue and be sued, to plead and be impleaded, to answer, and be answered unto, to defend and to be defended, in all and singular suits, causes, quarrels, matters actions and things, of what kind of nature so ever; and also to have, take, possess, acquire, and purchase lands … of this our realm of England … the said Governor and Company, and their successors, shall and may, forever hereafter have a common seal …

[F]or the better ordering and managing of the affairs and business of the said Company, and their successors, there shall be one Governor, one Deputy-Governor and ten Assistants, to be from time to time, constituted, elected and chosen, out of the freemen of the said Company … said officers shall apply themselves to take care for the best disposing and ordering of the general business and affairs of and concerning the lands … calling them together, to consult and advise of the business and affairs of the said Company. And that forever after hereafter, **twice in every year** … the Assistants and such of the freemen of the said Company, not exceeding six persons of Newport, four persons for each of the respective towns of Providence, Portsmouth and Warwick, and two places for each other place … to consult, advise and determine in and about the affairs and business of the said Company and Plantations … shall be called the **General Assembly** … to choose, nominate and appoint, such and so many other persons as they shall think fit … and to elect and constitute such offices and officers, and to grant such needful commissions, as they shall think fit …

twice in every year: The government would meet twice a year, or more if needed, and each town would have a certain number of representatives.

General Assembly: The legislative branch, which had powers to hold elections and create commissions.

[T]o make, ordain, constitute or repeal, such **laws** … as to them shall seem meet, for the good and welfare of the said Company, and for the government and ordering of the lands …

laws: The General Assembly could make laws, but they could not contradict the laws of England.

[T]o appoint, order, and direct … such places and courts of jurisdiction, for the hearing and determining of all actions … [and] to regulate and order the way and manner of all elections to offices … [and] to prescribe, limit and distinguish the numbers and bounds of all places, towns, or cities …

[And] to order, direct and authorize the imposing of lawful and reasonable fines, mulcts, imprisonments, and executing other punishments, pecuniary and corporal, upon offenders and delinquents, according to the course of other corporations within this our kingdom of England; and again to alter, revoke, annul or pardon, under their common seal, or otherwise, such fines, mulcts, imprisonments, sentences, judgements and condemnations, as shall be thought fit; and to direct, rule, order and dispose of, all other matters and things, and particularly that which relates to the making of **purchases of the native Indians**, as to them shall seem meet; whereby our said people and inhabitants in the said Plantations, may be so religiously, peaceably and civilly governed, as that by their good life and orderly conversation, they may win and invite the native Indians of the country to the knowledge and obedience of the only true God and Saviour of mankind; …

purchases of the native Indians: The government could regulate trade with Native communities.

We ... give and grant unto the said Governor and Company ... to nominate, appoint and constitute, such as so many commanders, governors, and military officers, as to them shall seem requisite ... for the **defense** and safeguard of the said Plantations ... to encounter, expulse, expel and resist, by force of arms, as well by sea as by land, and also to kill, slay and destroy, by all fitting ways ... all and every such person or persons as shall, at any time hereafter, attempt to enterprise the destruction, invasion, detriment or annoyance of the said inhabitants ... and upon just causes, to **invade and destroy the native Indians** ...

defense: The colony had the right to defend itself.

Nevertheless, our will and pleasure is, and we do hereby declare to the rest of our Colonies in New England, that it shall not be lawful for this is our said Colony of Rhode Island and Providence Plantations, in America, in New England, to invade the natives inhabiting within the bounds and limits of their said Colonies, without the knowledge and consent of the said other Colonies. And it is hereby declared, that it shall not be lawful to or for the rest of the Colonies to **invade or molest the native Indians** or any other inhabitants inhabiting within the bounds and limits hereafter mentioned, they having subjected themselves unto us, and being by us taken into our special protection, without the knowledge and consent of the Governor and Company of our **Colony of Rhode Island and Providence Plantations** ...

invade and destroy the native Indians: The colonists can "invade and destroy" Native Peoples in their homelands upon "just causes." It does not stipulate the terms of these "just causes," thus connecting the colony to the wider system of oppressive settler-colonialism.

invade or molest the native Indians: Rhode Island offered "protection" to Native people from invasion from other colonies. A decade later, Rhode Island allied with the other New England colonies *against* Native forces in King Philip's War. Williams tried to prevent this, but his diplomatic efforts failed when the Narragansett joined the war after the invasion and massacre of their village at Great Swamp.

[I]t shall be lawful to and for the inhabitants of the said Colony of Providence Plantations, without let or molestation, to pass and repass, with freedom, into and through the rest of the English Colonies, upon their lawful and civil occasions, and to converse, and hold commerce and trade, with such of the inhabitants of our other English Colonies as shall be willing to admit them thereunto, they behaving themselves peaceably among them; any act, clause or sentence ...

Colony of Rhode Island and Providence Plantations: New official name of the colony, which reinforced the fact that the two parts of the settlement, Rhode Island (Portsmouth and Newport on Aquidneck Island) and the mainland (Providence and Warwick), were one united colony.

In witness whereof, we have caused these our letters to be made patent. Witness ourself at Westminster, the eight day of July, in the fifteenth year of our reign.

By the **King**
HOWARD

King: King Charles II's royal seal approved the charter, but it would have been written by a court scribe.

HOWARD: Most likely Robert Howard, the king's Clerk of Patents.

DOCUMENT 13

Map of Providence town lots from tax list (1650)[9]

There are no original maps of Providence from the seventeenth century, and this map was created later using the 1650 tax list. The map illustrates how the lots were equal in size and placement, each having access to the Great Salt River (Providence River) leading into Narragansett Bay and a long and steep back lot. The map does not show how the town was in the midst of Indian country, surrounded by Narragansett and Wampanoag homelands.

Figure 13.1: Map of Providence

9 Map reproduction courtesy of the Norman B. Leventhal Map & Education Center at the Boston Public Library, Henry R. Chace (Henry Richmond). "Maps of Providence, R.I., 1650, 1765, 1770," Providence, RI, Nelson E. Osterberg (1914), https://collections.leventhalmap.org/search/commonwealth:3f4637626.

DOCUMENT 14

Mary Williams' role in managing the colony

For months and even years at a time, Mary Williams was the head of the Williams family.[10] Source (a) is the only known surviving copy of Mary's handwriting from 1650, when Mary addressed a letter to her absent husband. For unknown reasons, Mary never actually finished or sent the correspondence, and she even crossed out the address. Given the scarcity of paper, Roger used the reverse of Mary's unsent address to write to **John Winthrop, Jr.** Although Roger's letter to Winthrop, Jr. is one of hundreds that have survived, these few words on an unsent packet is the only known surviving copy in his wife's hand.

John Winthrop, Jr.: Son of John Winthrop and early governor of Connecticut colony.

When Roger returned to England in the 1650s to secure an updated charter, he longed for Mary to join him, but Mary refused. In excerpt (b) letters to **Gregory Dexter** (1652) and the Towns of Providence and Warwick (1653), Roger begs Mary to join him, but she remained steadfast in her decision to stay in Providence, likely because she needed to care for their children, manage the household, tend to their affairs, and keep the lively experiment alive. A bad initial crossing on the *Lyon* in the winter of 1631 may have tempered Mary's intention to cross the ocean again; moreover, war in Europe and the tense religious climate in England may have also put Mary off.[11]

Gregory Dexter: An important printer of controversial books and pamphlets, including Williams' *A Key*. After being imprisoned in England, he moved to Providence.

Excerpt (c) shows how Mary was central to clarifying the land disputes that rocked Providence in the 1660s. In 1661, when the town wanted to confirm the original agreement with the Narragansett Sachems in the 1630s, they looked to Mary Williams for her recollection. On 20 December 1661, Mary signed her **mark** on the confirmatory evidence regarding the 1638 agreement, thus reaffirming and ratifying the original vision for the settlement. The agreement described the original treaties with the Narragansett Sachems and how Providence was "a shelter for persons distressed of conscience" and how they sought "loving and peaceable neighborhood" with the "natives round and about us."

mark: Signing with a mark was not a sign of Mary's illiteracy, and other evidence reinforces that she could read *and* write.

Mary navigated many defining moments in her life without her husband, and perhaps the most terrifying was when she nearly died from an unknown illness in the early 1650s when Roger was away tending to Indian affairs. Mary survived, and Roger published the personal letter he sent to Mary in the wake of her illness as part of a pamphlet entitled *Experiments of Spiritual*

10 For more on Mary Williams, see Charlotte Carrington-Farmer, "More Than Roger's Wife: Mary Williams and the Founding of Providence," *The New England Quarterly* 97, no. 3 (Sept. 2024): 308–44.

11 Any letters that Mary sent to Roger while he was in England have not survived. However, clues from Roger's letters suggest that she did write. For example, one letter directly mentions his "wifes letter." See The Towns of Providence and Warwick to Roger Williams, after 22 March 1653, *Williams Corres.*, 1:380–82.

Health and Life (excerpt d). The irony of Roger being away when she nearly died, and then away again (this time in England on charter business) when he published the pamphlet in 1652, would not have been lost on Mary. The pamphlet reinforces not only Mary's literacy, but also hints at her own religious leanings. If her husband knew she would (presumably) appreciate him publishing a letter that he sent to her, this suggests that he valued her spiritual knowledge. The original letter was a private letter for Mary, but Williams dedicated the book to another woman, **Frances Wray Vane**. The book was styled as a devotional manual, a popular genre at the time, that provided spiritual lessons and consolation during difficult times.

Frances Wray Vane: Daughter of Sir Christopher Wray of Lincolnshire; she married Henry Vane in 1640. Williams stayed with Frances and her husband during his time in England.

a. Mary Williams' address to Roger Williams (ca. 1650)[12]

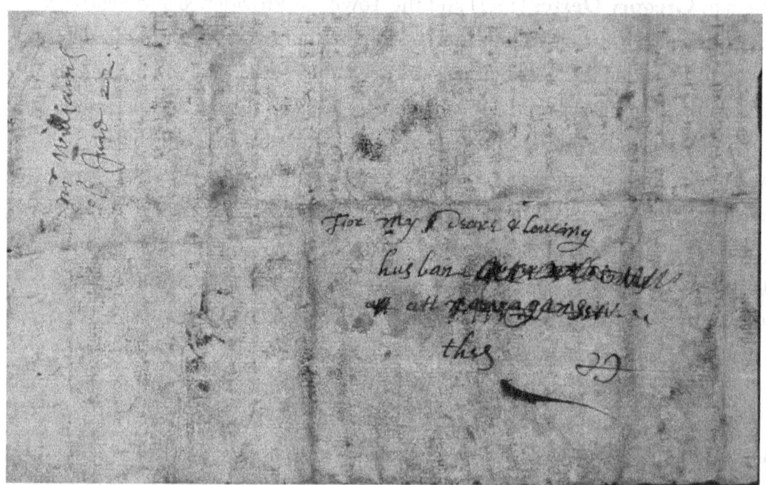

Figure 14.1: Mary Williams' address to Roger Williams

b. Roger Williams describes how he misses Mary in letters to Gregory Dexter and the Towns of Providence and Warwick (1652–53)

Roger Williams to Gregory Dexter (7 October 1652)[13]

Sir … in this dangerous **War with the Dutch**, the only safe Trading is to Bristol or those parts, for up along the Chanell in London Way is the greatest danger for although our Fleets be abroad, and take many French and Dutch,

War with the Dutch: The Anglo-Dutch Wars were a series of conflicts (many of them naval engagements) between the Dutch Republic and England in the mid-seventeenth century, primarily over trade and overseas colonies.

12 Mary's address was on the reverse side of an enclosure that Roger Williams included in the following correspondence: Roger Williams to John Winthrop Jr., 22 June 1650, *Winthrop Papers Special Collections*, P-350, Box 8, Massachusetts Historical Society, Boston, MA.

13 Roger Williams to Gregory Dexter, 7 October 1652, *Williams Corres.*, 1:366–67.

Yet they sometimes Catch up some of ours. Sir by my public Letters you will see how We Wrestle and how we are like Yet to Wrestle, in the hopes of an End ... For my self I had hopes to have got away by this ship but I see now the mind of the Lord to hold me here, **one Year Longer**. It is God's mercy, his very great mercy that We have obtained this Interim Encouragement from the Councill of State, that you may cheerfully go in the name of a Colony untill the **Controversy** be determined. The Determination of it, Sir, I fear will be a work of Time, I fear longer than we have Yet bene here ... I have no Thoughts of Return until Spring come twelve month. My Duty and Affection hath Compelled me [to acquaint] my **poor Companion** with it. I consider our many children, the dangers of the Seas and enemies and therefore I write not positively for her. Only I acquaint her with our Affaires. I tell her how joyful I should be of her being here with me until our Affaires were ended, and I freely leave her to wait upon the Lord for Direction, and according as she finds her Spirit free and Cheerful, so to come or stay. Sir if it please the Lord to give her a Free Spirit to cast herself upon the Lord I doubt not of Your love and faithful care in anything she hath occasion to use your help Concerning our children and Affaires during our Absence.

one Year Longer: Williams did not leave England for another 18 months.

Controversy: The Council of State had recently instructed Providence residents to continue under the 1644 patent until further direction. This was part of the uncertainty caused by William Coddington's patent, which had split the colony in two.

poor Companion: His wife, Mary Williams.

Roger Williams to the Towns of Providence and Warwick (1 April 1653)[14]

My dear and loving friends and neighbors of Providence and Warwick; our noble friend **Sir Henry Vane**, having [been] invited ... to accompany his lady to Lincolnshire, where I shall yet stay ... Sir Henry Vane and myself drew up, and the council by Sir Henry's mediation granted us, for the confirmation of the charter, until determination of the controversy. This determination you may please to understand is hindered by two main obstructions. The first is the mighty war with the Dutch ... Our second obstruction is the opposition of our adversaries, **Sir Arthur Haselrig** and **Colonel Fenwick** ... and all the friends they can make in parliament and council, and all the priests both presbyterian and independent, so that we stand as two armies ready to engage ... You may please to put my condition into your souls cases; remember, I am a father and an husband; I have longed earnestly to return with the last ship, and with these, yet I have not been willing to withdraw my shoulders from the burthen least it pinch others, and may fall heavy upon all; except you are pleased to give me a discharge. If you conceive it necessary for me to still attend this service, pray you consider if it not be convenient that my poor wife be encouraged to come over to me, and to wait together on the good pleasure of God for the end of this matter ... I write to my dear wife, my great desire of her coming while I stay, yet left it

Sir Henry Vane: (the younger) An English politician and former governor of Massachusetts Bay. As a proponent of religious tolerance, he supported Williams' vision for Providence. Vane returned to England and Williams wrote this letter from the Vane residence at Belleau, Lincolnshire.

Sir Arthur Haselrig: An important member of the Council of State and the Committee for Foreign Affairs, with significant power in Parliament; a formidable adversary for Williams.

Colonel Fenwick: Another influential challenger to Williams, who was part of a group who received a land grant west of the Narragansett River from the Earl of Warwick in 1632; Haselrig was his father-in-law. Fenwick was appointed as a member of the committee on plantations upon his return to England.

14 Roger Williams to the Towns of Providence and Warwick, 1 April 1653, *Williams Corres.*, 1:385–87.

to the freedom of her spirit, because of the many dangers, truly at present the seas are dangerous … although it pleased God himself, by many favors to encourage me, yet please you to remember, that no man can stay here as I do, leaving a present employment there, without much self-denial … I beseech … for you also, that no private respects or gains or quarrels may cause you to neglect the public and common safety, peace and liberties … So prays your most faithful and affectionate friend and servant … **P.S. My love to all my Indian friends**.

P.S. My love to all my Indian friends: Indigenous affairs and diplomacy occupied Williams' life, even when he was in England.

c. Confirmation of Land Evidence for Providence with Mary Williams' mark (1661)[15]

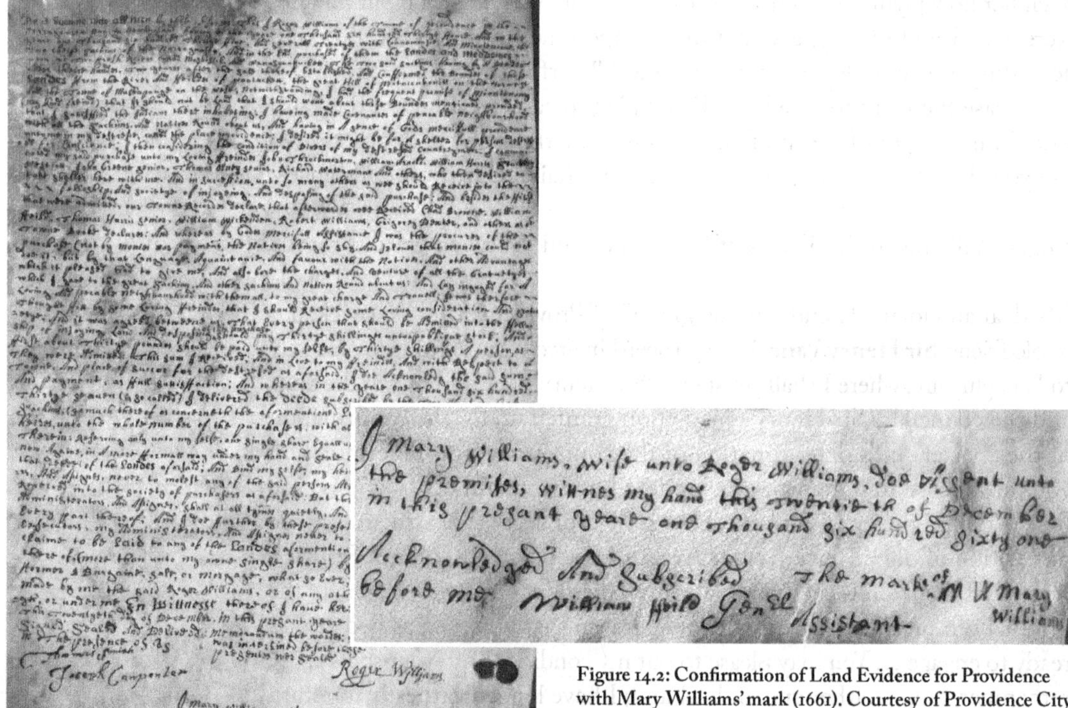

I Mary Williams, wife unto Roger Williams, doe assent unto the premises, wittnes my hand this twentieth of December in this present yeare one thousand six hundred sixty one
Acknowledged and Subscribed before me William Field Gen^ll Assistant
The mark of M W Mary Williams

Figure 14.2: Confirmation of Land Evidence for Providence with Mary Williams' mark (1661). Courtesy of Providence City Archives

15 Memorandum of original agreement for Providence, 20 December 1661, *Records of the Town of Providence*, RG 100, Providence City Archives, Providence City Hall, Providence, RI.

Transcription

I Mary Williams, wife unto Roger Williams, doe Assent unto the premises. Witness my hand this twentieth day of December in the present year one Thousand six hundred and sixty one. The mark of MW Mary Williams.

d. Letter to Mary Williams in *Experiments of Spiritual Health and Life* (1652)[16]

I confess ... it was but a private and sudden discourse, sent in private to my poor Companion and **Yoak-fellow**, occasioned by a sudden sickness threatening death, into which, and from which it pleased the Lord most graciously to cast and raise her ... And the truth is, the most of it was penned and wrote (so as seldom and never such discourses were) in the thickest of the naked Indians of America, in their very wild houses, and by their barbarous fires, when the Lord was pleased this last year (more than ordinarily) to dispose of my abode and travel amongst them ... The contents of this Discourse ... under the first are contained the Arguments of Spiritual Life, wherein the Weakest and the Sickest Child of God may find its **Spiritual Life apparent**, though over-cast and eclipsed with Spiritual Weaknesses and Distempers. Under the second Head, Arguments of the strength and vigor of the Spirit of Life and Holinesses: In which the strongest and the eldest in Christ, may find Experiments of Spiritual Heath, and Christian Activity ... Under the third Head are proposed some Means wherein the Spirit of God usually breathes for the preserving and maintain of a truly Spiritual and Christian Health and Cheerfulness ... The Letter which the Author sent with this Discourse to his Wife M.W. upon her recovery from a dangerous sicknesses. My Dearest Love and Companion in this **Vale of Tears**, Thy late sudden and dangerous Sickness, and the Lords most gracious and speedy raising thee up from the gates and jaws of Death ... so I hope, and earnestly desire, they may be ... as a warning from Heaven to make ready for a sudden call to be gone from hence, to live the rest of our short uncertain span, more as strangers, longing and breathing after another ... To cast off our great cares and fears and desires about this candle of this vain life, that is so soon blown out ... My dear Love, since it pleases the Lord so to dispose of me, and my affairs at present, that I cannot often see thee ... I now send thee that which I know will be sweeter to thee then the Honey and the Honey-comb, and stronger refreshment then the strongest wines or waters, and of more value than if every line and letter were thousands of gold and silver ... I send thee (though in Winter) an handful of flowers made up in a **little Posey**, for thy dear self, and our dear children, to look and smell upon, when I as the grass on the field shall be gone and withered.

Yoak-fellow: Close companion/spouse (i.e., his wife, Mary).

Spiritual Life apparent: Mary's spiritual struggles during her illness.

Vale of Tears: A Christian phrase and biblical reference to the trials and tribulations of life that are only left behind when one enters heaven.

little Posey: Williams' correspondence and spiritual interpretation of the illness, which were meant to provide comfort to Mary—not an actual posy of flowers.

16 Roger Williams, *Experiments of Spiritual Health and Life* (London, 1652).

DOCUMENT 15

Conflict with William Harris

William Harris and Roger Williams despised each other, and the decades-long dispute was both personal and political. The two not only hurled insults at each other, but they clashed over land boundaries. Williams had known Harris a long time, as they both arrived in Boston together on the *Lyon* in 1631. When Williams moved first to modern-day Rumford and then Providence, Harris followed, but by the mid-1650s their relationship had soured. Excerpts (a) and (b) explore how the disputes over land escalated in the 1660s and 1670s, spilling over into the political arena amid charges of abusing King Charles II. The land conflict with Harris pushed Williams to clarify the original boundaries of Providence, as Harris went back to England multiple times to advocate for his land claim; see excerpts (c) and (d). Excerpt (e) offers a comprehensive overview of the Williams–Harris conflict and gives a taste of some of the more colorful insults the two men hurled at each other. Their conflict was never resolved. Harris was captured by pirates on his final trip to England and died shortly after his release. Many accounts focus on how Williams' colony was a place of refuge for the persecuted, but his conflict with Harris illustrates the difficulties Williams faced in founding, implementing, and maintaining his grand vision.

Remonstrance: A formal document stating a grievance. This remonstrance against William Harris was presented in June 1667 by Arthur Fenner, John Throckmorton, Thomas Hopkins, and Shadrach Manton.

Majesty's: King Charles II.

Mr [William] Carpenter: One of the first settlers in Providence and original member of the Baptist church. He held several important public offices, including commissioner, juror, and town meeting moderator.

Thomas Harris: Thomas Harris, brother of William Harris, who arrived in Providence sometime in 1638/39. He held several important public offices, including colony commissioner, colony deputy, and colony assistant.

a. Town of Providence to the General Assembly of Rhode Island (after 27 July 1667)[17]

And whereas ... the Said William Harris desists not from his furious riding over the heads of his peaceable Neighbors but with greater fury threatens to prosecute all of us for high Treason, for our late sending our humble **Remonstrance** and petition to our honored Governor and Council in behalf of our oppressed Neighbors. We are Necessitated by this furious and desperate assaulting of us, in such a high manner as for all our lives, humbly pray this honored Assembly ... to vouchsafe Your sense on whether it contain any title of such a high Crime, which William Harris Now threatens ... We humbly pray that since so many of his **Majesty's** loyal Subjects and our peaceable Neighbors have been so hurried up and down by **Mr [William] Carpenter**, William and **Thomas Harris**, under the cloak and Color of his Majesty's name and Authority ... We humbly pray this

17 Town of Providence to the General Assembly of Rhode Island, after 27 July 1667, *Williams Corres.*, 2:572–73.

honored Assembly to pass an Order, that at the least William Harris may be declared incapable of future public power and Employment, until he hath satisfied some **General Assembly** of this Colony for his proud and furious Contentions, against the peace both of the Town and Colony.

General Assembly: It met in an extraordinary session in July and discharged William Harris as an assistant, although he maintained a seat as a moderator in an insurrectionary town meeting.

b. Town of Providence to the Governor and Council of Rhode Island (31 August 1668)[18]

That having being informed, that William Harris ... is resolved to pursue his Charge of a **Riot** etc. against so many of our honest and innocent Neighbors. We thought it our duty (being orderly met according to Law) for the honor of Truth, the honor of his Majesty, and the peace of his Majesty's loyal and peaceable subjects, (now most unjustly and insolently oppressed) to present these few lines to Your prudent Considerations ... First as to the Accusers ... all of them jointly William Carpenter, William and Thomas Harris, they pretend his Majesty's name and service, but it is a Mantle or Cloak to **private Ends**: For there are many Evidences ... of their treacherous profession ... of their treacherous minds against his Majesty's gracious Charter and Authority in this Colony, and the Government of Liberties of it ...

Riot: William Harris accused Arthur Fenner and others of taking over the town meeting by rioting in the summer of 1667.

private Ends: Harris' scheme to extend the boundaries of Providence to obtain a large tract of land for himself and his followers.

William Harris, he now forces us to remember that it is about 24 years since, he was disenfranchised and cast out from the Assembly of his Neighbors in Town meeting, for **assaulting a Neighbor and blood shedding** in the Kings high way in the street ... Tis true he hath thrust himself oft into our Meetings ... but the truth is he intruded and usurped, for he was never orderly received in again, since his disfranchisement upon record ... Since that time he hath lived in the Woods until the year 1656 ... not fit for the Society of Men ... but ... he broke forth with an open flag of Defiance ... under his hand writing to the four Towns of the Colony **against Civil Government** ... His book is yet extant and traitorously vomits out his filth against all Governsments and Governors (of what Rank soever) all Lords and Masters, against all Lawes, and Lawmaking Assemblies, against all Courts, all Punishments, prisons, Rates and Records, as Thieves, Robbers, Hypocrites, Satyrs, Owls (court of Owls) Dragons and Devils, and Soldiers, Legions of Devils ... he openly professing before the Country here at Newport, that he had nothing to lose but an old Coat for the Hangman, and he would maintain his writings with his blood ...

assaulting a Neighbor and blood shedding: Harris (who was serving as town officer at the time) violently beat Adam Goodwin in the street in 1644. Williams described how Harris was disenfranchised, but this did not come to fruition and the records are unclear.

against Civil Government: Williams used Harris' attacks on civil government to bring a charge of treason against Harris in 1656/57.

Since that time upon hope of a great Lordship of Land, he hath tacked about, **licked up his Vomit** ... [and] turned his former traitorous practices,

licked up his Vomit: Biblical reference to Proverbs 22:6. "Like a dog that returns to his vomit is a fool who repeats his folly."

18 Town of Providence to the Governor and Council of Rhode Island, 31 August 1668, *Williams Corres.*, 2:579–83.

into 10 Years vexations plaguing and tormenting both Town and Colony and the whole Country, with *Law*, *Law Suits*, and restless Fires and Flames of Law Contentions ... his Tongue is as fowl as his pen with constant and loathsome Reviling of all that crosse him (fool, Knave, Rascal Jackanapes, Scoundrel etc.) None scape his dirt of Reproach and Threatening ... he proceeds in his furious tormenting of his poor Neighbors, with most unjust and **causeless Vexations** ... The Claim of this **Spot** William Harris got his son Andrew in a deceitful way against the protests of Mr. Field, Mr Ony, Mr Carpenter himself and the rest of the purchasers ...

causeless Vexations: In July 1667 the General Assembly dismissed Harris from office as a colony assistant and fined him.

Spot: A meadow, which Harris and Resolved Waterman both claimed. It was laid out to Waterman in April 1667.

We herewith present You ... a petition of Redress ... We humbly pray First that you will please to Stop such shameful abuse of His Majesty's Name and Authority, and such Shameful oppression of his Ma[jes]ties loyal and peaceable Subjects ... We pray Your Countenance and Assistance to ... proceed legal with William Carp, William and Thomas Harris for their treacherous speeches (and We suspect Actions) against his Majesty's gracious Charter, and the Liberties, and Government ... which it hath pleased God and King (to the Envy and Astonishment of all our Neighbors), So wonderfully to bestow upon us.

c. Roger Williams to John Whipple, Jr., 8 July 1669[19]

Neighbor Whipple ... I humbly hope that you shall never find me Selfe Conceited, nor Selfe Seeking! so (as to others) not pragmatical and a Busybody as you insinuate ... This my testimony against this Unrighteous and monstrous proceedings ... First the grant of as large Accommodations as any English in New England had, this the Sachims always promised me, and they had cause for I was as a Right hand unto them to my great Cost and travel, Hence I was sure of **Tocekeunquanit meadowes** and what could with any show of Reason have been desire ... But some (that never did this Towne nor Colony good and tis feared never will) cried out (when Roger Williams had laid himself down as a stone in the Dirt for after Commers to step over in Towne and Colony) **what is Roger Williams**: We know the Indians and the Sachims as well as he, We will trust Roger Williams no longer. We will have our Bounds Confirmed us, under the Sachims hands before us ... Hence arose to my Soule cutting and Grief ... **the Bounds** set under the hands of those great Sachims Caunounicus and Miantunnomu, and were set short ... because they would not intrench upon the Indians inhabiting round about us for the prevention of strife between us ... My clamors and crying shall be to God and Men ... but for little ease and that your Selves and they that Scorn and hate me most may (if the Eternal please) find Cooling.

Tocekeunquanit meadowes: Toskeunke Meadows were near the Pawtuxet River and were claimed by both William Harris and the town of Warwick.

what is Roger Williams: A phrase Williams' enemies taunted him with, which Harris likely started. Williams repeatedly quoted the insult.

the Bounds: Boundaries described in 1636/38 Providence land evidence, and the source of one of the main conflicts between Williams and Harris.

19 Roger Williams to John Whipple, Jr., 8 July 1669, *Williams Corres.*, 2:586–88.

d. Roger Williams to John Whipple, Jr. (24 August 1669)[20]

As to saying that I was a Right hand to the Sachims (and Consequently had and might have had whatever I might rationally desire for this plantation, had I not bene stopped by that Envious Voice What is Roger Williams: We will have present bounds Set us.): my meaning is, that the Report of the Nahigonsicks Riches, and Country, and Friendliness to me and other Heretics kindled many hostile purposes and preparations against them in the English (especially of the Massachusetts) that, after (by my means) **a peace** was made and a league between the English and Nahiggoniks ... I was continually sent for by the Sachims, consulted with, and requested to write Letters in their names, and my own name, to all the 4 Colonies about us (especially the Massachusetts) ... Hence by reason of my great expense of time, my labors and travels (having no horse) my hazards in Canoes and by Pequts and Monhiggins etc. the Natives called me their Right hand ... (though William Harris Scorned and envied saying any Body could write a Letter etc.) ...

a peace: Williams worked as a diplomat to forge an alliance with the Narragansett and Massachusetts Bay colony during the Pequot War.

By the Sachims grant to me of an abundant Sufficiency to myself and my Friends ... I never understood infinite and boundless matters ... Is it not this Notoriously known that William Harris urged ... other Sachims after him ... to Confirm only what Miantunomu had granted to Roger Williams which was under the Sachims hands ...

Your Selves yet lye bewitched ... I desire others may come to see ... that William Harris (if God so please) may Come to see it himself least (too late) he wish that he had never seen Providence, nor New England nor the world it Self ... there was hardly even in New England William Harris His Equal, for Mostrous Evils.

e. Roger Williams to an Assembly of Commissioners (likely on or before 17 November 1677)[21]

The answer of Roger Williams apart to ... the said William Harris falsely and simply accuses the said Roger Williams. First he [Harris] charges Roger Williams for taking the lands of Providence in his own name which should have been taken in the names of those that came up with him. 2. He sold the Land of Providence for more than it Cost him. 3. He promised Pautuxet

20 Roger Williams to John Whipple, Jr., 24 August 1669, *Williams Corres.*, 2:594–604.

21 Roger Williams to an Assembly of Commissioners, undated but likely on or before 17 November 1677, *Williams Corres.*, 2:749–53.

for 5 [pounds] … and took 20. He stirred up Providence men to rise tumultuously against Pawtuxet men … I [Roger Williams] answer … [i]t is no new thing for me to bear all sorts of Reproaches Slanders etc. from William Harris … His language of me (and all that displease him) hath bene a Fool an Asse, a simple Dunce, a knave, a liar a Thief, a cheater an hypocrite, a Drunkard, a Traitor, a whore monger with Indian Women etc. To all which I can humble appeal to the Father of Spirits that through his infinite Mercy I have now many Years (above **three scores**) abhorred the Appearances and occasions of any of these Evils and am not such a fool to think much to be called with the Prince of Life Christ Jesus Deceiver, Mad man, Drunkard, Glutton, Blasphemer, Traitor … this honored and prudent Assembly will see this Charge Unrighteous and Ridiculous.

three scores: Sixty years.

For first it is not true that I was employed by any, made Covenant with any, was supplied by any, or desired any to come with me into these parts. My Soules desire was to do the Natives good, and to that End to learn their **Language** (which I afterward printed) … Yet out of Pity I gave leave to William Harris then Poor and destitute to Come along in my Company … I promised William Harris land and others if it pleased God to vouchsafe it me. But God furnished my self with, or by advantages which William Harris Nor Scarce any in New England had.

Language: The Narragansett language, which Williams published in *A Key* in 1643.

1st A Constant Zealous desire to dive into the Natives language.

2 God was pleased to give me a Painful, Patient spirit to lodge with them in their filthy Smoky holes (even whiles I lived at Plymouth and Salem) to gain their Tongue etc.

3 I spared no Cost towards them and in Gifts to Ousamaquin Yea and all his, and to Cawnounicus and [his?] tokens and Presents etc. many years before I came in person to the Nahiganset; and therefore when I came I was welcome: to Ousamaquin and that Prince Canounicus who was the **most shy of all English** to his last breath.

most shy of all English: Canonicus did not trust the English colonists.

4 I was known to all the Wompanoogs and Nagisosiks [Narragansett] to be a public speaker and at Plymouth and Salem and therefore with them held as a Sachim.

5 I could debate with them (in a great Measure) in their own Language.

6 I had the favor and Countenance of that noble Soule Mr [John] Winthrop who all Indians respected.

7 I mortgaged my house and Land at Salem (worth some hundredths) for Supplies … therefore was it a simple business for me to put in any with my Selfe. All that came with me and afterwards were not engaged but Came and went at pleasure but I was forced to go through and Stay by it …

As to my selling of them Pawtuxit and Providence: It is not true that I was such a fool to sell either of them … The truth in the holy presence of the Lord is this: William Harris Pretending Religion, wearied me with desires that I would admit him and others into fellowship of my Purchase. I yielded and agreed that the place should be for such as were destitute (especially for Conscience) and that Each Person so admitted should pay 30s country Pay towards a Towne stock and myself have 30 [pounds] … toward my charges …

As to that simple charge that I bought Cheap and Sold dear William Harris cannot be ignorant that Caunownicus whom he calls (in the Declaration) the **Conqueror** of all these parts. He was not I say to be stirred with money to sell his land and to let in Foreigners. Tis true he received **presents and Gratuities** many of me: but it was not thousands nor ten thousands of money could have bought of him an English Entrance into this bay. Thousands Could not have bought of him Providence or Pawtuxit or Aquedenick or any other Land I had of him.

Conqueror: Harris compared Canonicus to a monarch selling their conquered lands.

presents and Gratuities: Williams repeatedly made the point that diplomatic reciprocity was central to the Narragansett Sachems allowing him to settle.

I made him and his Youngest brother's Son Miantunnomu gifts of 2 sorts: First former Presents from Plymouth and Salem. 2. I was here their Counselor and Secretary in all their Wars with Pequts Monhiggins Long Islanders Wampanoogse. They had my person my shallop and Pinnace and hired servant at etc. Command on all occasions, transporting 50 at a time, and lodging 50 at a time at my house. I never denied them ought they desired of me. Caunounicus laid me out Ground for a trading house at Nahigonset with his own hand but he never traded with me, but had freely what he desired Goods Mony etc. so that tis simple to imagine that many hundreds excused me to the last of that man's breadth whom (dying) sent for me and desired to be buried in my cloth of Free gift and so he was. My trading house which yielded me 100 [pounds] … profit per annum God knows that for the public peace sake I left and lost it above 20 year since when I went last for England.

But honored Gentlemen (Bench and Jury) I beg Your Patience for a word more. He declares that I stirred up Providence men against Pawtuxet. I answer I have bene always blamed for being **too mild** etc. The truth is **Chad Brown** a Wise and Godly soul (now with God) with my self brought the

too mild: Being "too mild" is an unlikely assessment of Williams' character, given the many controversies he was embroiled in.

Chad Brown: A member of the special committee on land and pastor at the first Baptist church.

murmuring after Commers and the first monopolizing 12 go a Ones by Arbitrators chosen out of our selves; and Pawtuxt was allowed only peace Sake to the first 12 and the 12 gave me a share which I accepted after the Arbitration ... If there be any Difference between William Harris and me, I humbly offer to End it by Arbitration which I humbly conceave also will be the only Medicine for this long and multiplied Disease.

QUESTIONS TO CONSIDER

1. Why was the 1636/38 land evidence for Providence so radical?
2. What were the founding principles for Providence and how was the town governed?
3. What were the key principles of the 1644 Parliamentary Patent and the 1663 Royal Charter?
4. The 1663 Royal Charter declared that Rhode Island would be a "lively experiment" in religious freedom and separation of church and state. How did this play out in reality?
5. Consider the following documents from an Indigenous perspective: 1636/38 land evidence, 1644 Parliamentary Patent, and the 1663 Royal Charter. What do these documents reveal about inter/intra tribal dynamics and the effects of European settlement in Indigenous homelands?
6. What roles did Mary Williams play in the founding of Providence?
7. Consider the insults that William Harris and Roger Williams hurled at each other. How do they connect to the wider conflict between the two? How did Williams use the conflict with Harris to reflect on his purpose for founding the colony and his relationship with Native Peoples?

PART IV

Indigenous Peoples

LANGUAGE, CULTURE, AND DIPLOMACY

DOCUMENT 16

Roger Williams, *A Key into the Language of America* (1643)[1]

Williams' life was defined by "Indian affairs," including his trade, business, and political interactions with his Ninnimissinuok neighbors. After over a decade of going to great lengths to learn the Narragansett language, he published *A Key into the* ***Language of America*** in London in 1643 amid the English Civil War. At a most essential level, the work is a Narragansett-English dictionary and phrase book, but Williams' ethnographic observations set it apart. Over 200 pages and through 32 chapters, the book covers Narragansett terms for and ideas about greetings, numbers, times of the day, seasons, weather, winds, hunting, the earth and its fruits, beasts and cattle, fowl, the ocean, fish, sports and games, paintings, eating and entertainment, clothing, sleeping habits, illnesses, death and burial rituals, kinship networks, marriage practices, news and information networks, travel, religion, heaven, the sun and moon and stars, government, wars, money, debt and trust policies, and trade. In short, Williams tried to capture not only the Narragansett language, but the entire world of the Narragansett Peoples. There were clear limits to his success in doing so, and Narragansett speakers and culture keepers today can help identify the limits of Williams' understanding and the cultural and linguistic errors he recorded. In *The Tomaquag Museum Edition of A Key into the Language* (2019), Lorén Spears (Narragansett) notes in her preface that "Language is integral to culture. Without language a piece of the culture is missing." The Narragansett language has been used since time immemorial, and Spears explains that despite "colonization, enslavement, massacres, detribalization, government-sanctioned genocide, attacks on sovereignty, historical and lateral traumas, we [Narragansett Peoples] are still here and we still use our language."[2] The excerpts below include images of the original publication interspersed with transcriptions covering different examples of the Narragansett language and culture that Williams observed.

***Language of America*:** Williams boldly claims in the title that the language of America is the language of the First Peoples, not that of European settler-colonists.

1 Roger Williams, *A Key into the Language of America* (London, 1643).

2 Dawn Dove, Sandra Robinson, Lorén Spears, Dorothy Herman Papp, and Kathleen J. Bragdon, eds., *The Tomaquag Museum Edition: Roger Williams, A Key into the Language of America* (Yardley, PA: Westholme, 2019), xi–xiii.

A KEY into the
LANGUAGE
OF
AMERICA:
OR,
An help to the *Language* of the *Natives* in that part of AMERICA, called *NEW-ENGLAND.*

Together, with briefe *Observations* of the Customes, Manners and Worships, *&c.* of the aforesaid *Natives*, in Peace and Warre, in Life and Death.

On all which are added Spirituall *Observations*, Generall and Particular by the *Authour*, of chiefe and speciall use (upon all occasions,) to all the *English* Inhabiting those parts; yet pleasant and profitable to the view of all men:

BY ROGER WILLIAMS
of *Providence* in *New-England.*

LONDON,
Printed by *Gregory Dexter*, 1643.

Figure 16.1: Title page

2 *Of Salutation.*

What cheare Nétop? *is the generall salutation of all English toward them,* Nétop *is friend.*

Netompaûog	*Friends.*

They are exceedingly delighted with Salutations in their own Language.

Neèn, Keèn, Ewò,	*I, you, he.*
Keèn ka neen	*You and I.*
Asco wequássin	
Asco wequassunnúmmis	*Good morrow.*
Askuttaaquompsìn?	*How doe you?*
Asnpaumpmaûntam	*I am very well.*
Taubot paumpmaúntaman	*I am glad you are well.*
Cowaúnckamish	*My service to you.*

Observation.

This word upon speciall Salutations they use, and upon some offence conceived by the *Sachim* or Prince against any: I have seen the party reverently doe obeysance, by stroking the Prince upon both his sholders, and using this word,

Cowaúnckamish & Cuckquénamish	*I pray your favour.*
Cowaúnkamuck	*He salutes you.*
Aspaumpmáuntam sachim	*How doth the Prince?*

Aspaum-

Of Salutation. 3

Aspaumpmáuntam Commíttamus?	*How doth your Wife?*
Aspaumpmaúntamwock cummuckiaûg?	*How doth your children?*
Konkeeteâug	*They are well.*
Táu bot ne paump maunthéttit	*I am glad they are well.*
Túnna Cowâum	*Whence come you.*
Tuckôteshana	
Yò nowaûm	*I came that way.*
Náwwatuck nôteshem	*I came from farre.*
Mattaâsu nóteshem	*I came from hard by.*
Wêtu	*An House.*
Wetuômuck nóte shem	*I came from the house.*
Acâwmuck notéshem	*I came over the water.*
Otàn	*A Towne.*
Otânick notéshem	*I came from the Towne.*

Observation.

In the Narigánset Countrey (which is the chief people in the Land:) a man shall come to many Townes, some bigger, some lesser, it may be a dozen in 20. miles Travell.

B 2 Obser-

Figure 16.2: Of Salutation

a Key: The title of the book evokes the language of opening doors and drew on the form of other contemporary linguistic manuals.

To my Dear and Well-beloved Friends and Country-men, in old and new ENGLAND. I present you with **a Key**; I have not heard of the like … since it pleased God to bring that mighty continent of America to light: Others of my Country-men have often and excellently and lately written of the Country (and none that I know beyond the goodness and worth of it). This Key, respects the Native Language of it, and happily may unlock some Rarities concerning the Natives themselves, not yet discovered. I drew the Materials in a rude lump at Sea, as a private help to my own memory, that I might not by my present absence lightly lose what I so dearly bought in some few years of hardship and charges among the Barbarians … I resolved … to cast those Materials into this Key, pleasant and profitable for All, but specially for my **friends residing in those parts**.

friends residing in those parts: A thinly veiled dig at other settler-colonists in Massachusetts Bay and beyond who had not made an effort to learn either Indigenous languages or about Native cultures.

A little Key may open a Box, where lies a bunch of Keyes …

With this I have entered into the secrets of those Countries, wherever English dwell about two hundred miles, between the French and Dutch Plantations; for want of this, I know what gross mis-takers myself and others have run into.

There is a mixture of this Language North and South, from the place of my abode, about six hundred miles; yet within the two hundred miles (aforementioned) their Dialects doe exceedingly differ; yet not so, but (within that compass) a man may, by this help, converse with thousands of Natives all over the Country: ... I shall touch upon four Heads:

First, by what Names they are distinguished.
Secondly, Their Original and Descent.
Thirdly, their Religion, Manners, Customs, &c.
Fourthly, That great Point of their conversion ...

First, those of the English giving: as Natives, Savages, Indians, Wild-men, (so the Dutch call them Wilden) Abergeny men, Pagans, Barbarians, Heathen.

Secondly, their Names, which they give themselves.

I cannot observe, that they ever had (before the coming of the English, French or Dutch amongst them) any Names to difference themselves from strangers, for they knew none; but two sorts of names they had, and had amongst themselves.

First, general, belonging to all Natives, as *Ninnuock*, *Ninnimissinnûwock*, *Eniskeetompaūwog*, which signifies Men, Folke, or People.

Secondly, particular names, perculiar to severall Nations, of them amongst themselves, as, *Nanhigganēuck*, *Massachusêuck*, *Cawasumsêuck*, *Cowweseūck*, *Quintikóock*, *Qunnipiēuck*, *Pequttóog*, &c.

They have often asked mee, why we call them Indian Natives, &c. And understanding the reason, they will call themselves Indians, in opposition to English, &c ... They say that their Great God *Cawtántowwit* created those parts, ... There they say (at the South-west) is the Court of their great God *Cautántowwit*: At the South-west are their Forefathers souls: to the South-west they go themselves when they die; From the South-west came their Corne, and Beanes out of their Great God *Cautántowwits* field: ...

Directions for the use of Language ... [*A Key*] is framed chiefly after the Narrogánset Dialect, because most spoken in the Country, and yet (with attending to the variation of the people and Dialects) it will be of great use in all parts of the Country ... Because of the Life of all Language is in the Pronunciation, I have been at the pains and charges Cause to the Accents, Tones, or sounds to be affixed ...

Chapter I Of Salutation …

What cheare: The informal seventeenth-century English greeting "What cheer," or what cheery (good) news do you bring; a modern day "What's up?"

What cheare Nétop? Is the general salutation of all English toward them, Nétop is friend … They are exceedingly delighted with Salutations in their own Language … they are remarkably free and courteous, to invite all Strangers in, and if any come to them upon any occasion, they request them to come in …

Pétitees—Come in …
Taûbotneanawayean—I thank you …

I have acknowledged amongst them an heart sensible of kindness, and have reaped kindness again from many …

Chapter II Of Eating and Entertainment …

Parched meal: Parched corn meal, which is dried with heat.

Téaquacumméich—What will you eat?
Nókehick—**Parched meal**

… a very ready and wholesome food, which they eat with a little water, hot or cold, I have travelled with near 200 of them at once, near 100 miles through the woods, every man carrying a little Basket of this at his back, and sometimes in a hollow Leather Girdle about his middle, sufficient for a man three or four days … With a spoonful of this meal and spoonful of water from the Brooke, have I made a good dinner and supper …

meal pottage: A thick corn meal porridge made from unparched corn.

mercies: Delicacies.

Aupúmmineanash—The parched corne …
Nasàump—A Kind of **meal pottage**, unparched

From this the English call their Samp, which is the Indian corn beaten and boiled, and eaten hot or cold with milk or butter, which are **mercies** beyond the Natives plain water, and which is a dish exceeding wholesome for the English bodies …

Whomsoever comes in when they are eating, they offer them to eat of that which they have … If any stranger come in, they presently give him to eat of what they have, many a time, and at all times of the night (as I have fallen in travel upon their houses) when nothing hath been ready, have themselves and their wives, risen to prepare me some refreshing …

It is a strange truth, that a man shall generally find more free entertainment and refreshing amongst these **Barbarians**, then amongst thousands that call themselves Christians.

Barbarians: Non-Christians.

Chapter III Concerning Sleep and Lodging

N[u]sowwushkâwmen—I am weary
N[u]kàtaquaum—I am sleepy …
Matànnauk, or Mattanàukanash—A finer sort of **mats** to sleep on[3] …

mats: Skilled Indigenous weavers made many different types of mats, some for sleeping and some for elaborate decorative purposes. The mats were made from bulrush, cattail, corn husk, and thinly woven barks. The finer materials were used on the inside and the courser on the outside.

Fire is instead of our bedclothes. And so, themselves and any that have occasion to lodge with them, must be content to turn often to the Fire if the night be cold, and they who first wake must repair the Fire.

Mauataúnamoke—Fix the fire

Chapter V **Of their relations** of consanguinitie and affinitie, or Blood and Marriage

Of their relations: Family relations.

Nnìn, nnínnuog—Man, **Men**
Weémat—A brother

Men: nnínnuog, meaning The People, i.e., the Narragansett Tribe.

… They hold the band of brother-hood so dear, that when one had committed a murder and fled, they executed his brother and 'tis common for a brother to pay the debt of a brother deceased …

Towiúwock—Fatherless children
There are no beggars amongst them, nor fatherless children unprovided for …

Their affections, especially to their children, are very strong; so that I have known a Father take so grievously to the loss of his child that he hath cut and stabbed himself with grief and rage …

Chapter VI Of the Family and businesse of the House

Wetu—An **House** …
Neésquottow—A longer house with two fires
Shwishcuttow—With three fires
Abockquósinash—The mats of the house
Wuttapuíssuck—The long poles …

House: Intergenerational families lived in a wetu during the summer months along the coast, and used longhouses that were further inland during the winter. The houses were insulated with mats and covered with bark.

3 For more on mats, see *The Tomaquag Museum Edition: Roger Williams, A Key*, 30.

commonly get and fix [the long poles], and then the women cover the house with mats, and line them with embroidered mats, which the women make, and call them Mannotaúbana, or hangings, which amongst them make as faire a show as Hangings with us.

Fire: Used for heating, cooking, and in prayers and ceremonies.

Nòte or Yòte—**Fire** ...
Púck—Smoke ...
Nippúckis—Smoke troubles me ...

Birching bark, and Chestnut bark which they dress finely, and make a Summer-covering for their houses ...

Two families will live comfortably and lovingly in a little round house of some fourteen or sixteen foot over, and so more and more families in proportion ...

Túckiu Sachim—Where is the Sachim?
Mat-apeù—He is not at home
Payáu—He is come ...
Tawhítch mat peyáyean—Why came, or came you not ...
Awaùn ewò—Who is that?
Nowéchiume—He is my **servant**

servant: An ambiguous and complicated term, especially as Williams refers to his Native "servant" in his correspondence. It could also mean accompaniment or someone who had a lower status (e.g., captives or wards).

... Commonly they never shut their doors, day or night, and 'tis rare that any hurt is done ... Instead of shelves, they have several baskets, wherein they put all their household stuff ... Their women constantly beat all their corn with hand: they plant it, dress it, gather it ... beat it, and take as much pains as any people in the world ... It is almost incredible what burdens the poor women carry of Corn, of Fish, of Beans, of Mats, and a child besides ...

Princes: Williams often uses European concepts of royalty to describe Indigenous leaders, but this concept did not directly translate to Narragansett culture. The Narragansett cared for the whole community and shared resources.

Many of them naturally **Princes**, or else industrious persons, are rich; and the poor amongst them will say they want nothing ...

Nqussútam—I remove my house
Which they do upon these occasions: From thick warm valleys, where they winter, they remove a little nearer to their Summer fields, when 'tis warm spring, then they remove to their fields where they plant Corn ... their great remove is from their Summer fields to the warm and thick woodie bottoms where they winter: They are quick in half a day, yea, sometimes at few hours warning to be gone and the house elsewhere ...

Chapter VII Of their persons and parts of body

... Obs. Hence they call a Blackmore (themselve are tawny, by the Sunne and their anointings, yet they are borne white.)

Suckáutacone—**A cole-black man.**
For, Sucki is black, and Waûtacone, one that wears clothes, whence English, Dutch, French, Scotch, they call Wautaconâuog, or **Coatmen**.

A cole-black man: A very dark-skinned man, presumably a reference to the enslaved Africans in New England. The first recorded enslaved Africans arrived in Massachusetts Bay in 1638; part of a direct trade for enslaved Pequot captives in the West Indies.

Coatmen: One who wears coats, i.e., European-style clothes.

Nature knows no difference between Europe and **Americans** in blood, birth, bodies, &c. God having of one blood made all mankind, Acts 17. and all by nature being children of wrath, *Ephes.* 2.

Americans: Williams refers to the First Peoples as Americans. The concept of European settlers being "American" came later in the Revolutionary War period.

More particularly:

Boast not proud English, of thy birth & blood,
Thy brother Indian is by birth as Good.
Of one blood God made Him, and Thee & All,
As wise, as faire, as strong, as personal ...

Chapter VIII Of Discourse and News

Aunchemokauhettíttea—Let us discourse, or tell news
... Their desire of, and delight in news, is great ...
Cowawwunnâunchim—Your news is true
Uppanáunchim—Your news is false[4]
... Their manner is upon any tidings to sit round, double or treble, or more, as their numbers be; I have seen near a thousand in a round ... Every man hath his pipe of their Tobacco, and a deep silence they make, and attention give to him that speaks ... in a relation of news ... with very emphatical speech and great action, commonly an hour, and sometimes two hours together ...

Michéme nippannawâutam—I shall never believe it
... [O]ne answered me when I had talked about many points of God, of the creation of the soul, the danger of it, and the saving of it, he assented; but when I spoke of the rising again of the body, he cried out, **I shall never believe this** ...

I shall never believe this: Lines such as this one provide a direct insight into how Narragansett Peoples rejected key elements of Christianity in their own words, in this case the resurrection.

4 *The Tomaquag Museum Edition: Roger Williams, A Key*, 51, identifies that Williams has the definitions for false and true news mixed up; this work follows their correction.

Obs. Canounicus, the old high Sachim of the Nariganset Bay (a wise and peaceable Prince) once in a solemn Oration to myself, in a solemn assembly, using this word, said, I have never suffered any wrong to be offered to the English since they landed; nor never will: he often repeated this word, Wunnaumwáyean, Englishman; if the Englishmen speak true, if he mean truly, then shall I go to my grave in peace, and hope that the English and my posterity shall live in love and peace together. I replied, that he had no cause (as I hoped) to question Englishmans, Wunnaumwaúonck, that is, faithfulness, he having had long experience of their friendliness and trustiness. He took a stick and broke it into ten pieces and related ten instances (laying down a stick to every instance) which gave him **cause thus to fear** and say; I satisfied him in some presently, and presented the rest to the Governors of the English, who, I hope, will be far from giving just cause to have Barbarians to question their Wunnaumwâuonck, or faithfulnesse …

cause thus to fear: Lines such as this provide insight into the devastating impact of colonization and the behavior of European settlers.

A waunagrs, suck—English-man, men.

This they call us, as much as to say, These strangers,

Waútacone-nûaog.—Englishman, men.
That is, Coat-men or clothed …

Táwhitch peyáhetit—Why come they hither?

Obs. This question they oft put to me: **Why come the Englishmen hither**? and measuring others by themselves; they say, It is because you want firing: for they, having burnt up the wood in one place, (wanting draughts to bring wood to them) they are fain to follow the wood; and so to remove to a fresh new place for the woods sake.

Why come the Englishmen hither: This observation gives an insight into how Native Peoples made sense of European migration through their own relocation practices. It does not address the imperialistic desire for land, labor, and religious conversion that drove settler-colonialism.

Matta mihtuckqunnúnno? Have you no trees? …

Wussúckquash—Write a Letter …

Obs. That they have often desired of me upon many occasion; for their good and peace, and the English also, as it hath pleased God to vouchsafe opportunity.

Chapter IX Of the time of the day

Obs. They are punctual in measuring their Day by the Sunne and their Night by the Moon and Stars … living in the open fields, occasions even the youngest amongst them to be very observant of the Heavenly Lights

Chapter X Of the Season of the Yeere[5]

… They have **thirteen months** according to the several moons, and they give to each of them significant names, as

Sequanakéewush—Spring month
Neepunnakéewush—Summer month
Taquontikéewush—Harvest month
Paponakéewush—**Winter month**

Chapter XI Of Travell

Máyi—**A way**

… Obs. It is admirable to see, what paths their naked hardened feet have made in the wilderness in most stony and rocky places …

Wechauatíttea—Let us accompany
Taûbot wétáyean—I thank you for your company
Obs. I have heard of many English lost, and have oft been lost myself, and my selfe and others have often been found, and secured by the Indians.[6] …

Obs. They are generally quick on foot, brought up from the breasts to running … they are so exquisitely skilled in all the body and bowels of the **Country** (by reason of their hunting) …
Naynayoûmewot—A Horse …

Obs. Having **no Horses**, they covet them above all Cattell, rather preferring ease in riding, then their profit and belly, by milk and butter from Cowes and Goats and they are loath to come to the English price for any …

thirteen months: Since time immemorial Narragansett Peoples and other Eastern Woodland communities have celebrated 13 thanksgivings throughout the year, one for each new moon. For example, in the early summer there is strawberry thanksgiving. Traditionally, communities gather on the full moon to celebrate this gift from the Creator with feasting, games, songs, and dance. These vibrant and important traditions continue today.

Winter month: Winter is traditionally a time for storytelling, as elders share stories and histories.

A way: A path. The legacies of these paths remain today; e.g., Narragansett Trail and Wampanoag Trail.

Country: Indigenous communities are still connected to the land and waters today and traditional practices of hunting, fishing, and harvesting continue as communities adapt to environmental changes.

no Horses: The first horses arrived in Massachusetts Bay from England in 1629. Horses were a valuable commodity, and the famed Narragansett Pacer was bred in Rhode Island later in the seventeenth century.

5 For more on thanksgiving traditions, see *The Tomaquag Museum Edition: Roger Williams, A Key*, 60.

6 For more on these traditions, see *The Tomaquag Museum Edition: Roger Williams, A Key*, 62–72.

Crow: Narragansett Peoples today continue to tell the story of Crow and the gift of corn and beans. When Williams wrote "they have a tradition," he acknowledged Indigenous oral histories.

Earth or Land: Narragansett Peoples are directly connected to "Mother Earth" and their homelands and ancestors. Oral traditions describe the importance of these connections—past, present, and future. Today, the Narragansett Food Sovereignty Initiative promotes the right of Narragansett Peoples to define their own agricultural, labor, fishing, food, and land policies.

bounds of their Lands: Indigenous tribes and nations had their own territories with natural boundaries, with winter and summer villages. As a communal people, Indigenous concepts of land were fundamentally different from the European idea of land ownership.

Christians have right to Heathens Lands: Williams wrote extensively on how it was wrong for Europeans to use a patent from a monarch to claim Indigenous lands as their own. The way he acquired the lands for Providence reflected this belief.

Corn: An important part of Indigenous diets and culture, both historically and today. Indigenous traditions of burning fields provide the nutrients to enrich the soil, along with using fish as fertilizer for growing corn, beans, and squash (known as the Three Sisters).

Chapter XII Concerning the Heavens and Heavenly Lights

... Obs. By occasion of their frequent lying [in] the Fields and Woods, they much observe the Stars, and their very children can give Names to many of them, and observe their Motions ...

Chapter XIII Of Fowle

... Kaukont, tuock—**Crow**, Crowes.[7]

Obs ... they have a tradition, that the Crow brought them at first an Indian Grain of Corn in one Ear, and an Indian or French Bean in another, from the Great God Kautántouwit's field in the Southwest from whence they hold came all their Corn and Beans.

Chapter XVI Of the Earth and the Fruits therof[8]

Aûke—**Earth or Land**

... The Natives are very exact and punctual in the **bounds of their Lands**, belonging to this or that Prince or People ... I have known them make bargain and sale amongst themselves for a small piece ... notwithstanding a sinful opinion amongst many that **Christians have right to Heathens Lands**, but of the delusion of that phrase, I have spoke in a discourse concerning the Indians Conversion ...

Obs. There be diverse sorts of this **Corn** and of the colors ... if the use of it were known and received in England (it is the opinion of some skillful in physick) it might save many thousand lives in England ... the Indian Corn keeping the body in a constant moderate looseness.

Aukeeteaûmen—To plant corn ...

Obs ... The women set or plant, weed, and hill, and gather and barn all the corn and Fruits ... When a field is to be broken up, they have a very loving sociable speedy way to dispatch it. All the neighbors men and Women forty, fifty, a hundred & c, join, and come in to help freely.[9]

---

7 For more on fowl and oral history, see *The Tomaquag Museum Edition: Roger Williams, A Key*, 79–82.

8 For more on Narragansett connections to the earth, see ibid., 83–90.

9 For more on fish as a fertilizer, see Nanepashamet, "It Smells Fishy to Me: An Argument Supporting the Use of Fish Fertilizer by the Native People of Southern New England," in Peter Benes, ed., *Algonkians of New England: Past and Present: Dublin Seminar for New England Folklife 1991* (Boston: Boston University, 1993), 42–50.

Chapter XVII Of Beasts

… Obs. The Indians say they have black Foxes … but never could take any of them: they say they are Manittoóes, that is God Spirits or **Divine powers**, as they say of everything which they cannot comprehend …

Anùm—A Dog

Yet the variety of their **Dialects** and proper speech within thirty or forty miles each other is very great, as appears in that word,[10]

Anùm—The Cowwest Dialect
Ayím—The Narraganset [Dialect]
Arúm—The Qunnippiuck [Dialect]
Alùm—The Neepmuck [Dialect]

Chapter XVIII Of the Sea

… Obs. **Mishoòn an Indian Boat**, or Canoe made of Pine or Oak, or Chestnut-tree. I have seen a Native go into the woods with his hatchet carrying only a Basket of Corn with him, & stones to strike fire when he had felled his tree (being a chestnut) he made himself a little House or shed of the bark of it, he puts fire and follows the burning of it with fire, in the midst of many places, his corn he boils and hath the Brook by him, and sometimes angles for a little fish, but so he continues burning and hewing until he hath within ten or twelve days (lying there at his work alone) finished and (getting hands) launched his Boat, with which afterward he ventures out to fish in the Ocean … Some of them will not carry well above three or four: but some of them twenty, thirty, forty men …

Chapter XIX Of Fish and Fishing

Namaùs, suck—**Fish**, Fishes

Obs. The Natives venture one or two in a Canoe with a harping Iron … sometimes they take them by their nets, which they make strong of Hemp …

Pótop-paûog—**Whales** …

10 *The Tomaquag Museum Edition: Roger Williams, A Key*, 92.

Divine powers: Contemporary Narragansett culture keepers acknowledge that Williams is attempting (but failing) to fully describe Indigenous beliefs in the sacredness of animals and the natural world.

Dialects: *The Tomaquag Museum Edition* of *A Key* addresses how interpreting the diverse dialects that Williams describes is complicated by linguistics, modern politics, and the historical record.

Mishoòn an Indian Boat: A dug-out canoe which Native Peoples used for travel, trade, hunting, fishing, and whaling in the rivers, estuaries, bays, and the ocean around their homelands. The traditional practice of making a mishoòn from a single pine, chestnut, oak, or birch bark tree and shaped using fire, stone axes, and other scraping tools made from animal bone, shell, and stone continues today in Indigenous communities throughout the Dawnland.

Fish: Today, the traditional abundance and harvest of fish including herring, salmon, and other early spring fish has been impacted by pollution, damming, and industrialization. Indigenous communities are currently spearheading environmental protections.

Whales: Indigenous Peoples throughout New England were involved in whaling prior to European colonization. The whale is especially sacred in Wampanoag culture as part of the creation of their homelands.

Which in some places are often cast up; I have seen some of them, but not above sixty foot long. The Natives cut them out in several parcels, and give and send far and near for an acceptable present or dish …

Chapter XX Of their nakedness and clothing …

English clothes: Native Peoples traditionally wore clothes and shoes made from animal skins and feathers.

Obs. Our **English clothes** are so strange unto them, and their bodies … so to endure the weather, that when (upon gift &c.) some of them have had *English* clothes, yet in a shower of rain, I have seen them rather expose their skins to the wet then their clothes, and therefore pull them off, and keep them dry.

Obs. While they are amongst the *English* they keep on the *English* apparel, but pull off all, as soon as they come again into their own Houses, and Company …

Chapter XXI Of Religion, the soule, &c

Manì, manittówock—God, Gods

Gods: The Narragansett believe in one Creator and acknowledge the spirit within all creations.

Kautántowwit: According to Narragansett beliefs, Kautántowwit made everything and a portion of Kautántowwit's spirit lives in all creations. Narragansett Peoples today continue to give thanks to the Great Spirit, Kautántowwit, and the gifts of the four Directions and from above and below.

Obs. He that questions whether God made the World, the Indians will teach him … that God made all, but the[m] in special … [T]heir God made them and the Heaven, and Earth where they dwell …

First they branch their God-head into many **Gods**.
Secondly, attribute it to Creatures …

Kautántowwit the great South-West God, to whose House all souls go, and from whom came their Corn, Beans, as they say … [they have] The Eastern God … The Western God … The Northern God … The Southern God[11] …

a Native: Penowanyanquis, a Nipmuck trader for the Narragansett.

murderous English: Arthur Peach, Thomas Jackson, Richard Stinnings, and Daniel Cross.

suffered Death: Williams played a key role as a diplomat in bringing Peach and the others to justice for the murder.

I was once with **a Native** dying of a wound given him by some **murderous English** … who robbed him and run him through with a Rapier … but dying of his wound, they **suffered Death** at new Plymouth, in New England, this Native dying called much upon Muckquachuckquand, which the other Natives I understood (as they believed) had appeared to the dying young many years before and bid him whenever he was in distress call upon him …

---

11 For more on Narragansett religious beliefs historically and contemporarily, see *The Tomaquag Museum Edition: Roger Williams, A Key*, 108–18.

They have a modest Religious persuasion not to disturb any man, either themselves English, Dutch, or any in their Conscience, and worship, and therefore say:

Aquiewopwaũwash. Peace, hold your peace … they will relate how they have it from their Fathers, that Kautantowwit made one man and woman of stone, which disliking, he broke them in piece, and made another man and woman of a Tree, which were the Fountains of all mankind …

They … are very observant of the English lives: I have heard them say to an Englishman (who being hindered, **broke a promise** to them) You know God, Will you lie Englishman? …

Chapter XXII Of their Government and Justice

Sâchim, maûog—**King**, Kings

Obs. Their Government is Monarchical, yet at present the chief government in the Country is divided between a younger Sachim, Miantunnômu, and an elder Sachim, Caunoúnicus, of about fourscore [80] years old, this young mans Uncle; and their agreement in the Government is remarkable:

The old Sachim will not be offended at what the young Sachim doth; and the young Sachim will not do what he conceives will displease his Uncle … Sachims, although they have an absolute Monarchy over the people, yet they will not conclude ought that concerns all, either Laws or Subsides, or wars, unless to which the people are averse, and by gentle persuasion cannot be brought …

Chapter XXI Of Marriage …

… [T]he **Women** bring in all the increase of the Field, &c the Husband … fishes, hunts … [the women] from their extraordinary great labor (even above the labor of men) as in the Field … in carrying of mighty Burdens, in digging clams, and getting other Shellfish from the Sea, in beating all their corn in Mortars …

Chapter XXVI Concerning their Coin

The Indians are ignorant of Europe's **Coin** … Their own is of two sorts, one white which they make of stem or stock of the **Periwinkle**, which they call Meteaûhock, when all the shell is broken off, and of this sort fix of their

broke a promise: Williams' record of these interactions gives a small insight into Native perspectives of settler-colonialism.

King: Writing for an English audience, Williams incorrectly describes the leadership title of Sâchim through the Euro-centric lens of a royal monarch.

Women: Narragansett Peoples are matrilineal, and the husband joins the wife's family and village.

Coin: Wampum has always been an important part of Indigenous spiritual, political, and cultural practices, which continue to this day. The European settler-colonists used wampum as a trade currency, with devastating consequences for Native economies. Wampum comes from the Wampanoag term wampumpeak (shell beads).

Periwinkle: *The Tomaquag Museum Edition* of *A Key* suggests that it was more likely whelk shell, as today the Narragansett use whelk and quahaug for white beads.

162 Of *their Trading.*

black counterfeited by a Stone and other Materialls: yet I never knew any of them much deceived, for their danger of being deceived (in these things of Earth) makes them cautelous.

Cosaúmawem.	*You aske too much.*
Kuttíackqussaûwaw.	*You are very hard.*
Aquie iackqussaũme.	*Be not so hard.*
Aquie Wussaúmowash.	*Doe not aske so much.*
Tashin Commêsim?	*How much shall I give you?*
Kutteaûg Comméinsh.	*I will give you your Money.*
Nkèke Comméinsh.	I *will give you an Otter.*
Coanombúqusse Kuttassokakómme.	*You have deceived me.*

Obs. Who ever deale or trade with them, had need of Wisedome, Patience, and Faithfulnesse in dealing: for they frequently say *Cuppànnauem,* you lye, *Cuttassokakómme,* you deceive me.

Misquésu Kunúkkeke	*Your Otter is reddish.*
Yò aúwusse Wunnêgin	*This is better.*
Yo chippaúatu.	*This is of another price.*
Augausaúatu.	*It is Cheap.*
Múchickaúatu.	*It is deare.*

Wuttun-

Figure 16.3: Of their Trading

small Beads (which they make with holes to string the bracelets) are currant with the English for a penny. The second is black, inkling to blue, which is made of the shall of a fish, which some English call Hens, Poquaûhock, and of this sort three make an English penny ... The Indians bring down all sorts of Furs, which they take in the Country, ... this Money the English, French, and Dutch, trade to the Indians, six hundred miles in several parts (North and South from New England) for their Furs and whatsoever they stand in need of from them: as Corne, Venison ... Their white they call Wompam (which signifies): their black Suckáubock (Súcki signifying blacke) ...

Chapter XXV Of their Trading

... Amongst themselves they trade their Corn, skins, Coats, Venison, Fish &c. and sometimes come ten or twenty in a Company to trade amongst the English. They have some who follow only making of Bowes, some Arrows, some Dishes, (the Women make all their earthen Vessels) some follow fishing, some hunting, most on the Sea-side make Money ... They are marvelous subtle in their Bargains to save a penny, And very suspicious that English men labor to **deceive them**.

deceive them: Another example of Native perspectives on the negative impact of settler-colonialism, which included Europeans counterfeiting wampum and flooding the market.

Chapter XXVIII Of their Huntings

... The Natives **hunt** two ways: First, when they pursue their game (especially Deer, which is the general and wonderful plenteous hunting in the Country) ... Second, They hunt by Traps of several sorts.

hunt: Traditional hunting practices continue today with traps, bow and arrow, and guns. Intergenerational families often hunt together and share the harvest, giving thanks for the life of the animal through ceremony and prayer.

Chapter XXVIII Of their Gaming

... Their Games (like the English) ... are of two sorts, private and public ... A Game like unto the English Cards, yet instead of Cards they play with strong Rushes ... they [also] have a kinde of **Dice** which are Plum stones painted, which they cast in a Tray with a mighty noise and sweating. Their public Games are solemnized with the meetings of hundreds, sometimes thousands ... This Arbor or Play house is made of long poles set in the earth, four square, sixteen or twenty foot high, on which they hang great store of their stringed money have great staking, town against town, and two chosen out of the rest by course to play ... this kind of Dice in the midst of all their

Dice: These games continue today using painted stones, plum pits, or seeds.

Abettors, with great shouting and solemnity: beside, they have great meetings of foot-ball playing, only in summer, town against town, upon some sandy shore, free from stones, or upon some sort of heathy plot because of their naked feet at which they have great staking, but seldom quarrel ... But their chief ... for sport and game, is (if there land be at peace) toward Harvest, when they set up a long house called Qunnekamuck Which signifies Long house sometimes as hundred some times two hundred foot long upon a plain near the Court ... where many thousands, men and women meet ...

Of theire Warre & c.

... Obs. Their Wars are far less bloody, and devouring then the **cruel Wars** of Europe; and seldom twenty slain in a pitched field ...

cruel Wars: The idea of complete slaughter of a people was an alien concept to the Native Peoples of Southern New England in the 1640s.

Chapter XXX Of their paintings

... 1, They paint their Garments & c. 2. The men paint their Faces in War. 3. Both Men and Women **for pride** & c ... their red painting which they most delight in and is both the Bark of the Pine, as also a red Earth ...

for pride: Historically and contemporarily, Narragansett Peoples paint their faces for ceremonial purposes.

196 Of *Sicknesse.*

of Friends, and Neighbours, a poore empry visit and presence, and yet indeed this is very solemne, unlesse it be in infectious diseases, and then all forsake them aud flie, that I have often seene a poore House left alone in the wild Woods, all being fled, the living not able to bury the dead: so terrible is the apprehension of an infectious disease, that not only persons, but the Houses and the whole Towne takes flight.

Nummòckquese.	*I have a swelling.*
Mocquêsui	*He is swelled.*
Wàme wuhòck-Mockquêsui.	*All his body is swelled.*
Mamaskishaûi.	*He hath the Pox.*
Mamaskishaûonck.	*The Pox.*
Mamaskishaûmitch.	*The last pox.*
Wesauashaûi.	*He hath the plague.*
Wesauashaûonck.	*The plague.*
Wesauashaûmitch.	*The great plague.*

Obs. Were it not that they live in sweet Aire, and remove persons and Houses from the infected, in ordinary course of subordinate Causes, would few or any be left alive, and surviving.

Nmunnádtommin.	*I vomit.*
Nqúnnuckquus.	I *am lame.*
Ncúpsa.	*I am deafe.*

Npóckunnum.

Of *Sicknesse.* 197

Npóckunnum.	*I am blind.*
Npockquanámmen.	*My disease is I know not what.*
Pésuponck.	*An Hot-house.*
Npesuppaûmen.	*I goe to sweate.*
Pesuppaûog.	*They are sweating.*

Obs. This Hot-house is a kind of little Cell or Cave, six or eight foot over, round, made on the side of a hill (commonly by some Rivulet or Brooke) into this frequently the men enter after they have exceedingly heated it with store of wood, laid upon an heape of stones in the midle. When they have taken out the fire, the stones keepe still a great heat: Ten, twelve, twenty more or lesse, enter at once starke naked, leaving their coats, small breeches (or aprons) at the doore, with one to keepe all: here doe they sit round these hot stones an houre or more, taking *Tobacco*, discoursing, and sweating together; which sweating they use for two ends: First, to cleanse their skin: Secondly, to purge their bodies, which doubtlesse is a great meanes of preserving them, and recovering them from diseases, especially from the *French* disease, which by sweating and some potions, they perfectly and speedily cure: when they come forth (which is matter of admiration) I have seene

O 3 them

Figure 16.4: Of Sicknesse

Chapter XXXI Of Sicknesse …

Powwâw—Their Priest
Maunêtu—A Conjurer …

bewitch: Williams' Eurocentric bias and lack of understanding is evident when he describes Indigenous medicine people and their healing practices.

Obs. … These Priests and Conjurers … doe **bewitch** people, and not only take their Money, but doe most certainly (by the help of the Devil) work great Cures … [T]he poor people store up Money and spend both Money and goods on the Powwâw or Priests in these times, the poor people commonly die under their hands, for alas, they administer nothing but howl and roar, and hollow over them, and begin the song to the rest of the People about them who all join (like a choir) in Prayer to their Gods …

Chapter XXXII Of Death and Buriall[12]

black their faces: This tradition continues today.

… He hath some dead in house (whether wife or child &c) for although at the first being sicke, all the Women and Maides **black their faces** with soot and other blackings; yet upon the death of the sick, the father, or husband, and all his neighbors, the Men also (as the English were black mourning clothes) wear black Faces, and lay on soot very thick, which I have often seen clotted with their tears. This blacking and lamenting they observe in most doleful manner, diverse weeks and months, yea, a year, if the person be great and public … As they abound in lamentations for the dead, so they abound in consolations to the living and visit them frequently using this work Kutchímmoke, Kutchímmoke, Be of good cheere, which they express by stroking the cheek and head of the father or mother, husband, or wife of the dead … [T]hey abhor to mention the dead by name and therefore, if any man bear the name of the dead, he changes his name, and if any stranger accidently name him, he is checked, and if any willfully name him he is fined, and amongst States, the **naming of their dead** Sachims, is one ground of their warres.

naming of their dead: Narragansett culture keepers in *The Tomaquag Museum Edition* of *A Key* confirm that historically not naming the dead enabled their spirit to travel to the southwest to Cautantowitt's house.

12 For more on Narragansett beliefs about death historically and contemporarily, see *The Tomaquag Museum Edition: Roger Williams, A Key*, 169–72.

DOCUMENT 17

Traditional Indigenous Wetu (home), from Plimoth Patuxet Museums (n.d.)[13]

Williams described traditional Indigenous homes, known as a wetu (singular) or wetuash (plural in Wampanoag dialect) at length in *A Key into the Language of America* (1643). The images below are of a modern recreation of a wetu from the Patuxet Homesite at Plimoth Patuxet Museums.

Figure 17.1: Wetu exterior

Figure 17.2: Wetu interior

13 Plimoth Patuxet Museums, Patuxet Homesite Wetu, https://plimoth.org/for-students/homework-help/building-a-home.

DOCUMENT 18

Roger Williams' diplomacy following the murder of Penowanyanquis (1638)

In August 1638, a former soldier in the Pequot War, Arthur Peach, murdered a Nipmuck man, Penowanyanquis. Peach, who had been indentured to Plymouth's Edward Winslow, impregnated a woman out of wedlock and absconded with three other servants. However, the four men got lost in the woods north of Providence, and as they searched for food and shelter came across Penowanyanquis, a Nipmuck trader for the Narragansett, laden with newly acquired goods. Peach lured Penowanyanquis over to share tobacco, but quickly stabbed him through the leg and into the stomach. Williams and others tried to save Penowanyanquis, but he succumbed to his wounds. Before he died, however, Penowanyanquis related what had happened, which enabled Williams to mediate with Plymouth and Massachusetts Bay to bring Peach to justice.[14] In excerpts (a), (b), and (c), Williams describes the attack and addresses the issue of retribution.

a. Roger Williams to John Winthrop (ca. 1 August 1638)[15]

I am bold to write in hasty advertisement concerning late passages ... there hath been great hubbub in all these parts, as a general persuasion that the time was come of a general slaughter of natives by reason of a murder committed upon a native **within twelve miles of us**, four days since, by four desperate English ... at Pawatuckqut, a river four miles from us toward the [Massachusetts] bay, four Englishmen were almost famished. I sent instantly provisions and **strong water** ... [T]hey were one Arthur Peach of Plymouth, an Irishman, **John Barnes, his man, and two others** come Pascataquack, travelling to Qunnihticut, that they had been lost five days ... they having told me, they came from Plymouth ... .and lost their way to Weymouth, from whence they lost their way again towards us ... [A]fter they were gone, an old native comes to me, and tells me, that the natives round about us were fled, relating that those four had slain a native, who had carried three beaver skins and beads for Caunounicus' son, and came home with five fathom [of wampum] and three coats, that three natives which came after him found him groaning in the path; that he told them four Englishmen had slain him ... [I] went myself with two or three more to the wounded in the woods. The natives at first were shy of us, conceiving a **general slaughter** ... I assured them that Mr. Governor

within twelve miles of us: The attack took place at Misquamsqueece, modern-day Seekonk, MA.

strong water: Alcoholic beverages.

John Barnes, his man, and two others: Thomas Jackson, Richard Stinnings, and Daniel Cross.

general slaughter: They feared the colonists would slaughter them as the English had the Pequot at Mystic.

14 Glenn LaFantasie, "Murder of an Indian, 1638," *Rhode Island History Journal* 38 (1979): 67–77.

15 Roger Williams to John Winthrop, ca. 1 August 1638, *Williams Corres.*, 1:170–73.

knew nothing ... and that I had sent to apprehend the men. So we found that he [Penowanyanquis] had been run through the leg and belly with one thrust. We dressed him and got him to town next day, where Mr. James and Mr. Greene endeavored, all they could [to save] his life, but his wound in the belly, and blood lost, and fever following, cut his life thread. Before he died, he told me that the four English had slain him ... the English saw him in the [Massachusetts] bay and his beads, sitting in the side of a swamp ... Arthur called him to drink [i.e., smoke] tobacco, who coming and taking the pipe of Arthur, Arthur run him through the leg into the belly, when springing back, he struck at him, but missed him, and his weapon run into the ground, that getting from them ... they pursued him, till he fell down, when they missed him, and getting up again, when he heard them close by him, he run ... till he fell down again, when they lost him ... towards night, he came and lay in the path, that some passenger might help him ... Sir, I shall humbly crave your judgment, whether they ought not to be tried where they were taken. If they be sent any way, whether not to Plymouth. In case Plymouth refuse ... send them to us, what answer we may give ... This native, **Will, my servant**, shall attend your worship for answer.

Will, my servant: Likely the unfree Indigenous boy Williams picked out and had Winthrop rename the previous year.

b. Roger Williams to John Winthrop (14 August 1638)[16]

The natives, friends of **the slain** had consultation to kill an English man in revenge. Miantunnomu heard of it and desired the English would be careful on the highways, and sent himself expresses threatening to them etc. and informed them that Mr. Governor would see Justice done. **Ousamequin**, coming from Plymouth told me that the 4 men were all guilty. I answered but one. He replied true One wounded him, but all lay in wait 2 days and assisted. In conclusion: he told me that **the principal** must not die for he was Mr Winslow's **man**: and also that the man [Penowanyanquis] was by birth a Neepmuck man: and so not worthy another man should die for him. I answered what I thought fit ... He that doth Violence to the blood of any person let him flee to the pit, let none deliver him. The Lord mercifully cleanse the Land from blood.

the slain: Penowanyanquis.

Ousamequin: Commonly known by his title, Massasoit, the powerful Sachem of the Pokanoket (Wampanoag).

the principal: Arthur Peach.

man: servant.

c. Roger Williams to John Winthrop (after 21 September 1638)[17]

Sir, at Plymouth, it pleased the Lord to force the prisoners to confess, that they all complotted and intended murder, and they were, three of them, (the **fourth having escaped**, by pinnace, from Aquedenick,) executed in

fourth having escaped: Daniel Cross escaped.

16 Roger Williams to John Winthrop, 14 August 1638, *Williams Corres.*, 1:176–77.

17 Roger Williams to John Winthrop, after 21 September 1638, *Williams Corres.*, 1:182–85.

the presence of the natives who went with me. Our friends confessed, that they received much **quickening** from your own hand.

quickening: Encouragement.

DOCUMENT 19

Narragansett "Submission" to King Charles I (1644)[18]

Amidst a changing landscape in the Dawnland in the 1640s and Williams' own appeal to the English Parliament for a patent, the Narraganset Sachems "submitted" to King Charles I in 1644. A surface-level reading of the document depicts the Narragansett Nation as weak—renouncing land, possessions, and sovereignty to an English king thousands of miles across an ocean. In practice, this was not the case; the Narragansett Nation were a powerful sovereign nation, and they made this alliance for their own diplomatic and strategic advantage to short-circuit local interference from competing settler-colonists and tribes around the region. In 1643 Miantonomi had been captured and executed by the Mohegan following a raid. The resulting conflict over debt and land likely impacted Canonicus' and Pessicus' (Miantonomi's brother) decision to allow Samuel Gorton to take the "submission" to England. Gorton had his own agenda in trying to protect his settlement at Warwick. The English settler-colonists who are mentioned in the agreement were part of a group involved in a fraudulent purchase of land from Pumham, Sachem of Shawomet. Pumham, who was under the jurisdiction of the Narragansett Nation, appeared as a witness to Miantonomi's land evidence to Samuel Gorton in 1642. Pumham and Soconoco, Sachem of Pawtuxet, challenged Miantonomi and the Narragansett Nation by submitting themselves and their lands to the Massachusetts Bay Colony. Subsequently, both leaders complained to Massachusetts authorities about transgressions by Samuel Gorton and his followers with some success in 1645. This context frames the complex alliances that were shaped in the 1640s, with Williams getting a patent from the English Parliament the same year the Narragansett allied with the king; both unions emerged against the backdrop of competing local conflicts from other Indigenous tribes and English settlements.

Know all men, colonies, peoples, and nations, unto whom the same hereof shall come, that we, the chief sachems, princes or governors of the Narragansett (in that part of America now called New England) together with the joint and unanimous consent of all our people and subjects, inhabitants thereof, do upon serious consideration, mature and deliberate advice and counsel, great and weighty grounds and reasons moving us

18 "Submission of the Chief Sachem of the Narragansett to Charles I," *Native Northeast Portal*, https://nativenortheastportal.com/annotated-transcription/digcoll3983.

thereunto, whereof one most effectual unto us is that noble fame we have heard of, that great and mighty prince, Charles, King of Great Britain, in that honorable and princely care he hath of all his servants and true and loyal subjects, the consideration whereof move and bend our hearts with one consent, freely, voluntarily, and most humbly, to submit, subject, and give over ourselves, peoples, lands, rights, inheritances, and possessions whatsoever, in ourselves and our heirs, successively forever, unto the protection, care, and government of that worthy and royal prince, Charles, King of Great Britain and Ireland, his heirs and successors forever, to be ruled and governed according to those ancient and honorable laws and customs established in that so renowned realm and kingdom of Old England.

We do, therefore, by these presents confess, and most willingly and submissively, acknowledge ourselves to be the humble, loving, and obedient servants and subjects of his Majesty, to be ruled, ordered, and disposed of, in ourselves and ours, according to his princely wisdom, counsel, and laws of that honorable state of Old England, upon condition of his Majesty's royal protection and **righting of us in what wrong is, or may be done onto us**, according to his honorable laws and customs, exercised amongst his subjects, in their preservation and safety, and in the defeating and overthrow of his and their enemies; not that we find ourselves necessitated hereunto, in respect of our relation, or occasion we have or may have with any of the Natives in these parts, knowing ourselves sufficient defense, and able to judge in any matter or cause in that respect, but have just cause of jealousy and suspicion, of some of his Majesty's pretended subjects; therefore, our desire is to have our matters and causes heard and tried according to his just and equal laws in that way, and order His Highness shall please to appoint; nor can we yield over ourselves unto any that are subjects themselves, in any case, having ourselves been the chief sachems, or princes, successively, of the country, time out of mind, and for our present and lawful enacting hereof, being so far remote from his Majesty, we have by joint consent, made choice of four of his loyal and loving subjects, our trusty and well-beloved friends, Samuel Gorton, **John Wickes**, **Randall Holden, and John Warner**, whom we have deputed and made our lawful attorneys or commissioners, not only for the acting and performing of this, our deed, in the behalf of his Highness but also for the safe custody, careful conveyance, and declaration hereof unto his Grace, being done upon the lands of the Narragansett at a court or general assembly called and assembled together of purpose for the public enacting and manifestation hereof. And for the further confirmation and establishing of this, our act and deed, we, the abovesaid sachems, or princes, have, according to that commendable custom of Englishmen, subscribed our names and set our

righting of us in what wrong is, or may be done onto us: King Charles will protect the Narragansett against any enemy.

John Wickes, Randall Holden, and John Warner: Associates of Samuel Gorton, who settled in Shawomet (Warwick, RI). They were accused by Gorton's enemies of a fraudulent purchase by the Pawtuxet settlers who convinced Pomham to make the claim. The three men were captured with Gorton and sentenced to hard labor and imprisonment before eventually returning to Shawomet.

seals hereunto, as so many testimonies of our faith and truth, our love and loyalty to that, our dread Sovereign, and that according to the Englishmen's account, dated the 19th day of April, 1644,

Pessicus, his mark, chief sachem and successor of that late deceased Miantonomo

The mark of that ancient Canonicus, protector of that late deceased Miantonomo during the time of his nonage

The mark of **Mixan**, son and heir of that abovesaid Canonicus

Witness: Witnessed by two of the chief counsellors to Sachem Pessicus, **Awashaw**, his mark, **Tomanick**, his mark, Indians

Certification: Sealed and delivered in the presence of these persons, **Christopher Helme**, **Robert Potter**, **Richard Carder**, English

Copy: A true copy of the act and deed of the voluntary and free submission of the chief sachem and the rest of the princes, with the whole people of the Narragansett unto the government and protection of that honorable state of Old England, set down here verbatim

Pessicus: The younger brother of Miantonomi, who rose to the position of Sachem (which he shared with Canonicus) after his brother's murder by the Mohegans in 1643. Both Pessicus and Canonicus sought revenge against the Mohegans, which put them at odds with the Commissioners of the United Colonies.

Mixan: Eldest son of the Narragansett sachem Canonicus I and married to Quaiapen.

Awashaw: Influential chief counselor and diplomat for Sachems Pessicus and Ninigret.

Tomanick: A chief counselor to Pessicus.

Christopher Helme: Migrated to Massachusetts in 1637 and then moved to Shawomet.

Robert Potter: Migrated to the Massachusetts Bay Colony in 1634 and moved to Portsmouth, RI, before settling in Shawomet in 1641. He was involved in the Pomham land controversy and served a few months in prison before returning to Shawomet.

Richard Carder: Settled in Boston, Portsmouth, and eventually Shawomet. He was accused by Gorton's enemies of a fraudulent purchase by the Pawtuxet settlers who convinced Pomham to make the claim. He was one of the eleven men captured with Gorton and sentenced to hard labor and imprisonment before eventually returning to Shawomet.

DOCUMENT 20

Roger Williams to the General Court of Massachusetts on issues of diplomacy (1654)[19]

Writing to the General Court of Massachusetts in 1654, Williams reflected on his work as a diplomat in trying to secure peace in the region. He also addressed efforts to stop the conversion of Native Peoples to Christianity, and how this tied to his work in England.

I ... upon the express advice of Your ever honored Mr Winthrop deceased I first adventured to being Plantation among the thickest of these Barbarians.

League: An alliance.

That, in the Pequot Wars it pleased Your honored Government to employ me in the hazardous and weighty Service of negotiating **League** between Your Selves and the Narigansetts: When the Pequt Messengers (who sought the Narigansetts League against the English) had almost ended that my work and Life together ... since that time ... I have been more or less interested and used in all the great Transactions of War or Peace between the English and the Natives, and have not spared, Purse, not Pains nor Hazards (very many times) that the Whole Land English and Natives might sleep in peace Securely ...

At my last departure for England I was importuned by the Nariganset Sachims and especially by Nenekunat, to present their petition to the high Sachims of England that they might not be forced from their Religion, and for not changing their Religion be invaded by War. For they said they were daily visited with Threatening by Indians that came from about the Massachusetts, that if they would not pray they should be destroyed by War ...

his Highness: Lord Protector Oliver Cromwell.

With this their Petition I acquainted (in private discourses) divers of the chief of our Nation, and especially **his Highness**, who in many discourses I had with him ... expressed a high Sprit of Christian Love ... and was often pleased ... with very many Questions and my Answers about the Indian affairs of this Country ... and after all Hearings of Yourselves and us, it hath pleased his Highness and his Council to grant ... some expressly concerning the very Indians ...

---

19 Roger Williams to the General Court of Massachusetts Bay, 5 October 1654, *Williams Corres.*, 2:408–13.

I humbly pray Your Consideration whether it be ... not only possible but very easy for the English to live and die in peace with all the Natives ... for ... are not all the English of this Land (generally) a persecuted people from their Native Soil, and hath not God of peace and Father of Mercies made these Natives more friendly in this Wilderness then over Native Countrymen in our own land to us? Have they not entered League of Love, and to this day continued Peaceable Commerce with us? Are not our Families and Townes grown up in peace amongst them? ... I have bene and am a friend to the Natives ...

the Narigansetts and the **Mauquawogs** are the 2 great Bodies of Indians in this Country ... and they both yet are friendly and peaceable to the English ... The Narigansets as they were the first, so they have bene long Confederates with You, they have bene true in all the Pequot Wars ... Their late famous long-lived Caunounicus so lived and died in the same most honorable manner and solemnity (in their Way) as you laid to sleep Your Prudent Peacemaker Mr Wintrop did they honor this their Prudent and Peaceable Prince.

Mauquawogs: Mohawks.

QUESTIONS TO CONSIDER

1. What can we learn about Roger Williams' views on Indigenous Peoples from *A Key into the Language of America*? How and why is this source useful to tribal members, historians, anthropologists, and linguists today? What are some of the limits of using this document to learn about the Narragansett and other Native Peoples?

2. How does the murder of Penowanyanquis highlight tensions after the Pequot War? What role did Roger Williams play in bringing Arthur Peach to justice?

3. Consider the Narragansett "Submission" to King Charles I. How and why may the Narragansett have interpreted this document as an alliance rather than submission?

4. What do the documents reveal about the complexity of inter-tribal politics, concepts of sovereignty, competing colonial enterprises, and the meaning of royal power? How can scholars use these documents to reframe Indigenous perspectives of power and diplomacy?

5. Examine Roger Williams' work as a diplomat among the Indigenous Peoples of Southern New England. How did his role change as the seventeenth century progressed?

6. Throughout his life Roger Williams claimed to be a "friend" to the Indigenous Peoples of New England. To what extent was that true?

CONVERSION

Williams' own religious journey impacted how he viewed conversion efforts. Having witnessed state persecution of religious dissenters in England and being banished from Massachusetts Bay, Williams was opposed to any false conversions. He made it clear that "forced Worship stinks in God's Nostrils."[20] By the end of the 1630s, Williams had become increasingly convinced that a valid baptism required knowing consent. Williams was (re)baptized as a fully consenting adult in 1638, and helped to found the first Baptist church in America in Providence.[21] As Williams embraced the Baptist faith, he not only questioned the validity of infant baptism, but also missionary efforts to convert Natives to Christianity.[22]

---

20 Roger Williams, letter to Major John Wilson and Governor Thomas Prence, 22 June 1670, *Williams Corres.*, 2:617.

21 Charles Hartman (Historian and former Pastor at the First Baptist Church, Swansea) argues that the Providence congregation followed the "General" Baptist tradition, and the Baptist's political influence flowed throughout Providence and South East Massachusetts into the eighteenth century. Charles Hartman, email correspondence with the author, July 2024.

22 For more on Baptists in Rhode Island, see J. Stanley Lemons, *Retracing Baptists in Rhode Island: Identity, Formation, and History* (Waco, TX: Baylor University Press, 2019); William G. McLoughlin, *New England Dissent, 1630–1833: The Baptists and the Separation of Church and State* (Cambridge, MA: Harvard University Press, 1971); William G. McLoughlin, *Soul Liberty: The Baptist Struggle in New England, 1630–1833* (Hanover, NH: University Press of New England, 1991).

DOCUMENT 21

Roger Williams, *Christenings make not Christians* (1645)[23]

Williams explored the issue of false conversions at length in his 1645 work, *Christenings make not Christians*. As the title suggests, Williams believed that simply baptizing someone did not make them Christian. He published this work in opposition to increasing efforts in Massachusetts Bay to convert the Ninnimissinuok. Part of Williams' objection was rooted in his acknowledgment of Indigenous Peoples having their own (if incorrect) religion, but also his assessment of European Christianity. Williams argued that European Christians (both Catholic and Protestant) were no more faithful to the "true" message of Christ than Indigenous Peoples—hence conversion was false, as it was from one "damnable" religion to another.

Heathen Dogs: An offensive term for Native Peoples. "Heathen" implied non-Christian and "dog" that someone was not economically self-sufficient, had no hope of redemption (as animals had no souls), and were in Satan's cohort (dog is God spelled backwards).

How oft have I heard both the English and Dutch (not only the civil, but the most debauched and profane) say, These **Heathen Dogs**, better kill a thousand of them then we Christians should be endangered or troubled with them … They have spilt our Christian blood, the best way to make riddance of them, cut them all off, and so make way for Christians.

I shall therefore humbly intreat my country-men of all sorts to consider, that although men have used to apply this word Heathen to the Indians that go naked, and have not heard of that One-God, yet this word Heathen is most improperly, sinfully, and unchristianly so used in this sense …

[T]hey [the Indigenous Peoples] are intelligent, many very ingenuous, plain-hearted, inquisitive, and … prepared with many convictions …

[F]or the Catholics conversion, although I believe I may safely hope that God hath in his Rome, in Spain, yet if Antichrist be their false head … yea consequently their preachings, conversions, salvations (leaving secret things to God) must all be of the same false nature like wise.

If the reports … be true, what monstrous and most inhumane conversions have they made; baptizing thousands, yea ten thousand of the poor Natives, sometimes by wiles and subtle devices, sometimes by force compelling them to submit to that which they understood not, neither before nor after such their monstrous Christenings …

23 Roger Williams, *Christenings make not Christians* (London, 1645).

For our New-England parts, I can speak it uprightly, and confidently, I know it to have been easy for myself, long here this, to have brought many thousands of these Natives, yea the whole country, to a far greater Antichristian conversion then ever was heard yet in America …

why have I not brought them [Indigenous Peoples] to such a conversion as I speak of? I answer, woe be to me, if I call light darkness, or darkness light; sweet bitter, or bitter sweet; woe be to me if I call that conversion unto God, which is indeed subversion of the souls of Millions in Christendom, from one false worship to another …

it must not be, (it is not possible it should be in truth) a conversion of People to the worship of the Lord Jesus, by force of Arms and swords of steel …

But so did never the Lord Jesus bring any unto his most pure worship, for he abhors as all men, the very Indians doe an unwilling Spouse, and to **enter into a forced bed** …

enter into a forced bed: Williams is comparing forced conversion to the rape of a person's soul.

it is out of question to me, that I may not pretend a false conversion, and false state of worship, to the true Lord Jesus …

If any now say unto me, Why then if this be Conversion, and you have such a **Key of Language**, and such adore of opportunity, in the knowledge of the Country and the inhabitants, why proceed you not to produce in America some patterns of such conversions as you speak of?

Key of Language: Reference to Williams' knowledge of the Narragansett language and his book, *A Key into the Language of America*.

I answer, first, it must be a great deal of practice, and mighty pains and hardship undergone by myself, or any that would proceed to such a further degree of the Language, as to be able in propriety of speech to open matters of salvation to them …

Secondly my desires and endeavors are constant (by the help of God) to attain a propriety of Language.

Thirdly … my worthy Countrymen in the Bay of Massachusetts and elsewhere, that I received not long since expressions of their holy desires and proffers of assistance in the work …

DOCUMENT 22

John Eliot's translation of the Bible into Wôpanâak, *Mamusse Wunneetupanatamwe Up-Biblum God* (1663)[24]

Given Williams' views on converting Natives to Christianity, it is unsurprising that he objected to the work of the Bay Colony's chief missionary, John Eliot. Eliot, like Williams, arrived in Bay Colony in 1631. Eliot began preaching to Indigenous Peoples in the 1640s, and he quickly realized that learning the local Wôpanâak Algonquian dialect would help his efforts. He first published a basic primer and Bible extracts, then published the entire New Testament in Wôpanâak in 1661. He followed this with the combined Old and New Testament in 1663, with a second edition in 1685. Often referred to as the "Eliot Indian Bible," it was not only the first Bible printed in any language in North America, but it was the largest single printing venture of the early colonial period. Williams was strongly against Eliot's translation of the Bible, as he feared human error in translation, language issues, and false conversions.

Eliot's Bible translation was part of his larger missionary efforts, which Williams also opposed. This included setting up "Praying Towns" which sought to erase Indigenous cultures and identities, as inhabitants were forced to live in English-style houses and follow strict rules. Eliot published various accounts of his missionary efforts, including *A Brief History of the Progress of the Gospel amongst the Indians in New England* (1671). In recent years, Wampanoag Peoples have used Eliot's work to revive the spoken language with the goal of returning language fluency to the Wampanoag Nation as a principal means of expression. Following visions from her ancestors, Jessie Little Doe Baird (Mashpee Wampanoag), studied linguistics at MIT and received a MacArthur fellowship, which pioneered the **Wôpanâak Language Reclamation Project**. Today, the program is thriving and is bringing back the language "one student at a time."[25]

Wôpanâak Language Reclamation Project: Using seventeenth-century documents produced to erase their religion and culture, the Wôpanâak Language Reclamation Project is one of many efforts to counter the legacy of colonization.

24 John Eliot, *Mamusse Wunneetupanatamwe Up-Biblum God* (Cambridge, MA, 1663). Images produced by the British Library at Early English Books Online.

25 See the PBS documentary about efforts to revive the Wôpanâak language, *We Still Live Here: Âs Nutayuneân* (2011).

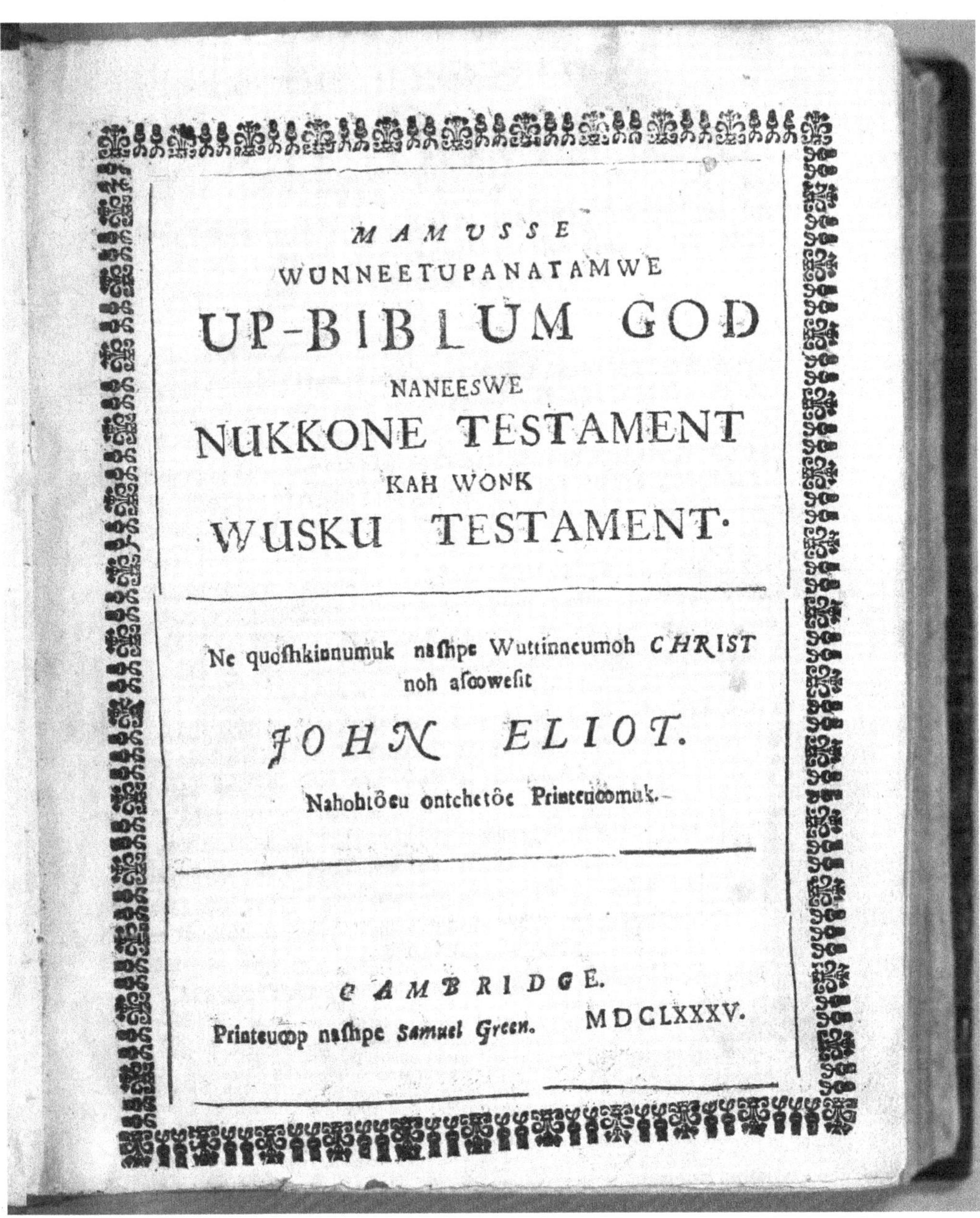

MAMUSSE
WUNNEETUPANATAMWE
UP-BIBLUM GOD
NANEESWE
NUKKONE TESTAMENT
KAH WONK
WUSKU TESTAMENT.

Ne quoshkinnumuk nashpe Wuttinneumoh CHRIST
noh asoowesit

JOHN ELIOT.

Nahohtôeu ontchetôe Printeuoomuk.

CAMBRIDGE.
Printeuoop nashpe Samuel Green. MDCLXXXV.

Figure 22.1: Cover page of 1685 edition of the Old and New Testament

Kestecun mattaok Chap. I. nequttatahshikquinut

NEGONNE OOSUKKUHWHONK *MOSES*

Ne asowetamuk
GENESIS.

CHAP. I.

1 The creation of heaven and earth &c:
26 Of man in the image of God. 29 The
appointment of food.

Eske kutchissik *a* ayum
a Psal. God Kesuk & Ohke.
33.6. 2 Kah Ohke mô-
& 136. matta kuhkenaunu-
& Acts neunkquttinnoo kah
14.15. monteagunninno, &
& 17. pohkenum woskeche
24. Heb. moonôi, kah wun
11. 3. Nashauanittoomoh-
God popomshau wos-
keche nippekontu.
b 2 Cor. 3 Onk noowau God, *b* Wequaiaj, kah
516. mô wequai.
4 Kah wunnaumun God wequai ne en
wunnegen: Kah wutchadchaube ponumun
God noeu wequai kah noeu pohkenum:
5 Kah wutussowetamun God wequai Kesukod, kah pohkenum wutussowetamun
Nukon: kah mô wannonkooook kah mô
mohtompog negonne kesukod
6 Kah noowau God *c* Sepakehtamoudj
c Psal. noeu nippekontu, kah chadchapemoudj na-
136.5. shauweit nippe wutch nippekontu.
Jer. 10. 7 Kah ayimup God sepakehtamóonk, kah
12. & wutchadchabeponumunnup nashaueu nippe
51.15. agwu, uttiyeu agwu sepakehtamóonk, kah
nashaueu nippekontu uttiyeu ongkouwe se-
pakehtamôonk, kah mónkô n nih.
8 Kah wuttissoweetamun God *d* sepakeh-
d Jer. 51. temóonk Kesukquash, kah mô wunnonkoo-
15. ook, kah mô mohtompog nahohtoeu kesukok
9 Kah noowau God moémooidj nippe ut
agwu kesukquash pasukqunnu, kah pah-
e Psal. kemoidj nanabpeu, kah mónkô n nih.
33.7. 10 Kah wuttissoweétamun God nanabpi,
& 126.5 Ohke, kah moémoo nippe wuttissowetamun
Job 38.8. Kehtoh & wunnaumun God neen wunnegen
11 Kah noowau God dtannékej ohke moskeht, mosketh skannémunúook skannémunash
kah meechummué mehtugquash meechummuook meechummuonk nishnoh pasuk neane wuttinnussuonk, ubbuhkuminuook ut
woskeche ohke, kah mónké n nih.
12 Kah ohke dtannegeuup moskeht, kah
mosket skannemunnúook skannemunash, nish
noh pasuk neane wuttinnussuonk, kah mah-
tug meechummuook, ubbuhkuminuoouk
wuhhogkat nishnoh pasuk neane wuttinnussuonk, kah wunnaumun God ne en wunnegen
13 Kah mo wunnonkooook, kah mo mohtompog shwekesukod
14 Kah noowau God, *f* Wequanantega- f Deut.
nuohettitch ut wussepakehtamooonganit ke- 4.19.
sukquash kah pohshehettich ut nashauwe ke- Psal
sukod, kah ut nashauwe nukkonut, kah kuk- 136.7
kinneasuonganuhettich, kah uttoocheyeu-
hettich, kah kesukodtuoo wulhettich, kah
kodtummoowulhettich.
15 Kah n nag wequanantéganoohettich
ut sepaketamoowonganit kesukqut wequa-
sumókettich ohke, onk mo n nih.
16 Kah ayum God neesunash missiyeuash
wequanantéganash, wequananteg mohsag na-
nanumunumoo kesukod, wequananteg peasik
nananumoomoo nukon, kah anogqsog
17 Kah ut ponuh God wussepakehtamooonganit kesukquash, woh wequasumwog
ohke.
18 Onk woh *g* wunnanumunneau kesukod kah nuhkon, kah pohshemoo nashaueu g Jer
wequai, kah nashaueu pohkenum, kah wun- 31.35.
naumun God ne en wunnegen
19 Kah mô wunnonkoook kah mô mohtompog yaou quinukok
20 Kah noowau God, Moonahettich nippekontu pomantamwae ponomutcheg, kah
puppinshaussog pumunahettich ongkouwe
ohket woskeche wussepakehtamooonganit
kesukquash.
21 Kah kezheau God matikkenunutcheh
Pootâopoh, kah nishnoh pomantamoe óâas
noh pompâmayit uttiyeug moonacheg nip-
pekóntu, nishnoh pasuk neane wuttinnussuonk, kah nishnoh oonuppohwhunin puppin-
shaash, nishnoh pasuk neane wuttinnussuonk,
kah wunnaumun God neen wunnegan.
22 Kah oonanumoh nahhog God noowau, h Gen.
Mishéneetuónittegk, *h* kah muttaanook, kah 8.17.
numwapegk nippe ut kehtohhannit, kah & 9.1.
puppinshasog muttaanhettich ohket.
23 Kah mo wanonkooook kah mo mohtompog napanna audtahshikquinukok,

24 Kah

Figure 22.2: 1685 edition opening page of the Book of Genesis from the Old Testament

DOCUMENT 23

Roger Williams on Indigenous baptism and conversion in "code" (ca. 1680)[26]

Towards the end of his life, Williams wrote a shorthand essay in the margins of a book he owned.[27] Virtually every square inch of blank space in the book's 234 pages is filled with shorthand. Williams was familiar with shorthand from his teenage years in London recording sermons and speeches for Sir Edward Coke. He adapted and customized his **own shorthand** based on a system developed by John Willis in 1602. Housed in the John Carter Brown Library at Brown University, the shorthand remained unreadable for more than 300 years until Lucas Mason-Brown (an undergraduate mathematician at the time) deciphered it. Mason-Brown collaborated with historians Linford Fisher and Stanley Lemons to interpret the writing in the context of Williams' other works. Williams' notes have nothing to do with the book on which they were written, and he mostly likely wrote in shorthand to save paper (which had to be imported from England) to record his thoughts in a small space. The shorthand writing addresses three separate topics: cosmography, medicine, and baptism. The baptism section, which runs to 20 pages, includes an essay, "A Brief Reply to a Small Book Written by John Eliot," essentially a point-by-point counterargument to Eliot's stance on infant baptism. His shorthand reveals that Williams remained staunchly against any forced conversion, even in the wake of King Philip's War. Williams described how if missionaries used "treachery and seduction" it was a "sore" to Christ's gospel and led to false conversion. The images that follow show the shorthand covering all blank space in the margins.

own shorthand: Williams used his own symbols for words; for example, his word for friendship was the letter 'f' next to a drawing of a boat.

26 *An essay towards the reconciling of differences among Christians.* John Carter Brown Library, Providence, RI, DA6-E78t. Williams likely wrote this sometime between 1679 and 1683. Stanley Lemons, Linford Fisher, and Lucas Mason-Brown, Decoding Roger Williams: The Lost Essay of Rhode Island's Founding Father (Waco, TX: Baylor University Press, 2014).

27 The book has no title page, and the first page of printed text, "An Essay Towards the Reconciling of Differences Among Christians," is likely a subtitle. An unknown "Widow Tweedy" donated the book to the John Carter Brown Library in 1871.

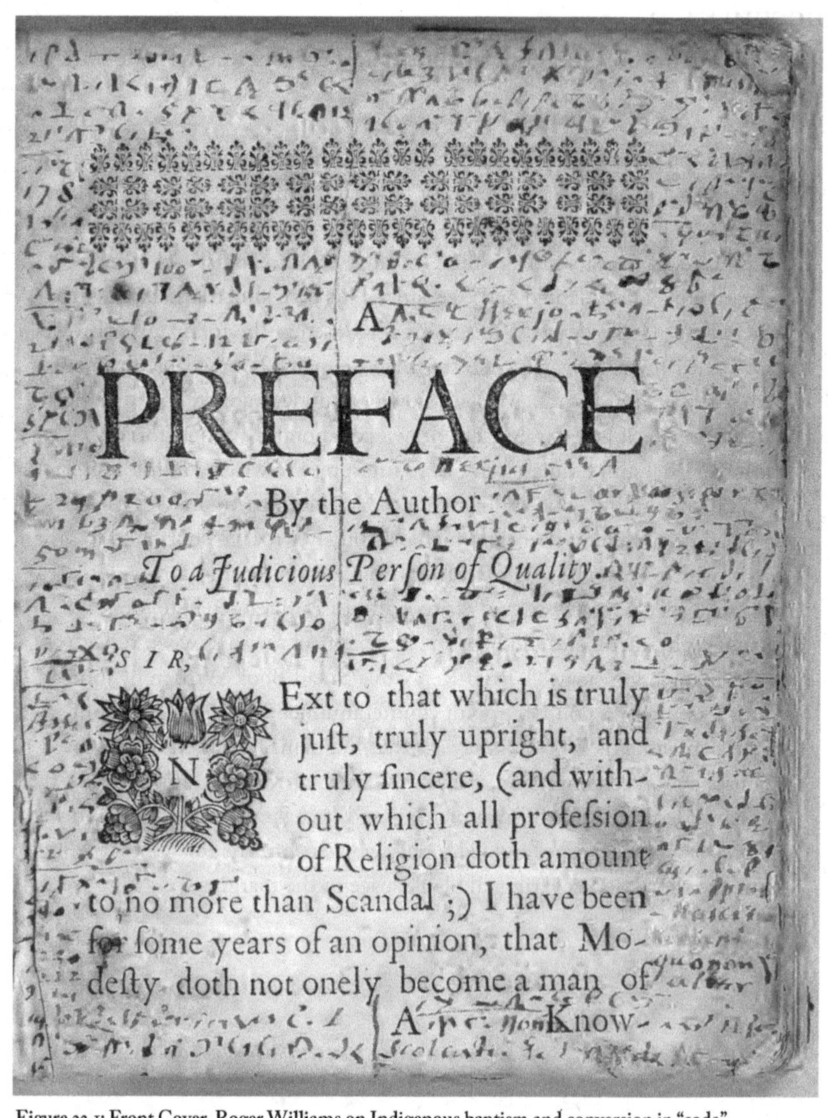

A

PREFACE

By the Author

To a Judicious Person of Quality.

SIR,

Next to that which is truly juſt, truly upright, and truly ſincere, (and without which all profeſsion of Religion doth amount to no more than Scandal;) I have been for ſome years of an opinion, that Modeſty doth not onely become a man of

A Know-

Figure 23.1: Front Cover, Roger Williams on Indigenous baptism and conversion in "code"

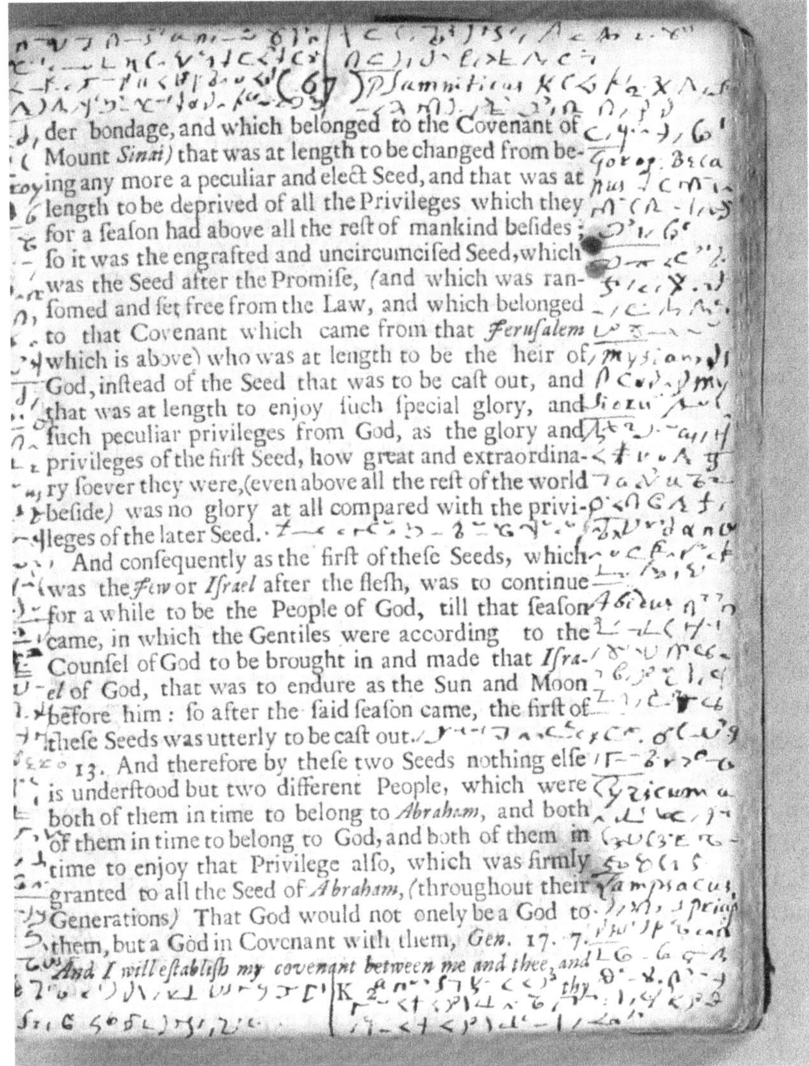

der bondage, and which belonged to the Covenant of Mount *Sinai*) that was at length to be changed from being any more a peculiar and elect Seed, and that was at length to be deprived of all the Privileges which they for a ſeaſon had above all the reſt of mankind beſides; ſo it was the engrafted and uncircumciſed Seed, which was the Seed after the Promiſe, (and which was ranſomed and ſet free from the Law, and which belonged to that Covenant which came from that *Jeruſalem* which is above) who was at length to be the heir of God, inſtead of the Seed that was to be caſt out, and that was at length to enjoy ſuch ſpecial glory, and ſuch peculiar privileges from God, as the glory and privileges of the firſt Seed, how great and extraordinary ſoever they were, (even above all the reſt of the world beſide) was no glory at all compared with the privileges of the later Seed.

And conſequently as the firſt of theſe Seeds, which was the *Jew* or *Iſrael* after the fleſh, was to continue for a while to be the People of God, till that ſeaſon came, in which the Gentiles were according to the Counſel of God to be brought in and made that *Iſrael* of God, that was to endure as the Sun and Moon before him: ſo after the ſaid ſeaſon came, the firſt of theſe Seeds was utterly to be caſt out.

13. And therefore by theſe two Seeds nothing elſe is underſtood but two different People, which were both of them in time to belong to *Abraham*, and both of them in time to belong to God, and both of them in time to enjoy that Privilege alſo, which was firmly granted to all the Seed of *Abraham*, (throughout their Generations) That God would not onely be a God to them, but a God in Covenant with them, *Gen.* 17. 7. *And I will eſtabliſh my covenant between me and thee, and*

Figure 23.2: Opening Page, Roger Williams on Indigenous baptism and conversion in "code"

QUESTIONS TO CONSIDER

1. What were Roger Williams' views on converting Native Peoples to Christianity? How and why did they evolve during his life?

2. How and why did Roger Williams' views eventually conflict with missionary efforts in Massachusetts Bay?

PEQUOT WAR

DOCUMENT 24

Roger Williams to John Winthrop and Henry Vane about battle tactics (1637)[28]

Between 1636 and 1638, the Pequot War raged in New England. The Pequot War (and later King Philip's War) were collectively part of the wars for New England. The Pequot not only fought the English settler-colonists, but also the Narragansett and Mohegan who sided with the settler-colonists. Williams played a key role as an intermediary and diplomat with the Narragansett during the war. In May 1637, Williams wrote to the Massachusetts leaders about battle tactics. In the excerpt below, he describes his work as a diplomat with the Narragansett and the different battle tactics in a letter to John Winthrop and Henry Vane. Williams also talks about a smallpox epidemic that had devastated some Native Peoples in the region.[29]

neighbour princes: Narragansett Sachems Canonicus and Miantonomi.

plague and other sicknesses: Previously, a smallpox epidemic had spread throughout Southern New England, killing many Native Peoples. Many settler-colonists interpreted this as the "hand of God" clearing the way for European colonization.

swamp: The tactic of women and children taking refuge in swamps during conflict was common among the Indigenous Peoples of Southern New England.

The latter end of the last week I gave notice to our **neighbour princes** of your intentions and preparations against the common enemy, the Pequts. At my first coming to them, Caunounicus ... was very sour, and accused the English and myself of sending the plague amongst them, and threatening to kill him especially. Such tidings (it seems) were lately brought to his ears by some of his flatterers and our ill-willers. I discerned the cause of bestirring myself, and staid the longer, and at last (through the mercy of the Most High) I not only sweetened his spirit, but possessed him, that the **plague and other sicknesses** were alone in the hand of the one God, who made him and us, who being displeased with the English for lying, stealing, idleness and uncleanness (the natives' epidemical sins), smote many thousands of ourselves with general and late mortalities. Miantunnomu kept his barbarous court lately at my house, and with him I have far better dealings. He takes pleasure to visit me, and sent me word of his coming over again some eight days hence. They pass not a week without some skirmishes, though hitherto little loss on either side. They were glad of your preparations, and in much conference with themselves and others ... I gathered these observations which you may please ... to consider ... That if any pinnaces come in ken, they presently prepare for flight, women and old men and children, to a **swamp** some three or four miles back ... They also conceive it easy for the

28 Roger Williams to Henry Vane and Deputy Governor John Winthrop, 1 May 1637, *Williams Corres.*, 1:72–74.

29 The illness did not have a significant impact on the Narragansett; consequently, the balance of power in the region changed.

English, that the provisions and munitions first arrive at Aquednetick, called by us Rhode-Island ... and then a messenger may be dispatched hither, and so to the [Massachusetts] bay, for the soldiers to march up by land to the vessels ... That the assault would be in the night, when they are commonly more secure at home, by which advantage the English being armed ... may enter the houses and do what execution they please ... That before the assault be given, an ambush be laid behind them and the swamp, to prevent their flight, etc. That it would be pleasing to all natives, that **women and children be spared** etc.

women and children be spared: In the end, women and children were not spared and many were slaughtered or enslaved. The Narragansett later expressed their horror at these practices, which went against their traditional way of waging war.

DOCUMENT 25

Roger Williams to Governor John Winthrop in the wake of the Mystic massacre (1637)[30]

The May 1637 massacre at Mystic was a defining moment in the war, when the settler-colonists and their allies surrounded and set fire to the Pequot village. Only a handful of the 500 men, women, and children who were inside the village survived, and many who escaped the fire were shot or stabbed. In the excerpt below, Williams is writing to Governor John Winthrop in the wake of this brutal attack and shares a Narragansett perspective on what should happen to the Pequot survivors.

Nanhiggonsicks: The Narragansett.

neighbors: The Narragansett.

be not enslaved: The Narragansett requested that Pequot survivors be not enslaved in the European sense of lifetime bondage.

Some 200 of these (since the slaughter at the Fort) came in revenge upon the **Nanhiggonsicks**: which the Nanhiggonsicks themselves knew not till these Pequts (now fallen to them) related it: for it pleased the Lord to Send a great mist that morning, that they durst not fight, and so returned …

I understand it would be very grateful to our **neighbors** that such Pequts as fall to them **be not enslaved**, like those which are taken in war: but (as they say is their general custom) be used kindly, and have houses and goods and fields given them: because they voluntarily choose to come in to them and if not received will to the Enemy turn wild Irish themselves.

30 Roger Williams to Governor John Winthrop, 21 June 1637, *Williams Corres.*, 1:86–87.

DOCUMENT 26

Roger Williams claims an unfree Indigenous child in letters to John Winthrop (1637)

The two excerpts below are letters that Williams wrote to John Winthrop in the summer of 1637. In them, Williams requests a specific boy, who was separated from his mother and siblings, and renamed by Winthrop—at Williams' request.[31] It is unclear whether the child was enslaved or indentured.[32] Excerpt (a) shows Williams' direct involvement in claiming an unfree Indigenous child, just one year after Providence was founded. In excerpt (b) Williams describes his role in returning **freedom-seekers** but goes on to request that the captives be treated as indentured servants, who were unfree for a set number of years, not for life. Whether this was heeded is unclear.

freedom-seekers: An unfree person who takes action to obtain freedom. Historians are increasingly using this term instead of fugitive, runaway, and escapee to challenge structures of power.

a. Roger Williams to John Winthrop (30 June 1637)[33]

It having again pleased the most High to put into your hands another miserable drove of Adams degenerate seed, and our **brethren by nature**: I am bold (if I may not offend in it) to request the keeping and bringing up of one of the children. I have fixed mine eye on this little one with the **red about his neck**, but I will not be preemptory in my choice, but will rest in your loving

brethren by nature: Biblical reference to Adam's degenerate seed, meaning that Indigenous People were "brethren by nature" and from the same seed as the English.

red about his neck: Either a birth mark or identifying mark from his captors. In an earlier letter, Williams described how colonists mistakenly attacked Narragansett Peoples, as these had no identifying signs/marks, and he requested some "yellow or red for their [Pequot] heads."

31 Israel Stoughton wrote to John Winthrop in June 1637: "by this Pinnace being Giggles ... you shall Receive 48 or 50 women and Children." Israel Stoughton to John Winthrop, 28 June 1637, *Winthrop Papers*, 3:435. It is unclear if the pinnace stopped in Providence, or if Williams identified the boy during a diplomatic mission to Narragansett, near modern-day Wickford, RI. *Williams Corres.*, 1:89 (notes 1 and 2). The following year, Williams referred to "Will," his "native ... servant," likely the same boy. For more on Indigenous enslavement and the meaning of "stolen relations," see "Stolen Relations: Recovering Stories of Indigenous Enslavement in the Americans," https://indigenousslavery.org. For the reference to Will, see Roger Williams to John Winthrop, ca. 1 August 1638, *Williams Corres.*, 1:170–73.

32 For more on slavery and servitude after the war, see Margaret Ellen Newell, *Brethren by Nature: New England Indians, Colonists, and the Origins of American Slavery* (Ithaca, NY: Cornell University Press, 2015); Katherine A. Grandjean, "The Long Wake of the Pequot War," *Early American Studies* 9, no. 2 (Spring 2011): 379–411; Michael L. Fickes, "'They could Not Endure that Yoke': The Captivity of Pequot Women and Children after the War of 1637," *New England Quarterly* 73, no. 1 (2000): 58–81; Andrea Robertson Cremer, "Possession: Indian Bodies, Cultural Control, and Colonialism in the Pequot War," *Early American Studies* 6, no. 2 (Fall 2008): 295–345; Kevin A. McBride, "The Historical Archaeology of the Mashantucket Pequots, 1637–1900," in *The Pequots in Southern New England: The Fall and Rise of an American Indian Nation*, ed. Laurence M. Haupman and James D. Wherry (Norman, OK: University of Oklahoma Press, 1993), 96–116; Lawrence M. Hauptman, "The Pequot War and Its Legacies," in *The Pequots in Southern New England*, 69–80; Ana Gonzalez interview with Lorén Spears (Narragansett), "Ep. 3: Roger Williams and the Pequot War," *The Public's Radio*, 5 November 2019, https://thepublicsradio.org/episode/ep-3-roger-williams-and-the-pequot-war.

33 Roger Williams to John Winthrop, 30 June 1637, *Williams Corres.*, 1:88–89.

pleasure for him, or any etc.[34] … Capt. Patrick also informs me of a great Itch upon the Soldiers to all **fowl upon** our neighbors [the Narragansett] … I much rejoice that as he says some of the chief at Qunnihticut Mr Heynes and Mr Ludlow are almost averse from killing women and children. Mercie outshines all the works and Attributes of him who is the Father of mercies.

fowl upon: Cause harm.

b. Roger Williams to John Winthrop (31 July 1637)[35]

Sir I here yet not of any of the runaway Captives at our neighbors [the Narragansett]. Yesterday I heard that 2 escaped from them to the Pequt. If any be or doe come amongst them I suppose they shall be **speedily returned**, or I shall certify where the default is. Sir, I desire to be truly thankful for the boy intended. His father was of Sasquakit where the last fight was: and fought not with the English as his mother (who is with you and 2 children more) certified me. I shall endeavor his good, and the common good, in him. I shall appoint some to fetch him: only I request that you would please to give a name to him. Sir concerning the Captives (pardon by wonton boldness) the Scripture is full of mystery, and the Old Testament of Types. If they have deserved Death, tis Sinn to spare. If they have not deserved Death then what punishment. Whether perpetual slavery. I doubt not but the Enemy may lawfully [be] weakened and despoiled of all comfort of wife and children etc.: but I beseech you well weigh if after a due time of training up to labor, and restraint, they ought not to be set free: yet so as without danger of adjoining to the Enemy.

speedily returned: The treaty that ended the war also included a clause to return freedom-seekers. Williams played a role in returning freedom-seekers, and when Pequot captives sought refuge with the Narragansett, he pressured Miantonomi to surrender them.

34 Roger Williams to John Winthrop, 2 June 1637, Williams Corres., 1:82–84.

35 Roger Williams to John Winthrop, 31 July 1637, *Williams Corres.*, 1:108–09.

DOCUMENT 27

Roger Williams to Governor John Winthrop on Pequot captives (1638)[36]

Following the war, the Pequot survivors were divided among Indigenous allies and settler-colonists, while others were sold into slavery around the Atlantic world. Survivors were stripped of their name and tribal nation affiliation, and accounts describe the horrors that some Pequot survivors endured, including starvation and brutal treatment. One unfree Pequot woman in Boston was raped, beaten, and burned. Williams described how "there are 2 Pequt Squaws, brought by the Nanhiggansick almost starved ... The biggest Mr Coles his native complains that she of all the natives in Boston is used worst, is beaten with firesticks ... I asked the biggest, who burnt her and why, she told me, Mr Pen because a fellow lay with her, but she saith, for her part she refused."[37] The excerpt is taken from a letter to John Winthrop of February 1638, in which Williams directly addresses his thoughts on what should happen to the rest of the Pequot captives. Williams later clarified that despite his close relationship with the Narragansett, he had "not yet turned Indian."[38]

Caunounicus and Miantunnoumu both desired that there might be a division made of these surviving Pequots (except the Sachims and murderers) and let their share be at your own Wisdoms. I shall humbly bold present mine own thoughts concerning a division and disposal of them. Since the most high delights in mercy, and great Revenge hath been already taken what if (the murtherers being Executed) the rest be divided and dispersed, (according as their numbers shall arise and divisions be thought fit) to become subject to yourselves in the Bay and Qunnticut wch they will easily doe in case they be Suffred to incorporate with the Natives in either places ... a tribute of **wolves heads** be imposed on them etc.

wolves heads: Wolves were a danger to the settler-colonists and this offered a practical solution; the eventual tribute was in wampum.

36 Roger Williams to Governor John Winthrop, 28 February 1638, *Williams Corres.*, 1:145–46.

37 Roger Williams to John Winthrop, 10 November 1637, *Williams Corres.*, 1:131–33.

38 Roger Williams to John Winthrop, 14 June 1638, *Williams Corres.*, 1:162–65.

DOCUMENT 28

Roger Williams reflects on his diplomatic efforts during the Pequot War in a letter to Major John Mason and Governor Thomas Prence (1670)[39]

In the excerpt below, written 33 years after the Pequot War, Williams reflects on the lengths he went to as a diplomat during the war. In a letter to Major John Mason and Governor Thomas Prence, Williams emphasizes the personal risks he took.

When the next Year after my Banishment, the Lord drew the Bow of the Pequt Warr against the Country ... I had my share of Service to the whole land in that Pequt Business, inferior to very few that acted ... upon Letters received from the Governor and Council at Boston, requesting me to use my utmost and Speediest Endeavors to break and hinder the League labored for by the Pequts against the Monhiggins and Pequts against the English ... the Lord helped me immediately put my Life into my hand, and **Scarce acquainting my Wife** to ship myself all alone in a poor Canoe, and to Cut through (a stormy Wind 30 miles in great Seas, every minute in hazard of Life) to the Sachims house. There days and nights my Business forced me to lodge and mix with the bloody Pequt Ambassadors, whose Hands and Arms (me thought,) reeked with the blood of my Countrymen murdered and massacred by them ... and from whom I could not but nightly look for their bloody Knives at my own throat also. When God wondrously preserved me, and helped me to break to pieces the Pequts negotiation and Design and to make and promote and finish my many Travels and Charges the English League with the Nahiggonsiks and Monhiggins against the Pequts: and that the English Forces marched up to the Nahiggonsik Country against the Pequts I gladly entertained at my house at Providence the **General Stoughton** and his officers, and used my utmost care that all his officers and Soldiers should be well accommodated with us. I marched up with them to the Nahigonsik Sachims and brought my Countrymen and the Barbarians, (Sachims and Captains) to a mutual Confidence and Complacency each in other ... upon Agreement, that I should keep at Providence as an Agent between the Bay and the Armie, I returned, and was Interpreter and Intelligencer, constantly receiving and sending Letters to the Governor and Council at Boston ... it was debated, whether or not I had Merited not only to be **recalled from Banishment**, but also to be

Scarce acquainting my Wife: Williams was frequently away from his wife Mary during their almost half century of marriage.

General Stoughton: Captain Israel Stoughton, a Massachusetts Bay magistrate, who commanded 160 men to round up Pequot Peoples after the Mystic massacre.

recalled from Banishment: Williams hypothesized whether his banishment should be revoked for his service as a diplomat during the Pequot War. It was not.

39 Roger Williams to Major John Mason and Governor Thomas Prence, 22 June 1670, *Williams Corres.*, 2:609–20.

honored with some Remark of Favor. It is known who hindered who never favored the Liberty of other mens Consciences. These things and ten times more I could relate, to show that I am not a stranger to the Pequt Wars.

QUESTIONS TO CONSIDER

1. What role did Roger Williams play as diplomat during the Pequot War? What do the primary sources reveal about the complicated relationships that Williams had with different Native leaders and Nations during the Pequot War?

2. What can we learn about Indigenous perspectives of the Pequot War from these sources? What can't we learn?

3. What happened to Pequot survivors after the war? What was Williams' position regarding Pequot captives?

KING PHILIP'S WAR

DOCUMENT 29

Roger Williams on the outbreak of conflict, in a letter to John Winthrop, Jr. (1675)[40]

King Philip's War erupted after years of tensions came to a head in June 1675, when three Wampanoag men were executed for the murder of John Sassamon, a Christian Indian. The war was part of the wider wars for New England, and in proportion to population it remains the deadliest war in American history. The New England colonies (Massachusetts, Plymouth, Connecticut, and Rhode Island) and their Mohegan and Pequot allies fought against an alliance of Native tribes and Nations, headed by King Philip (Metacom) of the Pokanoket band of Wampanoag. In the excerpt below, a letter to John Winthrop, Jr., Williams describes the start of the conflict and his diplomatic efforts to keep the Narragansett out of the war. Two days after sending this letter, he sent a follow up letter describing how "many wish that Plymouth had left the Indians alone at least not put to death the 3 Indians upon one Indians Testimony a thing which Philip fears … [and] leave the Monhiggins and Nahhiggonsicks to themselves."[41]

Negotiations with the Nahiggonsik [Narragansett] Indians … We had one meeting that night with Quaunochu, Miantunnomu's youngest Son, and upon the opening of the Governors Letters, he readily and gladly assented to all the Governor's desires and sent post to Mausup (now called Caunounicus) to the Old Queen [Matantuck], Ninicraft and Quawnipund, to give us a meeting … They being uncivil and barbarous and the old Queen (especially timorous) … We laid open the Governors Letters and accordingly they professed to hold no Agreement with Phillip in his rising against the English … if Phillip or his men fled to them yet they would not receive them but deliver them up unto the English. They question us why Plymouth pursued Phillip. We answered: He broke all Laws and was in Arms of Rebellion against that Colony and his ancient friends and protectors, though it is believed that he was the Author of the murdering of **John Sossiman** for revealing his plot to the Governor of Plymouth and for which the **3 Actors** were 2 weeks since Executed at Plymouth … though one brake the Rope

John Sossiman: John Sassaman, a member of the Massachusett Tribe who converted to be a Praying Indian.

3 Actors: The three Pokanoket men who murdered John Sassamon. Two were hung, but after the rope broke on the third man, Wampapaquan, he implicated Metacom and, after a brief reprieve, was shot.

40 Roger Williams to John Winthrop, Jr., 25 June 1675, *Williams Corres.*, 2:693–95.

41 Roger Williams to John Winthrop, Jr., 27 June 1675, *Williams Corres.*, 2:698–99.

and is kept in prison until their Court ... They demanded us why the Massachusetts and Rode Island rose, and joined with Plymouth against Phillip and left not Phillip and Plymouth to fight it out. We answered that all the Colonies were Subject to one King Charles and it was his pleasure and our Duty and Engagement for one **English man to stand to Death by Each other** in all parts of the World ... these 2 nations the Nahiggonsik and Monhiggons might be taken of from assisting Phillip (which passionately He Endeavors) and the English may more Securely and Effectually prosecute the quenching of this Philippian Fire ... Sir my **old bones** and Eyes are weary with Travel and writing to the Governors of Massachusetts and Rhode Island and your Selves.

English man to stand to Death by Each other: Williams describes his allegiance to the King of England and the other English colonies.

old bones: Williams was in his early seventies at the time.

DOCUMENT 30

Roger Williams to Governor John Leverett on the progression of the conflict, and Joshua Tift's account of his captivity (1676)[42]

Williams' diplomatic efforts to keep the Narragansett out of the war failed, and they allied with the Wampanoag, Nipmuck, Pacumtuck, Abenaki, and other Indigenous tribes and nations, while the Mohegan and Pequot fought with the English. The Wampanoag and their allies ended up fighting a war on two fronts, as they battled with the Mohawks to the west and the allied colonies to the east. Writing to Governor John Leverett in October 1675, Williams described how he was between "Fear and Hope" and humbly waited for the conflict to end.[43] Throughout the winter of 1675–76 the conflict escalated, and in December 1675 an army from Massachusetts, Plymouth, and Connecticut and their Native allies **attacked a Narragansett village**. Using Williams' former trading post, Coccumsusoc, as a launching point, the attack was a defining moment in the war, and approximately 650 Narragansett men, women, and children were killed, with hundreds more taken as captives. The war was devastating for the Ninnimissinuok, and not even Praying Indians were spared. Many were removed from their homes and imprisoned on barren islands in Boston harbor, where some died in bleak conditions from cold and hunger. In the excerpt below, a letter to John Leverett, Williams addresses the supply of guns from the French and diplomatic efforts to end the war. The focus of the excerpt is on Williams' description of how a settler, Joshua Tift (Tefft), was taken captive by the Narragansett. Tift lived close to the Great Swamp, and in this account, Tift recounts to Williams how he had been taken captive by the Narragansett. He claimed that he had no arms and that his life had been spared for agreeing to be enslaved. However, other sources describe how Tift had been a Narragansett encourager and conductor, shooting and injuring English soldiers. Shortly after Williams wrote this account, Tift was executed by **hanging and quartering** for treason.[44]

attacked a Narragansett village: Known as the Great Swamp Massacre, which took place in December 1675 near present-day South Kingstown, RI. The Rhode Island Historical Society returned the site to the Narragansett Indian Tribe in 2021.

hanging and quartering: Sometimes described as hung, drawn, and quartered. The 1647 order was likely used in Tift's case: "drawn upon a hurdell unto the place of execution, and there shall be hanged by the neck, cut down alive, his entrails and privie members cut from him and burned in his view; then shall his head be cut off and his body quartered." This was the customary punishment for traitors and rebels at the time.

This night I was requested … to take the Examination and Confession of an English man who hath bene with the Indians before and since the fight. His name is Joshua Tift … He was asked … how long he had bene with the Nahigonsiks: He answered about 27 days more or less. He was demanded

42 Roger Williams to Governor John Leverett, 14 January 1676, *Williams Corres.*, 2:711–14.

43 Roger Williams to John Leverett, 11 October 1675, *Williams Corres.*, 2:704–06.

44 John Bartlett, ed., *Records of the Colony of Rhode Island and Providence Plantations* (Providence, RI: A Crawford Green, State Printer, 1856), 1:160–61.

how he came amongst them. He said he was at his farm ... where he hired an Indian to keep his Cattle himself purposing to go to Rhode Island, but that day which he purposed and prepared to depart there came to his House Nananawtenu the Young Sachim[,] his Elder brother (Paupauquivwut) with their Captaine Quaquackis and a party of men and told him he must die. He said that he begged for his Life and promised he would be servant to the Sachim while he lived. He saith the Sachim then Carried him along with him having given him his Life as his Slave. He Said that he brought him to their Fort where was about 800 fighting men and about 200 houses. He Said the Indians brought 5 of his Cattle and killed them before his face. So he was forced to be Silent but prayed the Sachim to Spare the rest: who answered him what will Cattle now do you good, and the next day they Sent for the rest and killed them all ...

Being asked whether he was in the Fort in the fight, he Saith yes and waiting on his master the Sachim there until he was wounded (of which wound he lay 9 days and died) ... He Saith that if the Monhiggins and Pequts had bene true they might have destroyed most of the Nahiggonsiks, but, the Nahigonsiks parlayed with them in the beginning of the Fight so that they promised to shoot high which they did and killed not one Nahigonsik man except against their Wills. He saith that when it was duskish, Word was brought to the Sachims that the English were retreated. Upon this they Sent to the Fort to see what their Loss was, where they found 97 slain and 48 wounded ... they found 5 or 6 English bodies ...

[T]he Nahigonsiks powder is (generally) gone and spent but Phillip hath sent them word that he will furnish them enough from the French. He Saith they have carried New England Money to the French for Ammunition, but the money he will not take but Beaver or Wampum. He Saith the French have sent Philip a present vis a Brass gun and **Bandaliers** Suitable. He said also that the Nahigonsiks have sent 2 baskets of Wampum to the Mowhauks (Mauquawogs) where the French are for their favor and Assistance ... He saith that while they were in Consultation an Indian Squaw came in with a Letter from **the General**. ...

Bandaliers: Belts with pockets for holding ammunition.

the General: Josiah Winslow, governor of Plymouth Colony and commander-in-chief of the forces sent into Narragansett Country.

[H]e [Winslow] desired the Sachims would show themselves men and come and parley with him: that if they feared they might bring what Guard they pleased who might keep at a distance from ours who should not offer them any Affront, while the Sachims were at the House with the General from whom they should depart in peace if they came to no Agreement. Their Councilors said that the English did this only in policy to entrap the Sachims, as they had done Phillip many times ... Nananawtenu the young Sachim said he would not go but thought it best to use policy and to send word to the General that they would Come to him 3 days after. But Cawnounicus Said that he was old and would not lie to the English now, and said If you will fight ... tis folly for me to fight any longer ...

Their Chief Captain also said that He would not yield to the English so long as an Indian would stand with him. He Said he fought with the English and French and Dutch and Mowhauks and feared none of them, and said that if they yielded to the English they should be dead Men or slaves and work for the English.

DOCUMENT 31

Roger Williams to [Robert Williams?] on the burning of Providence (1676)[45]

The war wiped out close to half of the established New England towns, and had the tide of war not turned, the settler-colonists may have been pushed back to the Atlantic and New England may have been abandoned entirely. Native losses were equally devastating—with countless settlements destroyed. Amid the fighting, most of Providence (including the Williams family home) was burned to the ground. In this excerpt, Williams provides an update of the war in the spring of 1676, and describes his (failed) diplomatic efforts and the burning of Providence.

By **my Wife** I wrote to You some particulars of the Goings of God at Rehoboth. I thought fit to acquaint your dear Self, and my Dear Wife, and Children, and Friends, with the goings of the Most Hight at Providence ... All that we in Forts Men, Women, and Children were Saved. H[enry] Wright would trust God in his House. There they Killed Him with his own Hammer, Elizabeth Sucklin was preparing to go from Her own House to A Fort but delaying they Killed Her ... Our Town is about three Miles, at the one is A Fort ... This Morning we hear their Camp is between Notaquonckanit and Patuxet; and at this present We see smokes rise from Pawtuxet and from my Daughter Mercies House in the Woods ... In the afternoon of this burning Day of Gods Anger, and Indian that Knew **Vall** Called from the other Side of the Mill Hill that they two might speak together peaceably Without their Guns ... Word was brought me. I hasted out ... They then desired that we Would come to the point Without Arms as they would Do. The Town Cried out to us not to Venter. My Sons came Crying after me. Vall Went back. My Heart to God and the Country forced me to go on ... They met Without Arms. I asked who they were. They said Nahigonsets, and Cowwesets, and Wompano and Neepmucks, and Quanticoogs. I asked (for We heard so) Whether Phillip [was] amongst them. They said no; I asked where he was; They Said on this side Quniticut. I [asked] if the Nahigonsit Sachims were amongst them; they said they were at their Houses at Nahigonsit. I asked who Commanded Here: they said many Captains and Inferior Sachims, and Counsellors ... I asked Whither

my Wife: The letter to Mary Williams has not survived.

Vall: Valentine Whitman, a Providence resident, who worked as an Indigenous interpreter.

45 Roger Williams to [Robert Williams?] on the burning of Providence, 1 April 1676, *Williams Corres.*, 2:720–24. In the explanatory for note for this letter, LaFantasie explores the letter's provenance and authenticity.

they were bound. They Said to all the Tows about Plimoth ... I asked them Why they assaulted us With burning and Killing who ever were [kind?] Neighbors to them (and looking back) said I this House of mine now burning before mine Eyes hath Lodged kindly Some Thousands of You these Ten Years. They answered that we were their Enemies Joined with Massachusetts, and Plimouths, Entertaining, Assisting, Guiding of them, and I said we had Entertained all Indians being A Throughfare Town, but neither Wee nor this Colony had acted Hostility against them. I told them they were all this While Killing and burning ... They Confessed ... **we had forced them to it** ... that God was [with] them and Had forsaken us for they had so prospered in Killing and Burning us ... I told them they knew many times I had Quenched fires between the Bay and them, and Plimoth ... And now I did not doubt ... to Quench this and help to restore Quietness to the Land again. They Heard and Understood mee ... They desired me to come over the River to them and Debate matters at large ... I desired one of them to come over Saying they Had bin Burning all the Day on this side and were afraid of an old unarmed man. They Desired me to open my Cloak that they might See I had no Gun. I did so ... We had much repetition of the former particulars Which were debated ... He said You have driven us out of our own Countrie and pursued us to our Great Miserie ... [W]e are Forced to live upon you ... I said they were A Cowardly People ... We parted and they were so Civil that they called after me and bid me not go near the Burned Houses for their side might be Indians [that] might mischief me, but go by the Water Wide. My Dear Brother and Friends ... you must prepare Forts for Women and Children at Newport and on the Island or it will shortly be worse With You then us.

we had forced them to it: A rare insight into Native perspectives on the causes of the war, making it clear that the settler-colonists had provoked the war.

DOCUMENT 32

Roger Williams *et al.*, sale of Indigenous captives into slavery (1676)[46]

The Wampanoag and their allies suffered a symbolic blow when Metacom was killed in August 1676 at his Mount Hope base, in present-day Bristol, RI. Philip's severed head was then paraded through the streets of Plymouth and left on a pike for decades as a warning. Following the burning of Providence, the town came together for a meeting in August 1676 "under a tree by the water," and a committee was formed to work on the "disposal" of the Indians.[47] The following excerpts show how Rhode Islanders, including Roger Williams, agreed to sell Native captives into slavery around the Atlantic world. Williams' son, Providence, used his vessel to clear the town of "Indians" to the "great peace & Content" of inhabitants.[48] Others remained in bondage in New England households. Despite enslavement and forced removal, Indigenous Peoples are not vanished: they remain in their ancestral homelands. In recent years, Indigenous Peoples from New England have connected with descendants of their ancestors who were sold into slavery in the Caribbean with reunification powwows in Bermuda.

We whose names are hereunto subscribed having right to the said Indians, as by an act of the Committee doth appear, doe betrust, empower, and fully authorize Captain Arthur Fenner, William Hopkins and John Whipple Junior to hire and procure a boat to transport the said Indians where they may be sold, and to make sale and delivery thereof as fully, and as firmly, as if we were all personally present, and to do all such things as shall any ways belong to the transporting making sale or disposal of all and every of the said Indians as above said and to see all such charges as doth arise by the said Indians, after to them committed, defrayed out of the product of the same, and themselves reasonably satisfied for their pains, and then to make return of the remainder of the product of the said Indians to the said company. This being our real act and deed as witness our hands this 16 day of August 1676:

---

46 Roger Williams *et al.*, Sale of Indian Captives, 16 August 1676, Roger Williams Collection, Rhode Island Historical Society, Providence, RI.

47 So many Indigenous Peoples were sold into slavery in the seventeenth century that Barbados passed a law in 1676 to limit the number of enslaved Natives sent from New England. Linford Fisher, "'Dangerous Designes': The 1676 Barbados Act to Prohibit New England Indian Slave Importation," *The William and Mary Quarterly* 71, no. 1 (2014): 99–124.

48 Horatio Rogers, George Moulton Carpenter, and Edward Field, eds., *The Early Records of the Town of Providence* (Providence, RI: Snow & Farnham City Printers, 1895), 8:14.

Roger Williams
Daniell Abbott
John Morey
Henry Ashton
Nathaniell Waterman
Ephraim Pray
Joseph Woodward
Abraham Man
Eliazur Whipple
John Angell
James Olney
James Angell
Vallintine Whittman
Edward Bennett
Thomas Field
John Pray

QUESTIONS TO CONSIDER

1. What was King Philip's War and how was it part of the larger war for New England?
2. What different roles did Roger Williams play in the conflict?
3. What insights do the sources offer into Indigenous perspectives of King Philip's War?
4. How does Williams' involvement in the enslavement of Indigenous Peoples after the war complicate our understanding of him?

PART V

Religious Freedom

DEBATES WITH JOHN COTTON ON SOUL LIBERTY

DOCUMENT 33

Roger Williams, *The Bloudy Tenent of Persecution* (1644)[1]

Williams published his masterpiece on religious freedom, *The Bloudy Tenent of Persecution*, in 1644 in London when he was there on charter business. *The Bloudy Tenent* was part of a larger theological conflict that Williams had with Massachusetts Bay minister, John Cotton, which resulted in publication wars between the two combatants. Williams was at odds with Cotton on issues of the separation of church and state, conversion, and religious freedom, among others. John Cotton published *A Letter of Mr. John Cotton, Teacher of the Church in Boston in New-England, to Mr. Williams* in 1643, and Williams responded the following year with *The Bloudy Tenent*. Upon reading *The Bloudy Tenent*, Cotton wrote *The Bloudy Tenent, Washed and Made White in the Bloud of the Lamb* in 1647.[2] For Cotton, the dual responsibility of the magistrate was to protect the church from heretics and other enemies and enforce the "perpetual" laws. This meant that coercion was legitimate when Christians went astray, which in turn warranted the civil state to override their freedom.[3] Williams disagreed and responded in print in 1652 with *The Bloody Tenent Yet More Bloody by Mr. Cotton's Endeavour to Wash it White in the Blood of the Lamb*. In these publication wars, the two rivals examined key scriptural justifications for persecution, including Psalm 101, verse 8: "I will early destroy all the wicked of the land; that I may cut off all wicked doers from the city of the Lord."

---

1 Roger Williams, *The Bloudy Tenent* (London, 1644).

2 Cotton argued that "[w]hat persecution the Lord Jesus if he were on earth, would practice against those who would not receive him." For Cotton, "[t]he Answer is near at hand, and is written for the warning of all gain-sayers: Those mine enemies which would not that I should reign over them, bring them hither, and slay them before my face, *Luk. 19. 27.*" John Cotton, *The Bloudy Tenent, Washed and Made White in the Bloud of the Lamb* (London, 1647).

3 David Hall, *A Reforming People: Puritanism and the Transformation of Public Life in New England* (New York: Alfred A. Knopf, 2011).

As the full title *The Bloudy Tenent of Persecution, for cause of Conscience, discussed in A Conference between Truth and Peace* suggests, its 247 pages are framed as a discussion between allegorical speakers Truth and Peace. Williams cites lessons from "the lamentable experiences of former and present slaughters" and specific case studies to bolster his theories. The religious wars in Europe and the religious upheaval in England clearly demonstrated that persecution produced false converts who simply sought to evade punishment. Even those who stayed true to their faith and died for it simply became martyrs, which only served to harden their followers' resolve. Throughout, Williams argues that persecution goes against Christian charity, does not promote true conversion, and causes civil instability. The first part of the excerpt is from the preface, where Williams summarizes the book's twelve central arguments; this is followed by excerpts from the dialogue between Truth and Peace.

blood of so many hundred thousand: Religious wars, which pitted Catholic against Protestant countries.

First. That the **blood of so many hundred thousand** souls of protestants and papists, spilt in the wars of present and former ages, for their representative consciences, is not required nor accepted by Jesus Christ the Prince of Peace.

Secondly. Pregnant scriptures and arguments are throughout the work proposed against the doctrine of persecution for cause of conscience.

Mr. Calvin: John Calvin, a French theologian and pioneering reformer in Geneva during the Protestant Reformation in the sixteenth century.

Beza: Theodore Beza, a follower of Calvin; a French Protestant theologian and scholar who played an important role in the Reformation.

Thirdly. Satisfactory answers are given to scriptures and objections produced by **Mr. Calvin, Beza**, Mr. [John] Cotton, and the ministers of the New English churches, and other former and later, tending to prove the doctrine of persecution for cause of conscience.

Fourthly. The doctrine of persecution for cause of conscience, is proved guilty of all blood of the souls crying for vengeance under the altar.

Fifthly. All civil states with their officers of justice, in their respective constitutions and administrations, are proved essentially civil, and therefore not judges, governors, or defenders of the spiritual, or Christian, state and worship.

Sixthly. It is will and command of God that, since the coming of his Son the Lord Jesus, a permission of the most Paganish, Jewish, Turkish, or anti-christian consciences and worships be granted to all men in all nations and countries: and they are only to be fought against with that sword which only, in small matters, [is] able to conquer: to wit, the sword of God's spirit, the word of God.

Seventhly. The state of the land of Israel, the kings and people thereof, in peace and war, is proved figurative and ceremonial, and no pattern nor precedent for any kingdom or civil state in the world to follow.

Eighthly. God requires not an uniformity of religion to be enacted and enforced in any civil state; which enforced uniformity, sooner or later, is the greatest occasion of civil war, ravishing of conscience, persecution of Christ Jesus in his servants, and of the hypocrisy and destruction of millions of souls.

Ninthly. In holding an enforced uniformity of religion in a civil state, we must necessarily disclaim our desires and hopes of the Jews' conversion to Christ.

Tenthly. An enforced uniformity of religion in a civil state, confounds the civil and religious, denies the principles of Christianity and civility, and that Jesus Christ is come in the flesh.

Eleventhly. The permission of other consciences and worships than a state professeth, only can, according to God, procure a firm and lasting peace; good assurance being taken, according to the wisdom of the civil state, for uniformity of civil obedience from all sorts.

Twelfthly. Lastly, true civility and Christianity may both flourish in a state or kingdom, notwithstanding the permission of divers and contrary consciences, either Jew or **Gentile** ...

Gentile: Biblical term meaning someone who is not Jewish.

PEACE. Oh that my head were a fountain, and mine eyes rivers of tears to lament my children, the children of peace and light, thus darkening that, and other lightsome scriptures with such dark and direful clouds of blood.

TRUTH. Sweet peace, thy tears are seasonable and precious, and bottled up in the heavens. But let me add a second consideration from that scripture. If that scripture may now literally be applied to nations and cities in a parallel to **Canaan** and Jerusalem since the Gospel, and this Psalm 101 be literally applied to cities, towns and countries in Europe and America, not only such as assay to join themselves (as they here speak) in a corrupt church estate, but such as know no church estate, nor God, nor Christ, yea, every wicked person and evil-doer, must be hanged or stoned, etc., as it was in Israel. And if so, how many thousands and millions of men and women in the several

Canaan: Biblical reference to the "Promised Land."

kingdoms and governments of the world must be cut off from their lands, and destroyed from their cities, as this scripture speaks?

members of the Church of England: Williams thought it was hypocritical for puritans in Massachusetts Bay to criticize the Church of England and not formally separate from it.

mother whore: Meaning criticizing their home church, the Church of England.

Thirdly, since those persons in the New English plantations accounted unfit for church estate, yet remain all **members of the Church of England**, from which New England dares not separate ... what riddle or mystery, or rather fallacy of Satan is this?

PEACE. It will not be offense to charity to make conjecture. First, herein New England churches secretly call their **mother whore**, not daring America to join with their own mother's children, though unexcommunicate, no, nor permit them to worship God after their consciences ... If such members of Old England should be suffered to enjoy their consciences in New ... if, I say, they should set up churches after their consciences, the greatness and multitudes of their assemblies would decay, and withal the contributions and maintenance of their ministers, unto which all or most have been forced.

TRUTH. Dear Peace, these are more than conjectures. Thousands now espy, and all that love the purity of the worship of the living God should lament such halting. I shall add this, not only do they partially neglect to cut off the wicked of the land, but such as themselves esteemed beloved and godly by their own confession, because differing in conscience and worship from them, and consequently not to be suffered in their holy land of Canaan.

But having examined the Scripture alleged, let us now weigh their reasons. First, say they, the not cutting off by the sword, but tolerating many religions in a state would provoke God. Unto which I answer, first ... that no proof can be made from the institutions of the Lord Jesus that all religions but one are to be cut off by the civil sword ...

Secondly, I affirm that the cutting off by the sword other consciences and religions but one are to be cut off by the civil sword[,] other consciences and religions but one are to be cut off by the (contrarily) most provoking god, expressly against his will ... as also the bloody mother of all those monstrous mischiefs (where such cutting off is used) both to the souls and bodies of men ... Their civil New English state framed out of their churches may yet stand, subsist, and flourish, although they did (as by the word of the Lord they ought) permit either Jews, or Turks, or Anti-Christians to live amongst them, subject unto their civil government.

DOCUMENT 34

John Cotton, *The Bloudy Tenent Washed and Made White in the Bloud of the Lamb* (1647)[4]

Upon reading *The Bloudy Tenent*, John Cotton retaliated in 1647 with *The Bloudy Tenent, Washed, and Made White in the Bloud of the Lamb*, in which he critiqued Williams' arguments, Williams responding in print in 1652.[5] In the excerpt that follows, Cotton rebuts Williams' arguments on religious freedom, offers his interpretation of Indigenous land rights, and muses on the reasons behind Williams' banishment.

The great Questions of this present time are handled, viz. How far Liberty of Conscience ought to be given to those that truly fear God? And how far restrained to turbulent and pestilent persons, that not only raze the foundation of Godliness, but disturb the Civil Peace where they live? Also how far the Magistrate may proceed in the duties of the first Table? And that all Magistrates ought to study the word and will of God, that they may frame their Government according to it ... The Bloody Tenent (I mean the book styled by that name, tending to discuss an holy & wholesome truth of God, slanderously styled the *Bloudy Tenent*) was put forth against the Royall Law of the love of the Gospel ... This Title trespasses not only against the Creator of Christian love, which is wont to take even doubtful things in the fairest an sense: but even against the Law of truth ... It is true, where the Church is not, Cities and Townes may enjoy some measure of Civil Peace, yea and flourish in outward prosperity for a time, through the Patience and Bounty and Long-sufferance of God ... But when the Church cometh to be Planted amongst them, If then Civil States doe neglect them, & suffer the Churches to corrupt, and annoy themselves by pollutions in Religion, the staff of the Peace of the Common-wealth will soon be broken, as the Purity of Religion is broken in the Churches ... Therefore a Christian by departing from God, may disturb a *Gentile* civil State. And it is no preposterous way for the Governors of the State, according to the quality of the disturbance railed by the starting aside of such a Christian, to punish both it and him by civil censure ... Excommunication or any other Church-prosecution, cannot

4 John Cotton, *The Bloudy Tenent Washed and Made White in the Bloud of the Lamb* (London, 1647).

5 Williams responded in 1652 with a pamphlet titled *The Bloudy Tenent Yet More Bloudy by Mr. Cotton's Endeavour to Wash it White in the Blood of the Lamb; of Whose Precious Blood, Spilt in the Bloud of his Servants; and of the Blood of Millions Spilt in Former and Later Wars for Conscience Sake, That Most Bloody Tenent of Persecution for Cause of Conscience, upon, a Second Tryal Is Found More Apparently and More Notoriously Guilty, etc.*

… be called persecution … excommunication is … lawful persecution, if the cause be just offence, (as the Angell of the Lord is said to persecute the wicked Psalm 35.6.) …

A little before our coming, God had by pestilence, and other contagious diseases, swept away many thousands of the Natives who had inhabited the Bay of *Massachusetts*, for which the Patent was granted. Such few of them as survived **were glad of the coming of the *English***, who might preserve them from the oppression of the *Nahargansets*. For it is the manner of the Natives, the stronger Nations to oppress the weaker. This answer did not satisfy *Mr. Williams*, who pleaded, the Natives, though they did not, nor could subdue the Country, (but left it *vacuum Domicilium*) yet they hunted all the Country over, and for the expedition of their hunting voyages, they burnt up all the underwoods in the Country, once or twice a year, and therefore as Noblemen in *England* only for their game, and no man, might lawfully invade their Propriety: So might the Natives challenge the like Propriety of the Country here.

were glad of the coming of the *English*: Reference to the so-called "great dying," where thousands of Native Peoples throughout Southern New England perished between 1616 and1619 because of European diseases. Estimates range from 60 to 90 percent of Wampanoag Peoples dying, which changed the politics and power dynamics in the region. Cotton is suggesting that the Pokanoket Wampanoag (who signed a peace treaty with the Plymouth settlers in 1621) were pleased about the arrival of the English. Cotton's Eurocentric bias overshadows the complexity of inter- (and intra-) national and tribal politics.

It was replied unto him.

1. That the King, and Noblemen in *England*, as they possessed greater Territories then other men, so they did greater service to Church, and Common-wealth.

2. That they employed their Parkes, and Forests, not for hunting only, but for Timber, and for the nourishment of tame beasts, as well as wild, and also for habitation to sundry Tenants.

3. That our Towns here did not disturb the huntings of the Natives, but did rather keep their Game fitter for their taking; for they take their Deere by Traps, and not by Hounds.

4. That if they complained for any straits we put upon them, we gave satisfaction in some payments, or other, to their content.

5. We did not conceive that it is a just Title to so vast a Continent, to make no other improvements of millions of Acres in it, but only to burn it up for pastime.

But theses answers were not satisfying to him [Roger Williams], this was still pressed by him as a National sin, to hold to the Patent, yea, and a National duty to renounce the Patent: which to have done, had subverted the fundamental State, and Government of the Country. The second offence, which procured his Banishment, was occasioned as I touched before. The

Magistrates, and other members of the General Court upon Intelligence of some Episcopal, and malignant practices against the Country, they made an order of Court to take trial of the fidelity of the People, (not by imposing upon them, but) by offering to them an Oath of Fidelity: that in case any should refuse to take it, they might not betrust them with place of public charge, and Command. This Oath when it came abroad, he [Williams] vehemently withstood it, and dissuaded sundry from it ... because it was the establishment not of Christ, but of mortal men in their office ... Whereupon Mr. Williams took occasion to stir up the Church to join him in writing Letters of Admonition unto all the Churches ... Which Letters coming to the several Churches, provoked the Magistrates to take the more speedy course with so heady, and violent a spirit ...

And for the latter point: What persecution the Lord Jesus if he were on earth, would practice against those who would not receive him.

The Answer is near at hand, and is written for the warning of all gainsayers: Those mine enemies which would not that I should reign over them, bring them hither, and slay them before my face, Luk. 19. 27.

QUESTIONS TO CONSIDER

1. Identify the key arguments that Roger Williams and John Cotton make in *The Bloudy Tenent of Persecution* and *The Bloudy Tenent, Washed and Made White in the Bloud of the Lamb.*

2. How do the points that Williams makes in *The Bloudy Tenent of Persecution* connect to his other written works that advocate for religious freedom and separation of church and state?

FRAMING RELIGIOUS FREEDOM AND SEPARATION OF CHURCH AND STATE

DOCUMENT 35

Letters between Roger Williams and Anne Sadleir discussing issues of religious freedom and the Church of England (1652–53)[6]

Anne Sadleir, the eldest daughter of Sir Edward Coke, was born in 1584 in Huntingfield and married Ralph Sadleir in 1601. Sadleir knew Williams when he was a young boy working for her father. Excerpts (a) to (g) are from letters between Williams and Sadleir from 1652 to 1653 when Williams was in England on charter business. In excerpt (a) Williams discusses some of the controversies he's been caught up in and sends Sadleir a copy of *Experiments in Spiritual Health*. Excerpt (b) includes Sadleir's criticisms of Williams, which she recorded on the address packet. Excerpt (c) is Sadleir's initial response to Williams, in which she tells him she has not read his book and defends the Church of England. Excerpt (d) is Williams' follow up, where he discusses various books Sadleir has recommended for him and he sends her a copy of *The Bloody Tenent Yet More Bloody*. Excerpt (e) is Sadleir's increasingly terse response in which she reaffirms her love of the Church of England and informs Williams that she did not even open *The Bloody Tenent Yet More Bloody* because the title put her off. She instructs Williams not to contact her again. Excerpt (f), shows that Williams ignored her request and wrote back; he discusses his other works on minsters as hirelings, issues of religious toleration, and the monarchy. Excerpt (g) is Sadleir's final response, which implores Williams to leave her alone and to go back to where he came from.

a. Roger Williams to Anne Sadleir (in or after April 1652)

My much honored friend Mrs. Sadler,

The Never dying Honor and Respect, which I owe ... have emboldened me once more to inquire after **Your dear Husbands** and Your Life and Health and Welfare. This last winter I landed (once more) in my Native Country being sent over from some parts of New England with some Address to the Parliament[.] My very **great Business** and my very great straights of Time, and my very great Journey homeward to my dear Yokefellow and many children I greatly

Your dear Husbands: Anne married Ralph Sadleir, heir to the estate of Standon Lordship in Hertfordshire, in 1601.

great Business: Important business of renewing Rhode Island's previous parliamentary patent.

6 Anne Sadleir Correspondence with Roger Williams, R.5.5, Letters 30–36, Sadleir Collection, Wren Library, Trinity College, Cambridge University, UK.

fear will not permit me to present my ever obliged Duty and Service to you at Standon, especially if it please God that I may dispatch my Affaires to depart with the ships within **this fortnight** ... It has pleased the most High [God] to carry me ... through mighty Labors, mighty Hazards, and mighty Suffering, and to vouchsafe to use so base an Instrument (as I humbly hope) to glorify Himself, in many of my Trials and Sufferings both amongst the England and Barbarians. I have been formerly and since I landed occasioned to take up the 2 edged sword of God's Spirit, the Word of God and to appear in ... some Contests against the ministers of Old and New England ... as touching the true Ministry of Christ, and the Soul Freedom ... Since I have landed I **published 2 or 3 things** ... tis Controversial with which I will not trouble your Meditations. Only, I crave the Boldness to send you [*Experiments in Spiritual Health*, which includes] ... a Letter to my dear wife (upon the Occasion of her great sickness near Death) I sent her being absent myself among the Indians. And being greatly obliged to Sir Henry Vane Junior (once Governor of New England) and his Lady, I was persuaded to publish it in her name and humbly to present Your honorable hands with one or 2 of them. I humbly pray you to cast a serious eye on the holy Scriptures on which the Examinations are grounded ... I have bene oft glad in the Wilderness of America to have bene reproved for going in a Wrong Path and to be directed by a naked Indian Boy in my Travels ... What I have done and Sufferd (and I hope for the Truth of God according to my Conscience) in Old and New England, I should be a Fool in relating ... I confess I have many Adversaries, and also many Friends and divers Eminent ... My humble respects presented to Mr. Sadler.

this fortnight: Williams wanted to leave England within two weeks, but did not do so for another two years.

published 2 or 3 things: On this trip, Williams published *Fourth Paper, Presented by Major Butler*; *Experiments of Spiritual Health and Life*; and *Hirelings Ministry None of Christs*. *The Bloody Tenent Yet More Bloody* was likely still at press at the time of writing.

b. Anne Sadleir's note on Roger Williams' address packet (1652)

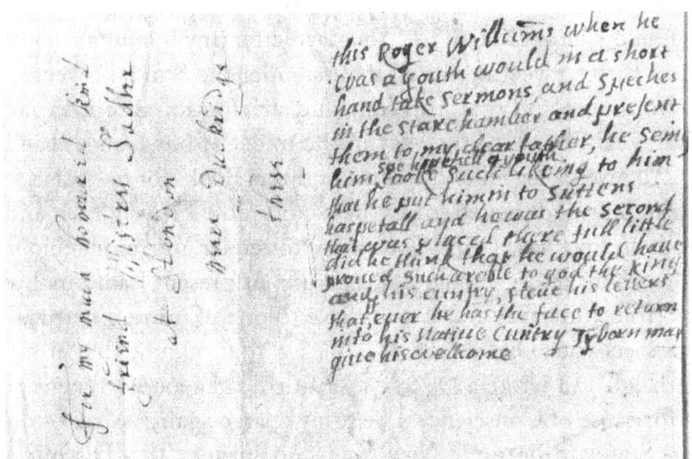

this Roger Williams when he
was a youth would in a short
hand take sermons and speeches
in the starchamber and present
them to my dear father, he seeing so hopefull a youth
him took such liking to him
that he put him in to Suttens
hospitall and he was the second
that was placed there full little
did he think that he would have
proved such a rebel to god the king
and his cuntry, I leave his letters
that ever he has the face to return
into his native cuntry Tyborn may
give his welcome

Figure 35.1: Anne Sadleir's note on Roger Williams' address packet (1652)
Source: Master and Fellows of Trinity College, Cambridge. Manuscript reference R.5.5, Letter number 31.

Select Transcription

Roger Williams … rebel to god the king and his country … that ever he has the face to return to his native country **Tyburn** may give his welcome.

Tyburn: Notorious execution site in London.

c. Anne Sadleir to Roger Williams (after April 1652)

Mr. Williams … I have given over reading many books, and therefore with thanks has returned yours. Those that I now read, besides the Bible, are first the **late Kings Book, Hookers Ecclesiasticall Policie, Reverend Bishop Andrews sermons** with his other divine meditations; **Dt. Jeremy Taylors** works, and **Dt. Thomas Jackson** upon the Creed. Some of these my dear father was a great admirer of and would often call them the glorious lights of the church of England. These lights shall be my guide, I wish they may be yours, for your new lights that are so much cried up, I believe in the conclusion, they will prove but dark lanthorns[,] therefore I dare not meddle with them. Your friend in the **old way**.

late Kings Book: *Eikon Basilike. The Pourtraicture of His Sacred Majestie* (London, 1649). "Eikon Basilike" (Greek) means "portrait of the king," and the book offers a positive portrait of the recently executed King Charles I.

Hookers Ecclesiasticall Policie: Richard Hooker was an English theologian and author of *Of the lawes of ecclesiasticall politie* (1599).

Reverend Bishop Andrews sermons: Lancelot Andrews, Bishop of Winchester, published many sermons prior to 1652.

Dt. Jeremy Taylors: Bishop of Down and Connor, Taylor published many works prior to 1652. He achieved fame as an author during the Protectorate of Oliver Cromwell and was known for his poetic style of expression.

Dt. Thomas Jackson: Master of Corpus Christi College, Oxford, and Dean of Peterborough, Jackson published commentaries on the Apostles' Creed.

old way: Church of England.

d. Roger Williams to Anne Sadleir (likely late spring 1652)

My much honored kind friend Mrs Sadleir,

My humble respects premised to Your much honored self and Mr Sadleir, humbly wishing You the saving Knowledge and Assurance of Life, which is Eternal, when this poor Minutes Dreame is over! In my poor span of Time I have bene often in the Jaws of Death, sinking at Sea, shipwrecked on shore, in danger of Arrows Swords and Bullets: And yet me thinks the most High and most holy God hath reserved me for some Service to his most glorious and Eternal Majesty … Your last letter (my honored friend) I received as a Bitter Sweeting (as all that is under the Sun is) Sweet in that I hear from You, and that You continue striving for Life Eternal: Bitter, in that we differ about the Way in the midst of our Dangers and Distresses … You were pleased to direct me to divers Books for my satisfaction. I have carefully endeavored to get them, and some I have gotten and upon my reading, I purpose (with Gods help) to render You an ingenious and Candid Account of my Thoughts Result etc. At present I am humbly bold, to pray Your Judicious and Loving Eye to **one of mine**. Tis true, I cannot but Expect your Distaste of it! … please You to know that at my last being in England I wrote a Discourse entitled, The bloodie Tenent of Persecution for cause of Conscience. I bent my charge against Mr Cotton especially, the Standard-bearer of New English Ministers. That Discourse he since answered and calls his booke The Bloodie Tenent made White in the Bloud of the Lambe. This joinder of mine (as I humbly hope) unwasheth

one of mine: Williams sent Sadleir a copy of his recently published *The Bloody Tenent Yet More Bloody*.

his Washings—and proves that in Soule Matters no Weapons but Soule Weapons are reaching and Effectual.

e. Anne Sadleir to Roger Williams (likely summer 1652)

Sir

I thank god my blessed Parents bred me up in the old and best religion and it is my glory that I am a member of the church of England as it was when all the reformed churches gave her the right hand. When I cast my eye upon the frontispiece of your book, and saw it entitled the bloody tenant I durst not adventure to look into it, for fear it should bring into my memory that much blood that has of late been shed, and which I would fain forget. Therefore I do with thanks return it. I cannot call to mind any blood shed for conscience, some few that went about to make a rent in our once well governed church, were punished but none suffered death. But this I know that since it has been left to every mans conscience to fancy what religion he list, there has more Christian blood been shed, then was in the **ten persecutions**, and some of that blood will I fear cry till the day of judgement. But you know what the scripture says, that when there was no King in Israel every man did that which was right in his own eyes, but what became of that the sacred story will tell you. Thus entreating you to trouble me no more in this kind and wishing you a good journey to your charge in new providence I rest your friend in the old and best way.

ten persecutions: The ten plagues on Egypt described in Exodus 2–3.

f. Roger Williams to Anne Sadleir (likely winter 1652/53)

My honored kind friend Mrs Sadleir

I greatly rejoiced to hear from you, although [you are] now an Opposite to me even in the highest points of Heaven and Eternity.

1. Two things your lines express: First your Confidence in Your own Old Way etc.
2. Civility, and Gentleness, in that (not being pleased to accept my Respects and Labors presented yet) you gently with thanks and your Reason return them.

I shall not be so sorry You differ from me, if yet the Father of Spirits please to vouchsafe you a Spirit of Christian Searching and Examination ... That you admire the Kings Book and Bishop Andrewes his Sermons and Hookers Policy etc ... I am far from wondering at it ... I now find that the church and Sanctuary of Christ Jesus, consists not of Dead but Living stones. Is not a parish or National Church forced (to the pretended Bed of Christs

Worship) by Lawes and Swords ... I find that (in respect of Ministerial Function and office) Such Ministers ... are all of Them, one as well another, False prophets and Teachers, So far as they are Hirelings and make a Trade and Living of preaching (John 10) as I have lately opened in my discourse of the **Hireling Ministrie none of Christs**. ... I have read the books You mention and the Kings book, which Commends 2 of them Bishop Andrews and Hookers yea and a third also Bishop Lauds. For the King [Charles I] I knew his person, vicious, a Swearer from his youth, and a oppressor and persecutor of Good Men (to say nothing of his own Fathers blood, and the blood of so many hundredth thousand English, Irish, Scotch, French, lately charged upon him). Against his and his blasphemous Fathers Cruelties, Your own Dear Father, and many Precious Men shall rise up shortly and cry for vengeance ... My honored friend: Since you please not to read mine, let me pray leave To request your reading of one Book of your own Authors, I mean the Liberty of prophesying pend by (so called) Do. **Jeremy Taylor** In the which is excellently asserted, the Toleration of differing Religions ... I do also humbly wish that you may please to read impartially **Mr Miltons** answer to the Kings book.

Hireling Ministrie none of Christs: Williams' recently published *Hirelings Ministry None of Christ* (1652), in which he made the theological argument with political implications that England and its colonies were not a favored nation of God nor a second Israel.

Jeremy Taylor: *A discourse of the liberty of prophesying* (London, 1647). The book examined the "Unreasonableness of Prescribing to Other Men's Faith and the Iniquity of Persecuting Differing Opinions."

Mr Miltons: John Milton, *Eikonoklastes* (London, 1649), which provided a justification for the execution of King Charles I.

g. Anne Sadleir to Roger Williams (winter 1652/53)

Mr. Williams

I thought my first letter would have given you so much more Satisfaction, that in that kind I should never have heard of you anymore, but it seems you have a face of brass, so that you **cannot blush**. But since you press me to it, I must let you know as I did before ... For the foul and false aspersions you have cast upon that king of ever blessed memory **Charles the Martyr**, I protest I trembled when I read them, and none but such a villain as your Selfe would have written them ... Thus you see I have the law, with the old and new testament on my Side ... For the blood you mention, which has been shed in these times which you would father upon the late king, there is a book called the History of independence[,] a book worth your reading, that will tell you by whom all this Christian blood has been shed ... For Miltons book that you desire I should read if I be not mistaken ... he had at that time **two or three wives** living. This perhaps were good Doctrine in new England, but it is most abominable in old England. For his book that he wrote against the late King that you would have me read, you should have taken notice of gods judgement upon him who stroke him with **blindness** ... God has begun his Judgment upon him here, his punishment will be here after in hell. But have you seen the **answer to it**. If you can get it I assure you it is worth your reading. I have also read Taylors book of the liberty of professing though it please me not yet I am sure it does you, or

cannot blush: Sadleir is accusing Williams of being shameless.

Charles the Martyr: Reference to King Charles I, following his execution in January 1649 after being found guilty of treason.

two or three wives: Milton published several works on divorce, including *The doctrine and discipline of divorce* (London, 1643). Sadleir was likely relying on rumor in claiming that Milton had multiple living wives. Milton married his first wife in 1643; she deserted him and died in 1650, and he did not remarry until 1656. When his second wife died, he waited five years to remarry in 1663.

blindness: By the autumn of 1651, Milton was almost, if not totally, blind.

else I [know] you [would] not have written [to] me to have read it. I say it and you would make a good fire. But have you seen his divine institution of the **office ministerial**. I assure you that is both worth your reading and practice. Bishop **Lauds book against Fisher** I have read long since, which if you have not done let me tell you that he has deeply wounded the pope, and I believe howsoever he be slighted, he will rise a Saint, when Seeming ones such as you are will rise devils. I cannot conclude without putting you in mind how dear a lover and great admirer my father was of the liturgy of the church of England, and would often say no reformed church had the like. He was constant to it both in his life and at his death. I mean to walk in his steps ... I will walk as directly to heaven as I can, in which place if you will turn from being a rebel, and fear God and obey the King there is hope I may meet you there. Howsoever trouble me no more with your letters for they are very troublesome to hear that wishes you in the place from whence you came.

answer to it: Follow up to the original defense of King Charles I, Joseph Jane's *Eikon aklastos, the image unbroaken* (London, 1651).

office ministerial: Jeremy Taylor's *Clerus Domini: or, A Discourse of the Divine Institution, Necessity, Sacrednesse, and Separation of the Office Ministerial* (London, 1651).

Lauds book against Fisher: William Laud's *A relation of the conference between William Laud and Mr Fisher the Jesuite* (London, 1639).

DOCUMENT 36

Roger Williams on religious freedom and separation of church and state, in a letter to the town of Providence (1655)[7]

Williams explored the idea of religious freedom in an open letter to the town of Providence in 1655. This letter was likely written in response to the political discord which rocked Providence throughout the winter of 1654–55. The town voted to establish a citizen militia and impose fines on those who refused to serve. There was significant opposition to the militia, including by Williams' brother, Robert. Williams wrote that he remained "studious of our common peace and liberty," arguing that liberty of conscience did not permit freedom from social obligation. The letter is one of Williams' most well-known pieces of correspondence and is sometimes referred to as the "Ship of State" letter because of the ship analogy Williams uses.

That ever I should speak or write a tittle, that tends to such an infinite liberty of conscience, is a mistake, and which I have ever disclaimed and abhorred. To prevent such mistakes, I shall at present only propose this case: There goes many a ship to sea, with many hundred souls in one ship, whose weal and woe is common, and is a true picture of a commonwealth, or a human combination or society. It hath fallen out sometimes, that both papists and protestants, Jews and Turks, may be embarked in one ship; upon which supposal I affirm, that all the liberty of conscience, that ever I pleaded for, turns upon these two hinges—that none of the papists, protestants, Jews, or Turks, be forced to come to the ship's prayers of worship, nor compelled from their own particular prayers or worship, if they practice any.

I further add, that I never denied, that notwithstanding this liberty, the commander of this ship ought to command the ship's course, yea, and also command that justice, peace and sobriety, be kept and practiced, both among the seamen and all the passengers. If any of the seamen refuse to perform their services, or passengers to pay their freight; if any refuse to help, in person or purse, towards the common charges or defense; if any refuse to obey the common laws and orders of the ship, concerning their common peace or preservation; if any shall mutiny and rise up against their commanders and officers; if any should preach or write that there ought to be no commanders or officers, because all are equal in Christ, therefore no masters nor officers, no laws nor orders, nor corrections nor punishments;—I

---

7 Roger Williams to the Town of Providence, ca. Jan. 1655, *Williams Corres.*, 1:432–33.

say, I never denied, but in such cases, whatever is pretended, the commander or commanders may judge, resist, compel and punish such transgressors, according to their deserts and merits. This if seriously and honestly minded, may, if it so please the Father of lights, let in some light to such as willingly shut not their eyes.

I remain studious of your common peace and liberty.

DOCUMENT 37

Roger Williams on issues of religious freedom, in a letter to Major John Mason and Governor Thomas Prence (1670)[8]

In his late sixties, an aging Roger Williams reflected on the colony and its original founding goals. The excerpt below is from a letter that Williams wrote in 1670 to John Mason and Thomas Prence. Here Williams addresses the founding goals of the colony as a haven for religious dissidents. He explains how forced religion not only goes against God's will, but also disrupts civil peace.

But here all over this Colony, a great number of Weak and distressed Soules and Consciences Scattered, flying hither from old and New Engl. The most high and only wise hath in his infinite Wisdom provided this Country and this Corner as a shelter for the poor and persecuted according to their Several persuasions. And thus that heavenly Man **Mr Hains** Governor of Connecticut (though he pronounced the Sentence of my long Banishment against me at Cambridge, then Newtown yet) said unto me, in his own house at Hartford (being then in some difference with the Bay) "I think Mr Williams I must now Confess to You, that the most wise God hath provided, and cut out this part of his World for a Refuge and Receptacle for all sorts of Consciences ..." I have offered and do, by these presents: to discuss by Disputation, Writing or printing among other points of Difference these 3 positions. First, that **forced Worship stinks in God's Nostrils**. 2. That it denies Christ Jesus yet to come, and makes the Church yet National, figurative and Ceremonial. 3. That in these flames about Religion ... there is no other prudent Christian Way of preserving peace in the World but by permission of differing Consciences.

Mr Hains: John Haynes, one of the founders of Connecticut, served as a magistrate and governor multiple times.

forced Worship stinks in God's Nostrils: One of Williams' famous lines describing how forced worship was abhorrent to God.

QUESTIONS TO CONSIDER

1. What did Williams and Anne Sadleir disagree about? What techniques did they use to try to persuade the other to see their perspective?

2. Identify how and why Roger Williams advocated for religious freedom and separation of church in state in his 1655 letter to the town of Providence and his 1670 letter to Major John Mason and Governor Thomas Prence.

---

8 Roger Williams to Major John Mason and Governor Thomas Prence, 22 June 1670, *Williams Corres.*, 2:609–20.

CONFLICT AND CONTROVERSY

DOCUMENT 38

Roger Williams to John Winthrop regarding the Jane and Joshua Verin freedom of worship and domestic violence controversy (1638)[9]

Jane and Joshua Verin followed Williams from Salem, and they built their house next door to the Williams family in 1636. Joshua did not attend the religious meetings held in Williams' house, but his wife did—against his wishes, and he violently beat her for this. The Verin case pitted the notion that wives were subordinate to their husbands against Providence's founding principle of religious freedom. In this excerpt, Williams describes how Joshua was disenfranchised for violating his wife's freedom of conscience and how he forced Jane to return to Salem with him.

Sir we have bene long afflicted by a young man, boisterous and desperate (Philip Verins son of Salem) who, as he hath refused to **hear the word** with us (which we molested him not for) this twelve month so because he could not draw his wife a gracious and modest woman to the same Ungodliness with him, he hath trodden her under foot tyrannically and brutishly: which she and we long bearing though with his furious blows she went in danger of Life at the last major vote of us discarded him from our Civil freedom, or disfranchise etc. he will have Justice (as he clamors) at other Courts. I wish he might for a fowl and slanderous and brutish Carriage, which God hath delivered him up unto. He will hale his wife with ropes to Salem, where she must needs be troubled and troublesome as differences yet stand. She is willing to stay and live with him or else where, where she may not offend etc. I shall humbly request that this Item be accepted, and he no way Countenanced until (if need be) I further trouble you.

hear the word: Pray with us.

9 Roger Williams to John Winthrop, 22 May 1638, *Williams Corres.*, 1:155–56.

DOCUMENT 39

Roger Williams on the Samuel Gorton controversy, in a letter to John Winthrop (1641)[10]

Samuel Gorton arrived in New England in 1637 and, just like Williams, conflict followed him and he hopped from place to place. After a brief stay in Boston, Gorton moved to Plymouth and then to Aquidneck Island (Rhode Island). In late 1640/early 1641 Gorton arrived in Providence with a small group of supporters. Initially, the Providence residents welcomed Gorton, but soon many began to begrudge his presence and his rapidly growing number of adherents. Williams was opposed to Gorton settling in Providence from the outset, and he expressed many of his concerns in the following letter. Evidence is scant on what specific issues were at the root of Gorton's conflict with the town, but his antiauthoritarian views undermined the town's political arrangements. Gorton's impassioned preaching style stressed religious individualism, which upheld the indwelling of the Holy Spirit in all believers. Gorton left Providence early in 1642, eventually settled along the Pawtuxet River at Shawomet (Warwick), and was involved in land conflicts in the region.

The following excerpt is one of the few direct references to Samuel Gorton that Williams made in his extant correspondence.

Master Gorton having foully abused high and low at Aquednick, is now bewitching and bemadding poor Providence, both with his unclean and foul censures of all the Ministers in this Country, (for which myself have in Christs name withstood him) and also denying all visible and external Ordinances in depth of **Familism**, against which I have a little disputed and written, and shall (the most High assisting) to death: As **Paul said of Asia**, I of Providence (almost) All suck in his poison, as at first they did at Aquednick. Some few and myself withstand his Inhabitation, and Towne privileges, without confession and reformation of his uncivil and inhumane practices at Portsmouth: Yet the tide is too strong against us, and I fear (if the framer of Hearts help not) it will force mee to little **Patience, and a little Isle next to your Prudence**.

Familism: Reference to sixteenth-century Familists (known as the Family of Love), a mystical religious group founded by Henrik Niclaes. In this context, Williams likely meant someone who believed in the direct and mystical infusion of the Holy Spirit.

Paul said of Asia: Likely a biblical allusion to Rom. 3:13: "Their throat is an open sepulcher; with their tongues they have used deceit; the poison of asps is under their lips."

Patience, and a little Isle next to your Prudence: Patience and Prudence Islands in Narragansett Bay.

10 Roger Williams to John Winthrop, 8 March 1641, *Williams Corres.*, 1:215–16.

DOCUMENT 40

Roger Williams on the persecution of Quakers, from *George Fox digg'd out of his burrows* (1676)[11]

George Fox, a founder of the Quaker movement, traveled throughout England, North America, and the Low Countries preaching the Quaker faith. Quakers believed that they were guided by an inner light, which compelled them to spread their messages of equality and a direct connection to God. Williams particularly hated what he saw as their socially deviant behavior. Although other places around the Atlantic imposed harsh penalties on Quakers as heretics, such as banishment, beatings, fines, whippings, imprisonment, mutilation, and death, they were welcome in Rhode Island.

In 1672 Fox visited Rhode Island, and Williams invited him to a public theological debate. In preparation, Williams wrote fourteen propositions which challenged core Quaker beliefs. Fox left the colony before Williams had a chance to debate him, but three of his followers, John Stubbs, John Burnyeat, and William Edmundson, debated with Williams. The first part of the debate centered on the first seven of Williams' propositions and took place at the Quaker meetinghouse in Newport in August 1672. Williams rowed all the way to and from Providence, no small feat for someone who had suffered ill-health and was approaching 70 at the time. A large crowd gathered and a spirited discussion ensued, lasting for four days. The final seven propositions were debated for a full day in Providence shortly afterwards. Williams' commitment to arguing points of scripture with the Quakers, both in person and in print, suggests that he believed their uncivil practice was the result of a genuine spiritual error. Williams hoped to offer them salvation by showing them their errors.[12] The following excerpt is taken from Williams' 1676 published account of the debate, *George Fox digg'd out of his burrows*. In it he describes the debate and his issues with the Quaker faith.

... Touching this most holy Spirit, and other heavenly Points in difference between the Protestants and the Quakers, I present your **royal eye** with a [landscape] ... of a Battle fought this last Summer in your Majesty's New-England, between some of the most eminent of the Quakers and myself,

royal eye: Williams dedicated the publication to King Charles II.

11 *George Fox digg'd out of his burrows* (Boston, 1676) was the only one of Williams' works to be published in Boston. Given that Quakers were outlawed in Boston, the Massachusetts Bay authorities supported Williams' attack. The following year Fox and Burnyeat responded with *A New-England Fire-Brand Quenched*.

12 Teresa M. Bejan, *Mere Civility: Disagreement and the Limits of Toleration* (Cambridge, MA and London: Harvard University Press, 2017), 76, 81.

three days at Newport on Rhode-Island, and one at Providence on the Main in the same Colony …

I am humbly bold to present it to your Royal Hand,

1. That your own precious Soul (infinitely more precious then thousands of Britain's or Worlds) may see the Grounds and Roots of these Protestant Disquisitions.
2. That your Majesty may see what your New-English Subjects are doing under the gracious Wing of your **wonderful Favor** to us &c …

wonderful Favor: Reference to Charles II granting Rhode Island's 1663 Charter.

I humbly importune your Majesty's continued Grace and Patience to this poor New-England which though a miserable, cold, howling Wilderness, yet eternal hath made it his Glory, your Majesty's Glory, and a Glory to the English and Protestant Name: …

I endeavored, but could not procure a Short-hand writer, so that I am forced to recollect Transactions from my Memory, and I believe (as in the holy presence of God) that I have not failed to present the true substance of passages without advantage to myself, or disadvantage to my Opposites …

I know that a great weight of your [Quaker] Opinions and Acting lie upon your believing your selves guided by the immediate Spirit of God: but I believe that I have proved that it is no more the Spirit of God, that speaks to and acts in you, then it was the true **Samuel** that spoke such heavenly words in the appearance of Sam. Mantle amongst a cloud of other witness you shall never persuade Souls (not bewitched) that the holy sprit of God would persuade your Women and Maidens to appear in public (streets & assemblies) **stark naked**, & c …

Samuel: Likely a biblical reference to 1 Samuel 19:24: "And he stripped off his clothes also, and prophesied before Samuel in like manner, and lay down naked all that day and all that night. Wherefore they say, Is Saul also among the prophets?"

stark naked: Quakers, including women, appeared naked in public places, including churches.

All that I can hope for (without Gods wonderful mercy) is to give my Testimony in my generation: for … few or none of you return. Yet I know Gods foundation is sure he knows who are his amongst you as amongst other persuasions …

I made this Offer following to George Fox, and any or all his Followers or Associates, then together at New-port on Rhode-Island. Tis true George Fox was at Providence some days before, and spoke publicly; and it was free for me publicly to have heard him, and opposed him … But … I resolved to try another way, and to offer a fair and full Dispute …

[T]he Propositions are these that follow.

First That the People called Quakers are not true Quakers according to the holy Scriptures.
2 That the Christ they profess is not the True Lord Jesus Christ.
3 That the Spirit by which they are acted is not the Spirit of God.
4 That they doe not **own** the holy Scriptures.
5 Their Principles and Professions, are full of Contradictions and Hypocrisies.
6 That their Religion is not only a Heresy in the matter of Worship, but also in the Doctrines of Repentance Faith. &c
7 Their Religion is but a confused mixture of Popery, **Arminianism**, **Socinianism**, Judaism &c.
8 The People called Quakers (in effect) hold no God, no Christ, no Spirit, no Angel, no Devil, no Resurrection, no Judgment, no Heaven, no Hell, but what is in man.
9 All that their Religion requires (external and internal) to make Converts and **Proselytes**, amounts to more than what a **Reprobate** may easily attain unto, and perform.
10 That the Popes of Rome do not swell with, and exercise a greater Pride, then the Quakers Spirit hath express, and doth aspire unto, although many truly humble Souls may be captivated amongst them, as may be in other Religions.
11 The Quakers Religion is more obstructive and destructive to the Conversion and Salvation of the Souls of People, then most of the Religions this day extant in the world.
12 The Sufferings of the Quakers are no true evidence of the Truth of their Religion.
13 That their many Books and writings are extremely Poor, Lame, Naked, and swelled up only with high Titles and words of Boastings and Vapor …

own: Recognize.

Arminianism: Seventeenth-century Protestant Christian theological movement, named for Jacobus Arminius, which countered the Calvinist doctrine of predestination, arguing that God's sovereignty and human free will were compatible.

Socinianism: Named after Faustus Socinus and Laelius Socinus, the sixteenth-century movement rejected the doctrine of the Trinity.

Proselytes: New converts to a faith.

Reprobate: Morally depraved person; someone beyond hope of salvation.

That the Spirit of their Religion tends mainly,
1 To reduce Persons from Civility to Barbarism.
2 To an Arbitrary Government, and the Dictates and Decrees of that sudden Spirit that acts them,
3 To a sudden cutting off of People, yea of Kings and Princes opposing them.
4 To as fiery Persecutions for matters of Religion and Conscience, as hath been or can be practiced by any Hunters or Persecutors in the world.

QUESTIONS TO CONSIDER

1. What does the Verin case show about the status of women and religious freedom in seventeenth-century Providence?

2. Who was Samuel Gorton and how and why did he clash with Roger Williams?

3. What were Williams' key criticisms of the Quaker faith? What can we learn about Williams' vision for Rhode Island through his dealings with the Quakers?

SELECT BIBLIOGRAPHY

PRIMARY SOURCES

Davis, James Calvin, ed. *On Religious Liberty: Selections from the Works of Roger Williams.* Cambridge, MA: Belknap Press of Harvard University Press, 2008.

Dove, Dawn, Sandra Robinson, Lorén Spears, Dorothy Herman Papp, and Kathleen Bragdon, eds. *The Tomaquag Museum Edition: Roger Williams, A Key into the Language of America.* Yardley, PA: Westholme, 2019.

LaFantasie, Glenn, ed. *The Correspondence of Roger Williams.* 2 vols. Providence, RI: Rhode Island Historical Society, 1988.

Miller, Perry, ed. *The Complete Writings of Roger Williams.* 7 vols. New York: Russell & Russell, 1963.

Note: all of Williams' published works are available on Early English Books Online.

SECONDARY SOURCES

Books

Barry, John. *Roger Williams and the Creation of the American Soul: Church, State, and the Birth of Liberty.* New York: Viking, 2012.

Bejan, Teresa M. *Mere Civility: Disagreement and the Limits of Toleration.* Cambridge, MA: Harvard University Press, 2017.

Brockunier, Samuel H. *The Irrepressible Democrat.* New York: Ronald Press Co., 1940.

Covey, Cyclone. *The Gentle Radical: A Biography of Roger Williams.* New York: Macmillan, 1966.

Fisher, Linford, J. Stanley Lemons, and Lucas Mason Brown. *Decoding Roger Williams: The Lost Essay of Rhode Island's Founding Father.* Waco, TX: Baylor University Press, 2014.

Gaustad, Edwin. *Liberty of Conscience: Roger Williams in America.* Valley Forge, PA: Judson Press, 1999.

Gilpin, W. Clark. *The Millenarian Piety of Roger Williams.* Chicago: University of Chicago Press, 1979.

Morgan, Edmond. *Roger Williams: The Church and the State.* New York: W.W. Norton & Company, 1967.

Warren, James. *God, War, and Providence: The Epic Struggle of Roger Williams and the Narragansett Indians against the Puritans of New England.* New York: Scribner, 2018.

Winslow, Ola Elizabeth. *Master Roger Williams: A Biography.* New York: Macmillan, 1957.

Articles and Book Chapters

Carlino, Anthony. "Roger Williams and His Place in History: The Background and the Last Quarter Century." *Rhode Island History Journal* 58 (2000): 34–71.

Carrington-Farmer, Charlotte. "More Than Roger's Wife: Mary Williams and the Founding of Providence." *The New England Quarterly* 97, no. 3 (Sept. 2024): 308–44.

Carrington-Farmer, Charlotte. "Roger Williams and the Architecture of Religious Liberty." In *Law and Religion and the Liberal State*, edited by Jahid Hossain Bhuiyan and Darryn Jenson. New York: Hart Publishing, 2020.

Field, Jonathan Beecher. "A Key for the Gate: Roger Williams, Parliament, and Providence." *The New England Quarterly* 80, no. 3 (Sept. 2007): 353–82.

Fisher, Julie. "Roger Williams and the Indian Business." *The New England Quarterly* 94, no. 3 (Sept. 2021): 352–93.

Haefeli, Evan. "How Special Was Rhode Island: The Global Context of the 1663 Charter." In *The Lively Experiment: Religious Toleration in America from Roger Williams to the Present*, edited by Christopher Beneke and Christopher S. Grenda. Lanham, MD: Rowman & Littlefield, 2015.

LaFantasie, Glenn. "A Day in the Life of Roger Williams." *Rhode Island History Journal* 46 (1987): 85–95.

Lemons, J. Stanley. "Roger Williams Was Not a Seeker but a 'Witness in Sackcloth.'" *New England Quarterly* 88, no. 4 (Dec. 2015): 693–714.

PERMISSIONS ACKNOWLEDGEMENTS

Figures 1.1–1.5	Janelle Jenstad, Greg Newton, and Kim McLean-Fiander, eds., *The Agas Map of Early Modern London* (Victoria, BC: University of Victoria, 2013–present), mapoflondon.uvic.ca/agas.htm. CC BY-NC-SA 4.0, https://creativecommons.org/licenses/by-nc-sa/4.0/.
Figure 9.1	1638 Deed for Providence, Unmarked Hollinger Box (Founding Documents), Providence City Archives, Providence City Hall, Providence, RI.
Figure 12.1	*Rhode Island Royal Charter*, 1663, Rhode Island Department of State House, https://www.sos.ri.gov/divisions/civics-and-education/for-educators/themed-collections/rhode-island-charter.
Figure 13.1	"Maps of Providence, R.I., 1650, 1765, 1770," Providence, R.I., Nelson E. Osterberg, (1914), https://collections.leventhalmap.org/search/commonwealth:3f4637626. Map reproduction courtesy of the Norman B. Leventhal Map & Education Center at the Boston Public Library, Henry R. Chace (Henry Richmond).
Figure 14.1	Roger Williams to John Winthrop Jr., 22 June 1650, *Winthrop Papers Special Collections*, P-350, Box 8, Massachusetts Historical Society, Boston, MA.
Figure 14.2	Memorandum of original agreement for Providence, 20 December 1661, *Records of the Town of Providence*, RG 100, Providence City Archives, Providence City Hall, Providence, RI.
Figures 17.1 and 17.2	Wetu interior and exterior. Courtesy of Plimoth Patuxet Museums.
Figures 23.1 and 23.2	*An essay towards the reconciling of differences among Christians*, DA6-E78t, John Carter Brown Library, Brown Digital Repository, Brown University Library, https://repository.library.brown.edu/studio/item/bdr:13453/.
Figure 35.1	Anne Sadleir Correspondence with Roger Williams, R.5.5, Letter 31, Sadleir Collection, Wren Library, Trinity College, Cambridge University, UK.

About the Publisher

The word "broadview" expresses a good deal of the philosophy behind our company. Our focus is very much on the humanities and social sciences—especially literature, writing, and philosophy—but within these fields we are open to a broad range of academic approaches and political viewpoints. We strive in particular to produce high-quality, pedagogically useful books for higher education classrooms—anthologies, editions, sourcebooks, surveys of particular academic fields and sub-fields, and also course texts for subjects such as composition, business communication, and critical thinking. We welcome the perspectives of authors from marginalized and underrepresented groups, and we have a strong commitment to the environment. We publish English-language works and translations from many parts of the world, and our books are available world-wide; we also publish a select list of titles with a specifically Canadian emphasis.

broadview press

This book is made of paper from well-managed FSC® - certified forests, recycled materials, and other controlled sources.